Marriages of Monmouth County, New Jersey, 1795–1843

Marriages of
Monmouth County, New Jersey,
1795–1843

❧ ❧

Compiled by
George & Florence Gibson

CLEARFIELD

Reprinted for
Clearfield Company, Inc., by
Genealogical Publishing Co., Inc.
Baltimore, Maryland
1992, 1995, 2005, 2006

NOTE

THE FOLLOWING LIST of marriages has been compiled from
the original marriage registers on file at the Monmouth
County Courthouse in Freehold, New Jersey. The date given
in each entry, set off to the extreme right, is to be taken as
the date of the marriage, except where it is preceded by the
word "recorded", which signifies the date the marriage was
recorded in the register and not the date of the marriage
itself.

MARRIAGES OF

MONMOUTH COUNTY, NEW JERSEY,

1795-1843

```
Aaronson, Clayton - Rebecca Stevenson.......   1-12-1815
Abraham, Charles - Helena A. Conover........   2-18-1818
Abraham, Lewis - Dorkis Gorden..............   2-18-1798
Abraham, Stephen - Letty Conover............   8-29-1818
Abraham, William - Lydia Mount..............   1-29-1826
Abrams, Simon - Lydia Bowne.................   4-17-1827
Acker, Daniel - Maragaret Thompson..........   9-31-1836
Ackerman, James - Sarah Corolen............. 10-28-1834
Ackerman, William - Mary A. Croxson......... 11-29-1829
Acre, Moses - Jane Johnston................. 11-23-1811
Acre, Stephen - Elizabeth Limman............   1-01-1812
Aker, Daniel - Juliann Cranmer..............   6-02-1833
Aker, William - Helene Tanner............... 10-27-1821
Akins, John - Emiline Logan.................   3-06-1836
Akinson, Moses - Charlotte Phillips.........   3-30-1814
Alcott, Thomas, Burlington, Co. -
    Jane Allen..............................   2-11-1829
Algor, Benjamin - Ruth Brand................ 11-25-1799
Algor, David H. - Abigail Thorn.............   9-26-1822
Algor, John - Hannah Layton.................   9-11-1813
Algor, John B. - Elizabeth Brand............ 11-20-1825
Algor, Jonathan - Mary Clayton.............. 3-08-1810
Algor, Thomas - Catherine Clayton........... 12-05-1803
Algor, Thomas - Nancy Ewing.................   1-27-1838
Algor, Westly - Abigail Shearman............ 12-15-1827
Allen, Charles - Ann Hopkins................   1-08-1830
Allen, Charles - Hannah W. Potter...........   9-28-1844
Allen, Cornelius - Elizabeth Smock.......... 1839-1841
Allen, Daniel - Eleanor Carr................ 10-08-1823
Allen, David - Beuley Price.................   1-12-1805
Allen, Ebenezer - Ann Little................   3-04-1828
Allen, Edmund W. - Sarah Throckmorton.......   6-16-1814
Allen, Elias - Ann Bruett................... 1834-1835
Allen, Ephraim - Lida Aumack................   8-03-1796
Allen, Ezekiel - Lydia Newman...............   4-05-1810
Allen, Gabriel - Rachel Dye.................   8-01-1837
Allen, Hamilton - Nancy Grant...............   3-10-1830
Allen, Isaac - Mary Connet..................   5-25-1825
Allen, Isaiah - Rebecca Rouze...............   5-26-1825
Allen, Jacob - Ann Smith....................   1-04-1818
Allen, Jacob - Margaret Gifford.............   2-16-1830
Allen, Jacob - Nancy Gifford.....(recorded).   6-04-1818
Allen, James - Abigail Rozell...............   1-23-1834
Allen, James - Ann Wooley...................   8-24-1806
Allen, James F. - Mary Allen................   4-28-1831
Allen, John - Elizabeth Woolley.............   1-26-1801
```

1

MARRIAGES OF MONMOUTH COUNTY, NEW JERSEY

Allen, John - Margaret Jones.................. 6-15-1820
Allen, John - Nancy Wilkerson................ 6-09-1799
Allen, John - Phebe Tindall.................. 7-11-1838
Allen, John L. - Rhoda Newman................ 6-25-1836
Allen, Jonathan T. - Rebeccah Hittle......... 4-12-1821
Allen, Joseph - Angeline Gifford............. 1-01-1840
Allen, Joseph - Nelly Doty................... 3-04-1798
Allen, Joseph D. - Phebe Ann Longstreet...... 2-28-1826
Allen, Lewis - Lydia Mount................... 5-13-1824
Allen, Nathan - Ann Van Brunt................ 3-14-1801
Allen, Richard L. - Charlotte Shearman....... 10-10-1834
Allen, Riley - Sarah Warren.................. 12-03-1806
Allen, Robert - Ann Hewlett.................. 3-08-1831
Allen, Robert - Elizabeth Howey.............. 1-05-1797
Allen, Samuel - Lydia Johnson................ 1-24-1839
Allen, Samuel - Mahala Ridgway............... 10-27-1827
Allen, Samuel - Rebecca Ann Allen............ 4-05-1836
Allen, Samuel F. - Hannah Wolcott............ 12-01-1814
Allen, Samuel - Fanna Wright................. 5-05-1804
Allen, Steven - Hannah Gifford............... 7-26-1826
Allen, Thomas - Lydia Johnson................ 3-25-1807
Allen, William - Ann Hendrickson............. 3-31-1838
Allen, William - Mary Michell................ 7-13-1804
Allen, William - Mary Mitchell............... 5-04-1809
Allen, William - Phebe Jonson................ 8-30-1817
Allen, William - Prudence Allen.............. 11-23-1831
Allger, Cornelius - Elizabeth Smock.......... 1839-1841
Alove, John - Alice Nickson..(both black).... 1-01-1831
Alten, John - Rebecca Poinset................ 1-25-1821
Alterson, William - Margaret Cornelius....... 12-18-1822
Ammerman, Isaac - Caroline Kerr.............. 1-27-1829
Anderson, Andrew - Martha Cattrell........... 1-09-1837
Anderson, Benjamin - Nancy Emmens............ 9-10-1807
Anderson, Charles - D. Harker................ 3-24-1842
Anderson, Daniel - Ann Hendrickson........... 12-31-1810
Anderson, David R. - Abigail M. Rogers....... 3-17-1825
Anderson, Elias - Hannah Cottrell............ 4-29-1839
Anderson, Elias - Zelpha Anderson............ 12-20-1812
Anderson, George Jr. - Elizabeth Dewitt...... 3-30-1797
Anderson, Jacob - Rebechah Stillwell......... 10-21-1812
Anderson, James - Elizabeth Anderson......... 9-14-1814
Anderson, James - Mary William............... 10-02-1803
Anderson, James - Penelope Camburn........... 2-16-1838
Anderson, James - Rachel Street.............. 10-18-1816
Anderson, Jeremiah Jr. - Nancy Stout......... 3-07-1797
Anderson, John - Eliza Emmons................ 4-25-1840
Anderson, John - Mrs. Jane Emly
  (both of Bucks Co. Pa.).................... 8-18-1834
Anderson, John, son of David - Mary Berk..... 6-22-1800
Anderson, John - Patience Wainright.......... 12-14-1797
Anderson, Joseph - Elizabeth Reynold......... 1-16-1837
Anderson, Joshua - Mary Vorhis............... 11-28-1812
Anderson, Mathis - Sarah Burk................ 10-03-1816
Anderson, Samuel J. - Sarah Bird............. 8-14-1822
Anderson, Thomas - Margaret Magire........... 8-07-1796

Anderson, William - Sarah Murdoch........... 8-11-1803
Andrews, James, of New York - Rachel Taylor... 7-31-1831
Andrews, Jesse - Hannah Bartlet............. 9-12-1796
Andrews, John M. - Cornelia White............ 9-13-1829
Andrews, Samuel - Mary Jackson............... 11-09-1827
Andrews, Thomas - Maria Allaire............. 6-05-1836
Antonides, Jacob - Elizabeth Zutphen......... 12-18-1800
Antonides Peter - Mary Lloyd................ 3-11-1797
Antonides, Vancentius - Sarah Bound......... 6-28-1797
Antonides, William - Gertrude Hays.......... 2-11-1828
Antonidus, Archibald - Diana Johnson........ 1-24-1833
Antonidus, David - Hetty Wilbur............. 4-13-1826
Antrim, Levi - Ann Pharo.................... 9-25-1796
Antrim, Thomas Esq. - Merriam Middleton...... 9-12-1835
Appelbee, Jacob - Mary Hopkins.............. 7-31-1795
Appelbee, Robert - Elizabeth Harvey......... 1796-1797
Applebee, Isaac Jr. - Charlotte Laurence..... 3-19-1829
Applebee, James - Eliza Layton.............. 1-14-1839
Applebee, John - Margaret Lawrence.......... 10-20-1827
Applebee, William - Sarah Price............. 10-23-1830
Applegate, Apollo - Mercy Phillips.......... 6-06-1819
Applegate, Charles - Mary Ann Horner........ 6-25-1837
Applegate, Charles - Rebecca Thomas......... 4-29-1835
Applegate, Clayton - Hannah Mount........... 6-04-1835
Applegate, Daniel - Eliner Haley........... 1-12-1811
Applegate, Daniel - Ussey Thompson.......... 8-26-1815
Applegate, David - Alice Hendrickson........ 3-12-1814
Applegate, Ephraim - Elizabeth Suidam....... 2-05-1807
Applegate, Forman - Elizabeth Clayton....... 5-06-1833
Applegate, George - Almira Cox.............. 3-05-1823
Applegate, Jacob - R. Reynolds............. 4-08-1842
Applegate, Jacob - Sarah Clayton............ 6-06-1835
Applegate, Jacob Jr. - Mary Luker........... 7-20-1796
Applegate, James - Charlotte Carson......... 1-06-1815
Applegate, James - Jane Snyder.............. 1834-1835
Applegate, John - Alchy Everingham.......... 2-28-1835
Applegate, John - Eliza Taylor.............. 4-21-1825
Applegate, John - L. A. Mirison............ 3-19-1840
Applegate, John - Nancy Anderson............ 4-02-1808
Applegate, John - Sarah Hudson.............. 1-19-1799
Applegate, John - Sarah Mallsborough........ 9-23-1804
Applegate, John D. - Mary Ann Hall.......... 10-07-1832
Applegate, John D. - Mary Grover............ 12-30-1820
Applegate, John H. - Ann Grant.............. 9-08-1838
Applegate, John L. - Mrs. Esther Hankins..... 9-29-1832
Applegate, Joseph - Ann Bray................ 1-05-1815
Applegate, Joseph - Catherine Luker......... 8-09-1814
Applegate, Joseph - Elizabeth Clayton....... 11-08-1818
Applegate, Joseph - Mrs. Rebecca Robinson.... 9-01-1836
Applegate, Lewis - Phebe Conk.............. 10-24-1840
Applegate, Matthias - Margaret Emmens....... 8-28-1836
Applegate, Peter - Meriah Covenhoven........ 5-21-1817
Applegate, Ruben - Mary Paister............. 12-23-1832
Applegate, Samuel - Hannah Fowler........... 1-30-1834
Applegate, Samuel P. - Lydia Tilton......... 7-21-1834

MARRIAGES OF MONMOUTH COUNTY, NEW JERSEY

Applegate, Thomas - Mariah Lewken............	1-20-1821
Applegate, Thomas, son of Thomas, -	
Sarah Baird daughter of Anthony..........	6-28-1798
Applegate, William - Ann Patterson..........	11-14-1822
Applegate, william - Ellen Seabrook..........	11-25-1835
Appleton, John - Jane Pullen................	2-10-1818
Araters, John - Rebecca Robertson...........	11-19-1826
Archer, Daniel - Theodocia Archer...........	2-07-1840
Archer, George - Cathren Mount..............	11-01-1814
Archer, George - Nancy Mount................	11-04-1796
Archer, George Jr. - Mrs. Ann Chambers......	12-23-1839
Archer, William - Sarah Grant...............	4-04-1840
Armstrong, Thomas - Ann Antonides,	
daughter of Sarah.......................	3-06-1800
Arnel, Joseph - Sarah Smith.................	7-29-1841
Arnold, Job - M. Malsbury...................	9-09-1831
Arnold, John - Ann Williams.................	11-08-1816
Arrance, William - Nancy Van Note...........	7-17-1824
Arrants, John - Catherine Plue..............	2-19-1832
Arrowsmith, Joseph - Sarah Van Brockle......	3-23-1815
Arrowsmith, Peter - Harriet Mc Lean.........	12-11-1823
Arrowsmith, Thomas - Ann Bedle..............	3-20-1839
Arrowsmith, Thomas H. - Ann E. Beadle.......	3-20-1839
Arrowsmith, Thomas V. - Elizabeth Walling....	11-27-1837
Arven, Michael - Mary Smith.................	1-26-1812
Asden, Charles - Theodosia Caward...........	7-05-1823
Ashly, John - Elizabeth Mc Cloud...........	1-28-1798
Ashton, Isaac - Ellen Garrison.............	3-06-1822
Ashton, James - Hannah Irons................	11-22-1834
Ashton, John - Olche Messler................	3-03-1821
Asloun, Samuel - Mrs. Ann Chamberlain.......	10-28-1809
Assur, Andrew, of New York - Lydia Cammet....	3-10-1828
Asy, Edward, of Burlington Co., New Jersey -	
Hannah Van Note.........................	11-17-1838
Atkinson, Joseph - Sarah Truax..............	4-09-1836
Atkinson, Robert - Sarah West.(both minors)..	
marriage recorded.......................	8-07-1834
Atterson, James - Charity Vorhees...........	8-05-1818
Atterson, Ralph - Rhoda Hulse..............	9-20-1818
Atterton, Ephraim - Merriam Tilton..........	3-03-1831
Aumack, Aron - Jane Robinson................	6-21-1825
Aumack, Daniel - S. Waydock.................	11-11-1824
Aumack, David - Mary Hampton................	3-26-1806
Aumack, Cornelius H. - Margaret Van Cleve....	5-10-1820
Aumack, J. - Betsey Bennett.................	6-23-1834
Aumack, John - Mary Morris..................	4-02-1807
Aumack, John L. - Nancy Campbell............	2-03-1819
Aumack, Peter - Mary Lokerson...............	5-21-1835
Aumack, Teunis - Mary Aumack................	11-26-1801
Aumack, William - Hannah Willber............	11-05-1814
Aumack, William - Sarah Stout...............	3-02-1806
Aumat, Garrett - Mary Dean..................	6-16-1797
Austin, Isaac - Pheby Strong................	9-05-1799
Austin, Nathan - Harriet Bennett............	12-25-1815
Avis, Elijah - Tinty Newbury................	12 25-1804

```
Ayres, Benjamin - Jane Miller...............  9-30-1815
Ayres, Charles - Susan Ann Collins..........  7-25-1829
Ayres, Daniel - Catherine Stillwell.........  2-02-1815
Ayres, Elijah - Elizabeth Bryan.............  3-23-1811
Ayres, Hezekiah - Mary Ann Conck............ 12-31-1818
Ayers, Jonathan - Lydia Wordell.............  2-19-1799
Ayres, Joseph - Mary Taleman................  9-12-1836
Ayres, Lewis - Elizabeth Logan..............  2-01-1824
Ayres, Lewis - Jane Leyton.................. 10-16-1825
Ayres, Richard - Jane Goodenough............  1-18-1817
Baily, Elias - Jerusha Roberts..............  7-11-1796
Baily, John - Sarah Vancleef................  1-30-1800
Baily, Joseph - Mary Morrell................  3-02-1825
Baily, Thomas - Catherine Beedle............ 11-15-1810
Bainbridge, Henry - Marie Helena Reed....... 11-30-1800
Baird, James - Ann Buck.....................  1-20-1820
Baird, James - Rebecca F. Ely...............  1-07-1834
Baird, John son of David - Sarah Davison....  1-05-1803
Baird, Moses - Elizabeth Raineer............ 12-25-1835
Baird, Rei - Sarah Clayton..................  2-11-1822
Baird, Thomas - Ellen Bilyer................ 12-11-1825
Baity, John - Mary Perrine..................  2-06-1840
Baker, Charles - Mary Ann Fenton............  9-01-1837
Baker, Frasure - Catherine Lane.............  6-12-1796
Baker, Stephen - Nancy Bennett..............  8-21-1830
Baker, William (Rev.) of Philadelphia, Pa. -
    Elizabeth Carhart.......................  9-20-1834
Balcom, Joseph - Sarah Bell................. 10-12-1833
Baldwin, Thomas - Rebecca Sutpin............  2-24-1798
Bamble, William - Sarah Herbert............. 10-28-1818
Baneson, John - Ann Mackmullin..............  1-10-1811
Banks, Bartholomew - Mary Hoffman........... 10-24-1829
Barber, Edward - Margaret Lucas.............  8-17-1809
Barber, John - Mary Allen................... 12-22-1826
Barcalow, Cornelius C. - Catherin Errickson..  3-29-1837
Barcalow, David - Elizabeth Allen...........  2-07-1835
Barcalow, Elisha - Amy Redfor............... 12-15-1816
Barcalow, John M. - Lydia Mount.............  2-12-1812
Barcalow, Nicholas - Jane Williamson........  1-14-1806
Barcalow, William - Hulda Bowne.............  2-26-1812
Bard, William - D. Budge....................  1-18-1840
Barefoot, Thomas - Hannah Branson........... 12-08-1818
Barkalew, William - Lydia Parker............  2-01-1798
Barkalow, Cornelius - Eunice Throckmorton....  3-11-1817
Barkalow, Cornelius - Mary Harbert..........  8-06-1800
Barkalow, Cornelius - Jedidah Erickson......  8-11-1799
Barkalow, Daniel - Mary Burtis.............. 11-30-1837
Barkalow, David - Mary Borden...............  3-03-1805
Barkalow, Derick - Deborah Francis..........  4-12-1825
Barkalow, John - Elizabeth Bond............. 12-21-1799
Barkalow, John - Mary Johnson............... 12-23-1818
Barkalow, John D. - Elizabeth Hendrickson...  3-02-1814
Barkalow, Mathias - Elizabeth Jeffery.......  9-18-1808
Barkalow, Mathias - Mrs. Elizabeth Emmons... 11-05-1835
Barkalow, Peter - Abigail Longstreet........  8-30-1818
```

5

```
Barkalow, Richard - Elizabeth Forman........  12-26-1838
Barkalow, Richard - Margaret Low............   2-14-1807
Barker, Gidian of New England - Meriah Logan.  12-28-1816
Barltson, Enos - Elizabeth Layor.............  12-15-1829
Barney, Bela - Deliah Oaks..................   12-25-1816
Barrcalew, Job - Sarah Corlies...............   3-05-1840
Barrett, William S. - Dinah Davis............   9-23-1835
Bars, John - Jerusha Mathews................   11-10-1834
Bartholf, John G. - Mrs. Christeana Haring...   6-24-1815
Bartleson, John - Catherine Throckmorton.....   2-05-1835
Bartlet, Nathan - Deliverance Hazelton.......   6-27-1802
Bates, Joel - Elenor Parmer..................   1-21-1833
Baxter, Charles H. - Elizabeth Throckmorton..   9-02-1830
Beabody, Jospeh - Hannah Van Cleef..........    3-15-1836
Beadle, Joel - Mary Willet..................   10-12-1800
Beamore, Daniel - Mary Ketcham...............   9-13-1838
Bean, Jesse of Pa. - Mary A. Ogden of Pa.....   7-16-1835
Beard, Thomas - Betsy Stout..................   4-09-1820
Beatty, James - Polly Patterson.............. 12-17-1796
Beatty, John T. - Susan Mc Keen.............   2-15-1829
Beck, Joseph E. - Hannah Forsythe...........  12-17-1835
Bedle, Aaron - Catherine Cottrell........... 12-12-1839
Bedle, Hendrick - Ellen Smith...............   6-13-1836
Bedle, Jeremiah - Delia Cuttrel.............   9-29-1834
Bedle, John - Lydia Bedle...................   4-18-1827
Bedle, William - Ann Morrell dg. of James.... 10-27-1831
Bedmon, Benjamin - Rachel Bennett...........   4-24-1823
Beedle, Elijah - Ann Wallen.................   7-31-1806
Beedle, James - Margaret Mount..............   3-31-1823
Beedle, Joel - Deborah Carrol...............   4-01-1823
Beedle, Thomas - Hannah Dorset.............. 12-14-1825
Beek, Edman - Johanah Claton................   8-05-1801
Beekman, Henry - Mary Antrim................  12-09-1831
Beers, John - Anne Tice.....................   3-12-1797
Beers, John - Hulda Morrell................. 11-18-1831
Beers, John - Rachel Butler.................   9-14-1834
Beers, Joseph - Eliza Bound................. 10-20-1822
Beers, Joseph - Nancy Mathews...............   3-29-1812
Beers, Thomas - Mary Ann Robertson..........   2-21-1805
Belden, Charles D. of N.Y. - Ann B. Conover..   2-29-1835
Bell, George - Lauretta Harris.............. 12-28-1838
Bell, Hugh - Sarah Woodward.................   3-06-1808
Bell, Nathan - Ester Cotteral.............. 11-22-1828
Bell, William - Mary Hulse..................   4-09-1842
Benedick, Theophilus - Mary Stillwagon dg. of
    Stephen.................................   2-12-1807
Benedict, Joseph - Ann Smith................   7-02-1835
Benjamin, John - Lucy Ann Conover...........   1-20-1827
Benjamin, John - Sary Ann Conover...........   1-20-1827
Bennet, Adrian - Ester Holmes...............   1-07-1806
Bennet, Albert - Rebecca Newell.............   5-15-1834
Bennet, Britton - Elnor Mc Clees............   5-09-1816
Bennet, Cyrenius - Ida Bennet...............   2-10-1802
Bennet, Daniel - Peggy Herbert dg. of David.. 12-29-1803
Bennet, David - Mary Green..................   9-24-1797
```

Bennet, Derrick - Elizabeth Bennet........... 12-31-1815
Bennet, Edwin - Elizabeth Bennet
　dg. of Stephen.......................... 10-22-1829
Bennet, Elija - Diademy Archer............... 11-06-1817
Bennet, Elisha - Sarah Johnston.............. 7-14-1804
Bennet, George W. - Angeletie Clayton........ 7-21-1830
Bennet, Hendrick - Elizabeth Hiers........... 1-02-1802
Bennet, Holmes - Elizabeth Crawford.......... 11-04-1829
Bennet, John - ---- Emmons................... 3-05-1834
Bennet, John - Margaret Horten............... 11-27-1806
Bennet, John - Sarah Vandine................. 7-10-1802
Bennet, John - Sarah Woolcott................ 11-13-1799
Bennet, Joseph - Maris Soper................. 1-08-1824
Bennet, Joshua of Pa. - Catherine Green...... 11-25-1802
Bennet, Logan - Mary Holmes.................. 2-03-1811
Bennet, Moses - Patience Emley............... 8-20-1806
Bennet, Peter - Hagar Williamson............. 11-02-1799
Bennet, Thomas - Jerushey Bailey............. 10-17-1802
Bennet, Thomas - Maria Shafto................ 7-08-1816
Bennet, Thomas - Phebe Harvey................ 7-16-1798
Bennet, William J. - Ann Schenck dg. of
　the late G. Schenck...................... 1-05-1830
Bennet, William - Harriet Larten............. 8-16-1834
Bennet, William - Jane Lefferson............. 12-18-1800
Bennet, William - Mary Davis................. 10-24-1809
Bennet, William - Miriam Dangler............. 10-14-1833
Bennet, William son of Henry - Sally Crawford
　dg. of David............................. 11-11-1806
Bennet, William - Sarah Lambertson........... 12-31-1795
Bennett, Benjamin W. - Rebecca Brown......... 10-14-1826
Bennett, Burtis - Louisa Johnson............. 12-31-1833
Bennett, Caleb - Anna Chambers............... 7-06-1800
Bennett, Caleb - Lydia Grover................ 12-25-1834
Bennett, Charles - Margaret Wallace.......... 2-11-1835
Bennett, Cornelius - Ellen Lambertson
　dg. of Thomas............................ 12-17-1831
Bennett, Crawford - Sally Schenck............ 1-09-1833
Bennett, Daniel - Frances Johnston........... 4-17-1816
Bennett, David - Catherine Heyer
　dg. of Peter............................. 3-21-1830
Bennett, Elihu - Mary Sherman................ 6-19-1840
Bennett, Garrett - Susan Moris............... 11- -1834
Bennett, Jacob - Phebe Elmer................. 8-18-1818
Bennett, James - Eliza Dangler............... 12-13-1829
Bennett, James - Elizabeth Morris............ 2-06-1833
Bennett, John - Elizabeth Van Marter......... 11-29-1797
Bennett, John - Mary Allen................... 3-29-1824
Bennett, John - Mary Ann Golden.............. 2-08-1828
Bennett, Joseph - Mary ----................. 8-27-1826
Bennett, Joseph - Theodosia Groves........... 9-21-1832
Bennett, Moses - Lucy Keemer................. 2-13-1840
Bennett, Moses - Sarah L. Imlay.............. 1-15-1823
Bennett, Peter - Mary White.................. 10-31-1822
Bennett, Samuel - Deborah Newman............. 10-20-1825
Bennett, Samuel - Martha Moore............... 5-05-1822

```
Bennett, Samuel - Sussannah Preston.........  10-15-1819
Bennett, William - Catherine Jonson.........   1-04-1821
Bennett, William - Idah Bills...............   2-17-1833
Benson, James of Pa. - Keziah Cook..........   5-02-1805
Benson, Perry - Mary Woodly.................  12-14-1826
Benson, William - Margaret Anderson.........  12-25-1836
Bent, Samuel - Rachel Bray (wid.)...........  11-25-1816
Bergen, Elia - Phebe Rue....................  10-02-1833
Bergen, Peter C. - Lydia Anderson...........  12-16-1813
Bergen, Reuben - Mary Hyres.................   4-09-1826
Bergen, William - Susan Reed................   1-18-1837
Berger, John (Rev.) - Matilda Henderson.....  11-10-1812
Berlin, David - Amy Carmen..................  12-10-1796
Berry, Lawrence - Blessing Newman...........   9-02-1826
Berry, Samuel - Mary Emans..................   1-31-1807
Bert, Alexander - Lydia Hendrickson.........   5-20-1803
Berton, John S. - Elizabeth Pittenger.......   1-04-1827
Bessonet, John P. - Mary White..............  10-24-1799
Besteds, Lewis - Eleanor Vannote............   1-20-1802
Betts, Samuel P. - Gertrude Conover.........   9-29-1829
Betts, Thomas - Elizabeth Tester............  12-31-1832
Betts, Walter - Rebecca Abraham.............   9-21-1809
Betzel, John of Pa. - Lydia Stevens.........   8-02-1813
Bevis, Samuel - Sarah Holmes................  10-15-1820
Biddle, Garret - Euphemia Roberts...........   4-29-1830
Biddle, Joel - Louisa Stillwell.............  11-21-1822
Biles, Henry - Martha Dilling (both black)...  9-02-1832
Biles, Stephen - Mary Thompson..............   9-16-1815
Bills, James - Mary Ann Hays................   8-13-1831
Bills, James - Mary Gilhan..................   1-07-1813
Bills, James - Rachel P. Bills..............  11-04-1837
Bills, John - Elizabeth Johnson.............   2-07-1807
Bills, John Jr. - Lucy Miller...............   7-13-1839
Bills, Johson - Ann Thompson................  11-05-1842
Bills, Jonah - Harriet Casner...............   5-01-1830
Bills, Peter - Joan Conk....................  12-31-1835
Bills, Price B. - Emily Savage..............   7-13-1826
Bills, Thomas - Mary Wardell................   1-06-1806
Bills, Thompson - Eliza A. Miller...........   8-24-1839
Bills, William - Mrs. Catherine Oakerson....   8-26-1826
Billu, Francis son of Asher - Hannah Rogers
   dg. of Samuel............................   3-17-1831
Bilyeu, Peter - Mariah Ogbourn..............  11-25-1801
Bim, Sico - Judith Schenck (both black).....   4-26-1831
Bin, Joseph - Catherine Britton.............   8-03-1826
Bingham, Luther (Rev.) - Juliann Davis......   4-01-1840
Bir, Joseph - Catherine Britten.............   8-03-1828
Bird, James - Margaret Bareford.............  12-25-1815
Bird, John - Ann Giberson...................   5-06-1798
Birdsall, Daniel - Catherine Loper..........  10-10-1833
Birdsall, John - Phebe Collins..............   3-02-1824
Birdsall, Seth - Amanda Hogan...............   1-07-1838
Birdsall, William - Elizabeth Hartshorne....   7-21-1832
Birdsell, Burnet - Merrilu Webb.............   2-05-1835
Birlew, ---- - Emiline Hance................   8-05-1832
```

```
Bishop, Anthony - Martha Huntzinger.........  12-31-1808
Bishop, James - Phebe Ketchum...............  11-07-1835
Bishop, Joseph - Tisha Carr.................   2-22-1826
Blackman, Joseph - Elizabeth Blackman.......  11-17-1802
Blackstock, William - Jane Chambers.........  11-10-1821
Blair, John - Rebecca Crawford..............  12-19-1829
Blake, John M. - Elizabeth Holeman..........   8-21-1834
Blake, Joseph - Ami Ann Johnson.............   5-06-1834
Blakely, Thomas of N.Y. - Lydia Vandyke.....   7-20-1803
Blatner, Randolph of Germany - Mary Ann Hale.  8-09-1825
Block, Paul - Mary Mc Fadin.................  11-10-1832
Bloodgood, Joseph - Mary Hart...............  10-23-1802
Blowers, George - Elanor Taylor.............   9-01-1831
Bobel, Frederick of N.Y. - Ann E. Morriss
    of New York............................  12-31-1835
Bodine, John - Mary Ann Imley...............  12-23-1834
Bodine, Tunis - Nancy Haywood...............  12-09-1821
Boeman, Benjamin - Phebe Burnee.............   4-09-1819
Bogar, William - Melhiah Crane..............   5-14-1805
Bogart, William - Elizabeth Soper...........   1-02-1832
Boger, John - Catherine Emmons..............   8-07-1814
Bognar, Joseph - Mary Harvey................  11-21-1818
Bogun, George - Zilpha Ann Crammer..........   7-25-1825
Boice, Cornelius P. - Elizabeth Thomas......   4-20-1839
Boice, Ira - Micah Smock....................   3-08-1827
Boker, Thomas - Phebe Catheart..............   1-12-1811
Bolman, Samuel - Eliza Harman...............   1-02-1843
Bond, Hugh - Mary Borden....................   8-28-1802
Bond, James - Delilah Bown..................   1-05-1806
Bond, James - Sarah Brown...................   7-28-1842
Bond, John - Lydia Emmons...................   9-24-1831
Bond, John - Sarah Van Kirk.................  10-15-1838
Bonham, William - Phebe Webb................  10-26-1833
Bonnel, George - Lydia Wilson...............  12-20-1838
Bonnel, John - Sarah Headley................   7-23-1800
Bonnel, Joseph - Sarah Britton..............   9-24-1831
Bonnel, Joseph R. - Elizabeth Britton.......   1-21-1822
Bonnell, John - Harriet Lippincott..........  1827-1828
Bonnell, Samuel - Hannah Rogers.............   1-01-1800
Boram, James - Elizabeth Getman.............  11-22-1838
Borden, Aaron - Sarah Ann Summers...........  11-12-1838
Borden, Ames - Mrs. Jemima Schenck..........  10-29-1808
Borden, Francis - Hannah L. Holmes..........   4-22-1839
Borden, Francis - Margaret Parker...........  10-21-1797
Borden, Isaac of N.Y. - Abby West...........   9-16-1840
Borden, James - Nancy Tunison...............   1-03-1814
Borden, John - Elizabeth Lindly.............   4-20-1826
Borden, Joseph - Huldah Combs...............   4-02-1835
Borden, Richard - Alice White (recorded)....   2-03-1834
Borden, Richard - Catherine T. Williams.....   2-10-1835
Borden, Thomas - Mrs. Mary Jackson..........  11-21-1802
Borden, Thomas - Susan Colies...............   4-16-1827
Borden, Tiley - Hannah Chambers.............   3-09-1817
Borden, William - Angeline Dennis...........   3-05-1829
Borden, William - Anna M. Stout.............   7-29-1822
```

```
Borden, William - Hannah Sammons.............    1-13-1828
Borden, William - Mary Havens................    3-20-1834
Borden, William - Rebecca Patterson..........    3-16-1837
Bordine, William - Elizabeth Strickland......   10-03-1839
Bostwick, Obadiah - Anne Cornell.............    2-14-1800
Boud, Cady - Rachel Dawall...................    2-08-1821
Boud, Richard - Lydia Right..................    8-17-1806
Boud, Thomas - Beuley, Borden................   12-31-1803
Boude, James - Elizabeth Maxson..............    5-12-1821
Boude, Joseph - Mary Crammer.................    3-05-1835
Bouman, Samuel - Margaret Anderson...........    2-02-1822
Bound, John - Sarah Hewett...................    6-17-1797
Bound, Joseph - Sarah Johnson................    5-01-1827
Bowdey, Thomas - Scynthia Scott..............    9-11-1841
Bower, Benjamin - Amy Rogers.................    1-02-1828
Bower, John - Ann M. Vanderbeek..............    4-14-1840
Bower, Joseph of Burlington Co., N. J. -
    Elizabeth Green..........................    5-04-1806
Bowers, John - Elizabeth Jeffry..............    1-06-1834
Bowers, Stephen - Eliza Bergen...............    3-16-1836
Bowker, John - Elenore Matthews..............    8-22-1840
Bowker, John - Elizabeth A. Page.............    9-15-1840
Bowker, Joseph - Nancy Paul..................    3-07-1829
Bowker, Michael - Lucretia Applegate.........   11-17-1805
Bowker, Samuel - Eliza May...................    1-12-1831
Bowker, Samuel Jr. - Rachel Soper............    2-04-1821
Bowles, Abraham - Mary Crawford (both black).   11-28-1839
Bowman, Andrew - Henrietta Rue...............    5-13-1838
Bowman, James - Elizabeth Thorp..............   12-24-1795
Bown, Andrew - Mary Worth....................    1-08-1800
Bown, Phillip - Phebe Poinset................   10-16-1800
Bowne, ---- - Abigail Willet.................    2-25-1798
Bowne, Andrew - Elizabeth Mathias............    8-22-1811
Bowne, Andrew - Sarah Warrell................    2-11-1809
Bowne, Charles - ---- Schanck................    5-12-1840
Bowne, Edward - Elizabeth Parker.............    1-17-1834
Bowne, Jacob - Elizabeth Covert..............    4-07-1825
Bowne, James - Mary Creig....................   12-22-1812
Bowne, James - Sarah Vansant.................   12-08-1801
Bowne, John - Anne Abraham dg. of James......   11-29-1808
Bowne, John - Rebekah Horner.................    5-11-1795
Bowne, Joseph - Anna Applegate...............    3-07-1799
Bowne, Peter - Amelia Asy....................    5-29-1816
Bowne, Peter - Anna Thomson..................   12-13-1796
Bowne, Spafford - Ann Denice.................   11-27-1822
Bowne, Thomas - Sarah Craig..................   12-31-1823
Bowns, Richard - Mary Haleman................    4-19-1828
Bowzer, Daniel - Elizabeth Jackson...........   12-24-1803
Bowzer, James - Elizabeth Shinn..............    1-10-1838
Boyd, James of N. Y. - Deborah C. Crox.......    2-09-1832
Boyd, John - Fanny Jeffery...................    6-16-1816
Boyd, Robert - Elizabeth Spence..............    9-22-1796
Boyer, Isaac - Tinty Newbury.................    2-18-1798
Boyle, Thomas - Mary McCandlish..............   10-31-1842
Bozerth, Samuel - Sarah Grant................    8-02-1817
```

```
Brady, James - Amelia Tilton................  7-31-1820
Brand, David - Rebeckah Alger...............  3-23-1813
Brand, Jeremiah - Lydia Halsey..............  8-22-1827
Brand, Malen - Mary Williams................ 12-18-1828
Brand, Mason - Ann Liming...................  1-03-1817
Brand, Samuel - Deborah White...............  2-01-1806
Brand, Samuel - Jane E----..................     1828
Brand, Samuel Jr. - Mary Ann Shearman.......  3-01-1825
Brand, Thomas Jr. - Mary Southard...........  8-29-1809
Brand, Tobia - Elizabeth Brown.............. 12-09-1841
Brand, Tobias - Elizabeth Brown.............  3-16-1811
Brand, White - Deborah Newman............... 12-31-1822
Brand, William - Abigail Newman.............  1-29-1806
Branes, Joshua - Ann Pembrook............... 11-30-1841
Brannen, Thomas Jefferson - Elizabeth Pearce. 1-06-1833
Branson, Ivans - Henrietta Solomon.......... 12-01-1834
Branson, Joseph - Lydia Wolcott.............  1-03-1807
Branson, Thomas - Levina Shinn.............. 10-02-1817
Branson, William - Margaret Finly........... 12-27-1820
Brant, Thomas of N.Y. - Hannah Patterson....  2-14-1824
Bratt, Egbert - Sarah Graveline.............  9-24-1805
Bray, John - Hannah Crawford................  9-23-1823
Bray, Joseph - Mary Bray....................  4-17-1831
Bray, Nicholas - Lydia Walling..............  1-22-1831
Bray, Samuel - Elizabeth White..............  7-10-1827
Bray, Samuel - Hope Applegate.:.............  1-30-1812
Bray, William - Mary Truax..................  5-15-1831
Brayman, Jessee - Hannah Baird.............. 11-06-1810
Brensor, Thomas - Elwyne Gill...............  9-12-1826
Brewer, Aron - Rachel Wilbur................  4-06-1815
Brewer, Benjamin - Jemima Trofford..........  1-03-1807
Brewer, Cornelius - Jane Williamson.........  2-10-1798
Brewer, Cornelius - Lydia Hurley............ 12-30-1815
Brewer, Daniel - Elizabeth Van Note.........  1-08-1831
Brewer, Elias - Elizabeth Anderson..........  8-  -1820
Brewer, Elias - Mrs. Elizabeth More.........  5-26-1810
Brewer, Elias - Henrietta Emley.............  1-28-1841
Brewer, Garret - Lucretia Luyster...........  1-15-1824
Brewer, George - Lyda Hulit.................  8-03-1810
Brewer, Gilbert - Hannah Vorhees............  4-20-1823
Brewer, Hendrick - Elizabeth McKaninny......  2-15-1815
Brewer, Hendrick - Lydia Hendrickson........  3-16-1802
Brewer, John - Ann Bowker................... 3-14-1811
Brewer, John - Clemine Horner...............  6-04-1810
Brewer, John - Elizabeth Freeman............  7-10-1821
Brewer, John - Satiha Parker................ 11-20-1802
Brewer, John - Unity Miers.................. 11-17-1825
Brewer, John D. - Elizabeth Freeman.........  3-15-1820
Brewer, John J. - Eliza Jeffery.............  3-24-1814
Brewer, John Jr. - Lydia Little.............  3-25-1819
Brewer, Johnson - Louisa Allen.............. 11-19-1836
Brewer, Joseph - Elizabeth Morris........... 12-06-1804
Brewer, Joseph - Franscynthe Heyer..........  5-26-1820
Brewer, Joseph - Hannah Hankins............. 10-04-1823
Brewer, Peter - Nancy Hankings.............. 12-08-1796
```

```
Brewer, Robert - Phebe Bird..................  9-09-1804
Brewer, Tyle - Dabre Tise...................  5-22-1812
Brewer, William - Hannah Hulce..............  12-28-1820
Brewster, Lewis of New York City -
  Louisa Provost...........................  5-21-1837
Brian, Joseph - C. Britton..................  8-03-1826
Brick, Joseph W. - Mary Allen dg. of
  Riley of Burlington, N.J.................  11-05-1836
Bridgman, Thomas of N.Y. - Martha Eastman....  3-08-1832
Briggs, Daniel - Sarah Ann Stillwell
  dg. of John..............................  3-07-1832
Brills, Abraham - Harriet Johnson...........  6-25-1824
Brimley, William - Catherine Ann Vancleave...  12-22-1832
Brinckerhoff, Abraham Jr. - Catherine Remson.  9-01-1814
Brinley, Asher - Nancy Slocum...............  1-26-1805
Brinley, George - Elizabeth White...........  11-20-1796
Brinley, Henry - Ann Aumont.................  4-07-1813
Brinley, Henry - Mary Robins................     1813
Brinley, Lewis - Eliza McElson..............  10-30-1837
Brinley, Samuel - Ann Grant.................  6-02-1800
Brinley, Sylvanus - Rebecca Niveson.........  1-20-1827
Brinley, Sylvester - Hannah Britton.........  2-11-1819
Brinley, Vincent - Sarah Ann Smith..........  1-15-1824
Brinley, William - Rachel Chamberlain.......  3-09-1798
Brittain, Thomas - Ann Mathews..............  4-07-1796
Britton, Abraham - Lucy Ealy................  11-13-1833
Britton, Benjamin - Rody Wilgus.............  9-17-1814
Britton, Benjamin S. - Rebecca Cornelius....  2-02-1822
Britton, Bennet - Rebecca Newman............  1-01-1831
Britton, Charles - Lydia Lippincott.........  3-18-1806
Britton, Daniel - Rachel Foster.............  10-13-1830
Britton, Ezra - Amy Applegate...............  5-22-1830
Britton, Isaac - Lydanna Lippincott.........  11-21-1830
Britton, James - Abigail Garwood............  6-05-1830
Britton, James - Eley Jeffery dg. of John....  5-08-1820
Britton, James - Mary Cotral................  10-18-1817
Britton, John - Elizabeth Throckmorton......  11-18-1813
Britton, Joseph - Mrs. Anne Estol...........  1-01-1814
Britton, Nathaniel - Lavinia W. Potts.......  11-07-1841
Britton, Nathaniel - Sarah Horner...........  8-07-1819
Britton, Richard - Elizabeth Malcome........  4-17-1827
Britton, Richard Jr. - Anne Stout...........  11-28-1802
Britton, Samuel - Ann Havens................  6-12-1821
Britton, Samuel - Ann Warren................  12-24-1795
Britton, Samuel - Mary Burch................  10-24-1799
Brock, Charles - Mary Stoutenborough........  11-21-1823
Brody, Nicholas - Margaret Arrant...........  12-28-1831
Bronson, Thomas - Elvyne Gill...............  9-13-1828
Brooks, William (Capt.) of Boston, Mass. -
  Eleanor Firman...........................  7-05-1807
Brotherton, William - Rachel Hutchinson.....  10-13-1808
Brower, Daniel - Ester Herr.................  10-27-1822
Brower, Isaac - Jane Brower.................  10-13-1836
Brower, Jacob - Amanda Scott................  2-25-1841
Brower, James - Margaret Lawrence...........  7-27-1800
```

```
Brower, John - Elizabeth Burdge..............  1-08-1812
Brower, John - Hester Brown.................  3-29-1816
Brower, Robbins - Nancy Cleavenger...........  8-10-1800
Brower, William - Maria Fleming..............  12-06-1829
Brown, Abner - Hannah Burdshall..............  3-05-1802
Brown, Adam - Hester Jackson.................  3-22-1823
Brown, Alexander - Mary Britton..............  9-22-1814
Brown, Andrew - Catherine C. Caine...........  1-07-1842
Brown, Anthony - Sarah Corlis................  11-09-1816
Brown, Benjamin - Phebe Test.................  1-28-1838
Brown, Benjamin - Sarah J----................  12-24-1799
Brown, Caleb - Sarah Smith...................  5-04-1802
Brown, Charles - Hannah Polhemus.............  1-18-1811
Brown, Clarkson - Rachel Young of
    Burlington Co., N.J......................  3-18-1820
Brown, Clayton - Esther Smith................  7-17-1839
Brown, Clayton - Livinia Brown...............  11-20-1840
Brown, Clayton - Mary Brown..................  10-04-1831
Brown, Cornelius - Hannah Newbury............  4-06-1816
Brown, Cornelius - Mary Tice.................  4-25-1823
Brown, Daniel - Ann Fowler...................  10-18-1832
Brown, Daniel - Lucretia Rogers..............  1-08-1824
Brown, Daniel - Sarah A. Poland..............  2-18-1841
Brown, Edward - Mary Beers...................  1-16-1825
Brown, Enoch W. - Mahala Everingham..........  2-03-1831
Brown, Enos - Julian Real....................  3-10-1810
Brown, Ezekial - Sarah Buckalew..............  5-09-1797
Brown, Frederick - Margaret Mires............  8-25-1814
Brown, George - Elizabeth Gardner............  4-01-1815
Brown, George - Lydia Marks..................  9-12-1822
Brown, George - Rebecca Brindley.............  2-19-1820
Brown, Jacob - Ann Still (both black)........  9-29-1828
Brown, James - Phebe Nutt....................  12-18-1830
Brown, Japhet - Sarah Davis..................  3-10-1806
Brown, Jeremiah - Mrs. Rebeckah Shaftoo......  3-16-1820
Brown, Jess - Elizabeth Price................  12-23-1826
Brown, Job - Phebe Williams..................  10-03-1842
Brown, Joel - Nancy Francis..................  1-01-1831
Brown, John - Ann English....................  10-31-1842
Brown, John - Ann Hough......................  2-18-1838
Brown, John - Mary Pearce....................  1-15-1830
Brown, John - Sarah Williams.................  12-02-1826
Brown, John C.- Delia A. Brown...............  3-22-1828
Brown, John Jr. - Susanna Stevenson..........  11-12-1795
Brown, Jonathan - Ann Newman.................  3-24-1808
Brown, Jonathan - Deliverance Kittle.........  6-06-1839
Brown, Jonathan - Mary Lemmon................  11-22-1806
Brown, Joseph - Ann Pearce...................  6-29-1824
Brown, Joseph - Delilah Burdsall.............  4-02-1827
Brown, Joseph - Hannah Crum..................  1-16-1814
Brown, Joseph - Lydia Ann Perrine............  11-28-1831
Brown, Joshua - Mary Scoby...................  6-10-1801
Brown, Lewis - Eliza Wardell.................  2-23-1815
Brown, Lewis - Mary Burgee...................  2-16-1806
Brown, Lyle - Lydia Remine...................  11-29-1808
```

```
Brown, Mark - Emeline Rogers................  8-29-1833
Brown, Morris - Elizabeth Pearce.............  2-06-1832
Brown, Peter - Elizabeth Johnson.............  11-11-1802
Brown, Peter - Sarah Magill..................  12-30-1841
Brown, Robert - Elenor Taylor (both black)...  7-13-1834
Brown, Samuel - Betsey Birdsall..............  12-31-1828
Brown, Samuel - Betsy Forester...............  4-17-1797
Brown, Samuel - Rachel Gray..................  3-16-1810
Brown, Thomas - Ann Tilton...................  1-03-1821
Brown, Thomas - Elizabeth Longstreet.........  9-07-1841
Brown, Thomas - Elizabeth Loper..............  10-24-1803
Brown, Thomas Jr. - Eleanor Lain.............  1-12-1822
Brown, Tylee - Elizabeth Remine..............  3-30-1812
Brown, William - Elizabeth Britton...........  12-21-1828
Brown, William - Elizabeth Hulick............  10-19-1835
Brown, William - Elizabeth Letts.............  2-02-1828
Brown, William - Hannah Lloyd................  10-19-1826
Brown, William - Hannah McCarey..............  1-10-1835
Brown, William - Jemime Newbury..............  7-24-1817
Brown, William - Rachel Bunnill..............  11-18-1832
Brown, William - Susannah Owen...............  4-23-1800
Brown, Zebulon - Matilda Rodgers.............  11-28-1838
Bruen, Cyrus - Eliza Henderson...............  9-03-1818
Bruere, John H. - Anna Scoby.................  12-17-1818
Brundage, John - Alice Emmens................  6-13-1797
Buchalow, Augustus - Elizabeth Throp.........  11-05-1831
Buck, Alexander - Mrs. Ann Hendrickson.......  1-16-1834
Buck, Sylvester - J. A. Denice...............  1836
Buckalew, Joseph - Phebe Buckelew............  8-16-1802
Buckalow, David - Mary Borden................  3-03-1805
Buckelew, Jacob - Harriet Cook...............  12-07-1841
Buckelew, Joseph - Nancy Valentine...........  1-21-1819
Buckelew, Peter - Mary Buckalew..............  3-22-1810
Bucklew, Gilbert - Cathrin Warner............  1-01-1802
Bucklew, William - Rachel Cook...............  2-26-1831
Buckman, J. T. B. - Ann Crawford.............  1833-1835
Buckson, Joseph - Sarah Hendrickson..........  12-29-1830
Bugs, William of N.Y. - Louisa Huff..........  5-26-1828
Bunel, Thomas - Mary Ruel....................  6-29-1800
Bunley, Joseph - Zebe Brewer.................  6-17-1819
Bunnell, Thomas - Eliza Snowden..............  12-02-1815
Bunting, Aaron - Martha Shreve...............  1-21-1830
Bunting, Samuel - Rebeca Conover.............  12-07-1828
Burage, Richard - Hannah Fisher..............  2-27-1830
Burch, Joseph - Betsey Britton...............  5-24-1795
Burchell, Elijah - Ann Ralph.................  1-25-1797
Burd, Richard S. - Ann Hampton...............  7-01-1830
Burden, John - Eliza Lake....................  2-10-1827
Burden, Joseph - Hannah Mount................  8-30-1812
Burden, Richard - Sarah Chadwick.............  2-06-1797
Burdge, David - Sarah Ann Brown..............  11-09-1826
Burdge, John - Jane Tate.....................  10-26-1799
Burdge, John - Sarah Vannort.................  9-24-1807
Burdge, John Jr. - Elizabeth Woolley.........  12-31-1838
Burdge, Joseph - Elizabeth Longstreet........  3-13-1814
```

14

Burge, Merrich - Harriet Allen	7-31-1828
Burdge, Merrick - Sarah Pearce	3-18-1822
Burdge, Samuel - Susan Walling	1-25-1814
Burdge, William - Elizabeth Longstreet	4-09-1808
Burdsall, Samuel - Amy Bennett	1-26-1828
Burge, Hugh - Lydia Garrison	5-03-1823
Burge, Richard - Zilpha Price	7-31-1797
Burge, Uriah - Susanna DuBois (both of N.Y.)	10-30-1803
Burk, Alexander - Hope Evengrim	4-27-1799
Burk, John R. - Caroline Stout	8-08-1821
Burk, William - Martha Anderson	11-21-1807
Burke, Daniel - Zilpha Shinn	10-16-1808
Burke, Richard - Mary Anderson	1-13-1807
Burke, Samuel - Lucy Reed	3-19-1831
Burling, George - Susanah Rodgers	2-14-1811
Burling, John - Mrs. Catherine Hall (wid.)	9-03-1820
Burnett, Nathaniel H. - Ellenor Letts	2-16-1823
Burr, Elias - Elizabeth Arnold	11-19-1838
Burr, Elias - Sarah Arnold	3-27-1822
Burress, Archibald - Lydia Beedle	7-05-1802
Burrowes, Joseph - Mary Nap	10-05-1798
Burrowes, Richard - Mary Taylor	12-12-1822
Burrows, Edward - Catherine Crawford	8-22-1815
Burtes, Wykoff - Hannah Thompson	11-29-1838
Burtis, Daniel - Elizabeth A. Vanderveer	9-05-1839
Burtis, Peter - Margaret Thompson	9-04-1833
Bush, Oliver - Sary Ann Cornelia Roseveld	10-06-1812
Busson, James - Lydia Ireton	8-28-1828
Butcher, Israel - Harriet White	10-23-1815
Butcher, Jacob - Harriet White	10-25-1815
Butcher, Joseph - Caroline White dg. of Ezekiel	6-14-1828
Butcher, Joseph M. - Elizabeth Newell	1-15-1822
Butler, Charles - Deliverance Collins	10-22-1818
Butler, Charles of New York City - Eliza Tilton	12-14-1837
Butler, James F. - Rebecca Mount	8-31-1841
Butler, Joseph - Ann Higgins	4-26-1838
Buzbee, Loran - Abigail Woodman	11-13-1839
Byard, Zebulon C. - Harriet Rossell	12-27-1837
Bye, Robert - Sarah Tester	12-31-1832
Byern, Mahlon - Jane Nutt	3-06-1828
Byse, Daniel - Sarah Pees	4-26-1801
Cabe, George M. - Sarah Bennett	9-25-1828
Cafferty, Samuel - Margaret Bailey	12-10-1815
Cakely, Jeremiah - Charity Moore	11-24-1810
Callahan, William - Elizabeth Horner	3-13-1817
Callahen, William - Rachel Norton	3-23-1801
Camauck, Jesse - Hanna Biracalo	1-19-1826
Cambran, Hebron - Levinah Bayer	4-01-1810
Cambran, Joseph - Mary Carr	9-20-1810
Cammel, Benjamin - Jane Smith	2-07-1802
Camp, Samuel - Euphemy Perrine	12-06-1835
Campbell, Edward - Susannah Robert	3-03-1842
Campbell, John - Jammia Reed	6-07-1829

```
Campbell, Joseph - Margaret Lafetra.........  11-17-1830
Campbell, Neal - Edney Hurley...............   6-26-1831
Campbell, Thomas - Lydia Griffith...........   3-22-1820
Campbell, William - Hannah Bowne.............  5-21-1823
Campbell, William - Mary Field.............. 12-27-1828
Canada, Samuel - Hannah Wooley.............. 10-25-1830
Canfelt, William - Mary Conover.............   2-02-1836
Caralt, Joseph - Emeline Estle..............   9-22-1829
Carhart, Cornelius - Sarah White............   1-13-1816
Carhart, George - Ann Covert................   3-02-1836
Carhart, George - Mary Herbert..............   8-01-1808
Carhart, Joel - Ann Vanpelt.................   7-29-1827
Carhart, John - Catherine Cehso............. 10-27-1810
Carhart, Joseph - Deborah Brown............. 11-03-1838
Carhart, Joseph - Elizabeth Hoss............ 10-16-1821
Carhart, Joseph - Margaret Nowlin...........   8-19-1820
Carhart, Richard - Catherine Aumack.........   4-13-1817
Carhart, Samuel - Sarah Bedle...............   9-26-1821
Carhart, William - Rebekah Vanpelt..........   9-13-1814
Caris, Simon - Hannah Warren................ 10-29-1836
Carl, James - Rachel Morris.................   4-17-1797
Carle, Joseph Tharp - Sally Cook............ 10-10-1799
Carle, Thomas - Mehalah Hults............... 11-14-1839
Carman, Elijah - Abigail Allen..............   9-01-1804
Carman, Joseph - Patience Burge............. 11-17-1802
Carmer, John - Elener Clayton...............   7-19-1840
Carmichael, Elijah - Rachel Wilson.......... 12-09-1835
Carmon, William - Ann Van Cleave............ 12-11-1816
Carney, Joseph - Mary Williams (both black).. 10-08-1827
Carney, Lewis - Julia Baird.................   1-12-1842
Carp, Michael - Mary Herr dg. of David......   7-12-1824
Carpenter, Larrence - Leueresy Ann Rogers....   1-26-1828
Carr, Isaac - Mary Bennett.................. 11-07-1840
Carr, James - Mary Smith.................... 12-21-1820
Carrell, William - Rebecca Dun..............   3-23-1797
Carson, Alexander - Rachel Campman.......... 12-25-1798
Carson, Charles - Sarah Tinney.............. 12-10-1806
Carson, Dubury - Jane Vanderber.............   5-24-1820
Carter, Alperd - Charlott Fenton............   5-06-1838
Carter, Barton - Clenentine Hill............   3-20-1839
Carter, John - Ann Claypoole................   4-24-1832
Carter, John - Elizabeth Walling............   3-06-1825
Carter, Lewis B. - Lydia A. Parker..........   1-04-1832
Carter, Samuel - Theodotia Brittain.........   2-27-1804
Carter, Thomas - Sarah Beegle...............   1-24-1843
Carter, William - Ann Bird.................. 10-13-1841
Carver, Henry - Deborah A. Beer.............   9-04-1841
Casedy, John - Margaret Fitzemmons..........   5-15-1815
Casler, Michael son of Joseph -
     Elizabeth Hendrickson................... 11-14-1824
Casler, Peter - Ellinor Davis...............   2-05-1799
Casmith, Thomas (wid'r.) -
     Catherine Thompson......................   6-16-1809
Casner, Thomas - Sarah Worden...............   7-05-1800
Cato, Free - Lydia ----- (both black)........   9-01-1800
```

```
Caul, francis - Henrietta Bird
  (both of New York City)................. 10-27-1839
Cavileer, Charles (Cap't) - Mary Bates....... 4-20-1800
Cayton, Job - Mary Anderson................. 2-17-1808
Chacey, Henry - Jane Britton................ 3-15-1815
Chacy, John - Margaret West................. 3-06-1808
Chacy, John - Ann Hopping................... 1-15-1814
Chadwick, Daniel - Merribal Chadwick........ 5-27-1837
Chadwick, Elisha - Sarah Mary Cole.......... 7-30-1842
Chadwick, Francis (rev.) - Ann Parker
  dg. of Captain Joseph.................... 9-09-1835
Chadwick, Francis - Elizabeth Worthley....... 7-30-1805
Chadwick, John - Ann Longstreet............. 1-18-1828
Chadwick, Joseph - Nelly Harkinson.......... 12-11-1797
Chadwick, Samuel - Deborah Crusher.......... 4-23-1797
Chadwick, Thomas - Amelia Wood.............. 2-27-1809
Chadwick, Thomas - Amelia Woodmansee........ 2-22-1809
Chadwick, Thomas - Hannah Talman............ 4-02-1799
Chadwick, Thomas - Jane Longstreet.......... 3-17-1821
Chadwick, Thomas - Keziah Jones............. 4-07-1811
Chadwick, William - Eliza Ann Mount......... 3-14-1840
Chadwick, William - Merribeth Webbley........ 7-25-1802
Chadwick, William - Rachel Dunton........... 12-07-1823
Chadwick, Wilson - Frances Conrow........... 12-26-1829
Chaffee, Charles - Margaret Horner.......... 12-07-1834
Chaffee, John - Ann Curtis.................. 2-26-1814
Chaffee, Lorenzo - Susan Gaskill............ 1-19-1839
Chaffee, Thomas - Ann Curtis................ 2-26-1814
Chaffee, William - Lydia Wilgus............. 9-17-1809
Chaffey, James - Caroline Simson............ 1-31-1813
Chaffey, Job - Bertha Brown................. 2-27-1830
Chaffey, Job - Sally Ann Woodward........... 1-21-1837
Chaliner, Story - Elizabeth Dennis.......... 1-01-1801
Challender, John - Lydia Southard
  (both of Burlington, Co. N. J.).......... 10-01-1836
Challender, Thomas - Hannah Hopkins......... 9-18-1824
Chamber, Caleb - Martha Woodward............ 5-13-1841
Chamberlain, Aaron - Liddia Lippincott....... 12-18-1827
Chamberlain, Addie - May Shepherd........... 2-02-1826
Chamberlain, David Jr. - Evelinah Anderson... 3-17-1825
Chamberlain, Ezekiel - Mary Ann Kenby........ 2-16-1837
Chamberlain, Gideon - Rebecca Chamberlin..... 3-25-1805
Chamberlain, Gilbert - Elizabeth Irons....... 12-29-1805
Chamberlain, Henry - Mary Vanbrunt.......... 3-20-1800
Chamberlain, Isaiah - Mary Coleman.......... 10-08-1831
Chamberlain, James - Elizabeth Williams...... 2-15-1837
Chamberlain, Jesse - Elizabeth Stout........ 10-26-1803
Chamberlain, Jesse - Mahala Bennet.......... 5-08-1823
Chamberlain, Jesse - Prudence Longstreet..... 4-06-1826
Chamberlain, Jobe - Elizabeth Soper......... 6-09-1819
Chamberlain, John - Elizabeth Van Dyke....... 5-16-1840
Chamberlain, John - Mrs. Mary Mount......... 2-11-1843
Chamberlain, Joseph - Elizabeth M. Bowth..... 5-26-1827
Chamberlain, Joseph - Mary Brewer........... 4-01-1827
Chamberlain, Orrin - Charity Gray........... 3-16-1826
```

```
Chamberlain, Reuben - Sarah Clevenger........  10-08-1831
Chamberlain, Richard - Catherine Johnson.....   3-25-1815
Chamberlain, Richard - Emaline Clayton.......   2-22-1828
Chamberlain, Samuel - Elizabeth Coleman......  12-24-1840
Chamberlain, Thomas - Hannah Cox.............   1-02-1823
Chamberlain, William - Abigail Horner........   2-05-1834
Chamberlain, William - Ann Edward............   1-05-1832
Chamberlain, William - Anne Chamberlain......   1-26-1804
Chamberlain, William - Harriet Sayer.........   7-22-1824
Chamberlain, William - Lydia Worth...........   9-10-1800
Chamberlain, William Jr. - Elizabeth Crammer.   5-18-1820
Chamberlin, Daniel - Lydia Chamberlin........   3-26-1802
Chamberlin, Gideon - Edith Lippincott........   5-10-1828
Chamberlin, Henry - Rebecca Chamberlin.......  11-11-1829
Chamberlin, James - Sarah Ogborn.............  11-12-1795
Chamberlin, Joseph - Hannah Bonnell..........   8-02-1810
Chamberlin, Richard - Selence Richardson.....   4-06-1801
Chamberlin, Samuel - Nancy Tomblinson........   1-01-1802
Chamberlin, William - Mary Anderson..........   9-20-1832
Chamberlin, William - Phebe Bird.............   2-21-1807
Chamberline, Gabriel - Ann Phillips..........   7-07-1823
Chambers, Anderson - Amy Mathews.............   2-28-1835
Chambers, Benjamin - Martha Stricker.........   5-27-1798
Chambers, Benjamin - Pauline Anderson........   3-02-1815
Chambers, Caleb - Lydia Mathew...............  11-06-1842
Chambers, Ellick Andrew - Eliza Hopkins......   9-07-1812
Chambers, Ezekiel - Rhoda Hulse..............   2-14-1835
Chambers, James T. - Sarah Anderson..........  11-16-1831
Chambers, John - Sarah Francis...............  12-23-1820
Chambers, Lewis - Lucretia Horner............   2-20-1807
Chambers, Michael - Sarah Perker.............   7-25-1807
Chambers, Solomon - Ann Johnson..............   1-11-1812
Chambers, Thomas - Mary Carsen...............   4-14-1827
Chambers, Thomas Jr. - Elizabeth Applegate...   4-27-1796
Chambers, William - Catherine Newbury........  11-16-1798
Chambers, William - Hannah Newman............   5-25-1815
Chambers, William - Mary Brown...............   2-19-1839
Champman, Talbot of Camden, N. J. -
     Jane Lampson............................   2-12-1843
Chandeler, John - Margaret Doughty...........  11-18-1835
Chandler, Amos - Catherine Chadwick..........   2-12-1816
Chandler, Edward - Emmeline Wardell..........   7-20-1817
Chandler, Elijah - Rebecca Vunk..............   1-10-1816
Chandler, Martin - Adeline Morris............   3-15-1827
Chandler, Stephen - Rebekah Mount............  11-17-1813
Chaney, Elia - Sarah Kirby...................   2-13-1840
Chanie, Thomas - Phebe C---..................   7-03-1813
Chanler, Thomas - Hannah Cook................   7-15-1800
Chapeman, Joseph - Elizabeth More............   5-18-1820
Chapman, Henry of Camden, N.J. -
     Hannah Ann Lawson.......................   8-02-1841
Chapman, Isaac - Nancy McDaniel..............   2-16-1808
Chapman, Lewis - Mary Coperthwaite...........   1-30-1813
Chapman, William - Eleanor Heaviland.........   9-27-1828
Chasey, Daniel - Louicia Vandike.............   3-27-1797
```

MARRIAGES OF MONMOUTH COUNTY, NEW JERSEY

```
Chasey, Samuel - Charlotte Smith.............  3-15-1820
Chasey, Samuel - Zilphy Cooper...............  1-11-1832
Chasey, William - Hannah Lane................  6-11-1810
Cheeseman, Abijah - Hannah Parker............  2-05-1822
Cheeseman, Joseph - Parmelia Brody...........  2-18-1832
Chelor, Samuel - Phebe Southard..............  8-17-1818
Choleter, Thomas - Margaret Embley...........  6-11-1835
Chuman, William - Susan Twig.................  4-06-1837
Chumor, Joseph (wid'r.) - Mary Aumack........  2-12-1817
Church, William - Lydia Campbell............. 10-08-1835
Church, Zalmon - Jane Oliphant...............  3-24-1836
Chruchward, Richard - Rachel Cranmer......... 12-23-1834
Cining, Job - Ann Jeffrey....................  1-04-1817
Clain, John M. - Elizabeth Everingam.........  6-10-1809
Clark, Alexander - Hannah Hight.............. 10-05-1803
Clark, Benjamin - Rhoda Vanarsdalen.......... 10-02-1833
Clark, George - M. Pulhemus.................. 12-01-1821
Clark, James - Julia Woohiver................ 12-  -1839
Clark, James of N. Y. - Mrs. Lydia A. Conover  3-17-1838
Clark, Thomas - Mary Seabrooks............... 11-29-1835
Clark, Wesley - Phebe A. Gaskill.............  7-31-1841
Clark, William - Anna Longstreet.............  9-04-1802
Clarke, Joseph - Nancy Carney................  8-23-1800
Clay, Andrew M. - Rachel Van Note............  3-20-1834
Clay, Harleus - Catherine Hutchinson.........  3-24-1834
Claypoole, C. - Charlotte Hovile.............  9-01-1837
Clayton, Abraham - Margaret Hulse............  4-20-1836
Clayton, Asher - Ellen Anne Thompson.........  3-22-1832
Clayton, Conover - Elizabeth Lewis...........  3-13-1840
Clayton, Cornelius - Catherine Giberson...... 10-28-1831
Clayton, Cornelius - Charity M. Kerby........  2-16-1828
Clayton, David - Catherine Stricklin.........  1-07-1798
Clayton, David - Lettis Vorhees..............  1-02-1841
Clayton, David - Lucy Johnson................  2-03-1803
Clayton, David - Rachel Applegate............ 10-27-1834
Clayton, David - Rebecca Prine...............  3-07-1799
Clayton, David I. - Sarah Truax..............  6-29-1825
Clayton, Edward - Catherine Shepherd.........  3-07-1833
Clayton, Edward - Rebecca West............... 11-13-1796
Clayton, Ellison - Lydia Lefferson...........  2-05-1833
Clayton, Ezekiel - Gene Godferd..............  1-01-1814
Clayton, Garet - Rebecca Woodward............ 11-25-1810
Clayton, Henry - Matilda Cottrall............  1-28-1826
Clayton, James H. - Hannah Conover...........  8-07-1825
Clayton, Isaac - Phebe Vanhise............... 12-21-1822
Clayton, James - Sarah Hankinson.............  2-09-1804
Clayton, James D. - Ann Vancleaf.............  1-18-1827
Clayton, James J. - Alice Ann Covenhoven.....  5-25-1833
Clayton, James N. - Hannah Corlis............  3-02-1826
Clayton, Jeremiah - Sarah Midleton...........  6-30-1805
Clayton, Joel - Catherine Fields.............  2-18-1832
Clayton, Joel T. - Catherine McChesney....... 12-26-1804
Clayton, John - Anna Parker..................  8-08-1810
Clayton, John - Betsey Stout.................  1-09-1809
Clayton, John - Deborah Hager................ 11-19-1836
```

```
Clayton, John - Lucretia Strickland.........    2-06-1836
Clayton, John - Lydia Ann Van Note..........    2-03-1842
Clayton, John - Margaret Dennis.............    1-22-1822
Clayton, John - Margaret Hendrickson........    1-01-1839
Clayton, John - Mrs. Esther Emmons..........   12-11-1839
Clayton, John - Rachel Cook.................   12-04-1811
Clayton, John - Rebeccah Johnson............   12-19-1799
Clayton, John - Sarah Emley.................    2-22-1802
Clayton, John J. - Mrs. Alitia Hulshart.....    7-01-1826
Clayton, Jonathan - Ann Longstreet..........   11-14-1830
Clayton, Jonathan - Rachel Cook.............    8-08-1810
Clayton, Joseph - Mary Manes................    5-06-1797
Clayton, Joseph son of John - Mary Perrine
   dg. of Joseph...........................    1-02-1825
Clayton, Joseph (wid'r) - Nelly Hankinson...   12-11-1797
Clayton, Peter - Eleanor Conk...............    2-26-1842
Clayton, Peter - Elsey Stout................    8-15-1804
Clayton. Peter - Hannah Cook................   10-05-1817
Clayton, Richard - Phebe Emmons.............    2-24-1822
Clayton, Stephen - Hannah Simison...........    9-03-1829
Clayton, Thomas - Alice Jewell..............   11-26-1825
Clayton, Thomas - Mary Throckmorton.........   12-14-1826
Clayton, Thomas - Prudence Longstreet.......   10-06-1806
Clayton, Thomas - Rachel Dennis.............    5-12-1823
Clayton, Thomas - Ruhama Sempoor............    3-22-1838
Clayton, Thompson - Hannah Ann Herbert......    1-14-1836
Clayton, Watson - Deborah Polemus...........    3-20-1837
Clayton, William - Deborah Jackson..........    3-23-1805
Clayton, William - Eleanor Vorhees..........    5-18-1833
Clayton, William - Hannah Vancleaf..........    3-08-1827
Clayton, Zebulon - Eliza James..............    4-07-1818
Clayton, Zebulon - Elizabeth Asburn.........   12-27-1808
Clearman, John - Nancy Vanderveer...........    5-01-1805
Clevenger, Barzil - Ann Steelman............    4-30-1797
Clevenger, Joshua of Burlington Co., N. J. -
   Edith Larison...........................    1-19-1838
Clevenger, Thomas of Burlington Co., N. J. -
   Catherine Curtis........................    3-25-1832
Clevenger, Thomas - Mary Brown..............    9-23-1811
Clevenger, William - Margaret Blake.........   11-29-1805
Clifford, Jonathan - Rachel Brewer..........   10-29-1809
Climax, Gaspard - Jane Arrent...............    9-06-1842
Clinton, Peter - Mary Lyons.................    3-11-1813
Clinton, Reuben - Jane Slocum...............    9-22-1842
Clonk, William (Cap't.) - Sarah Moore.......    2-27-1839
Coal, William - Elizabeth Jones.............    1-17-1825
Cocheran, Israel - Harriet Slaigh...........    7-07-1832
Cochrane, George of N. Y. - J. Wallace......    4-06-1841
Cocks, Job - Mary Ware......................    9-11-1839
Coffman, Benjamin - Rebecca Smith...........    9-05-1796
Coggins, Harris - Caroline Vancleaf.........   11-28-1842
Cole, Abner - Rachel Hendrickson
   (both black)............................    8-27-1832
Cole, Daniel - Euphame Tinney...............    9-13-1798
Cole, George - Ann Dillin...................    9-25-1823
```

```
Cole, George A. - Mary Cole................. 1-06-1827
Cole, Hartshorn - Phebe Errickson........... 4-06-1816
Cole, James - Catherine Longstreet.......... 2-07-1822
Cole, John - Gertrude Luft both of
    Middlesex Co. N. J...................... 7-04-1838
Cole, John - Nancy Newland.................. 9-17-1799
Cole, Joseph - Mary Ann Emmons.............. 12-20-1823
Cole, Orin - Catherine Remine............... 12-22-1832
Cole, Samuel - Caroline Conover (both black). 4-08-1828
Coleman, James - Theodocia Hutchinson....... 3-13-1828
Coleman, William - Rachael Giberson......... 11-23-1831
Coll, James - Rachel Mauris................. 4-17-1797
Colliers, George - Lucy Parent.............. 12-31-1828
Collins, Benjamin - Mariah Mills............ 8-19-1821
Collins, Charles - T. Herring............... 12-03-1842
Collins, George - Rebecca Warren............ 7-12-1813
Collins, James - Elizabeth Harkell.......... 2-08-1827
Collins, Job - Teresa Smith................. 1-22-1832
Collins, Joseph of Kentucky -
    Margaret Jackson........................ 9-04-1836
Collins, Zebulon - Esther Wilson............ 11-20-1824
Combs, Aaron - Hannah Vandeveer............. 8-25-1830
Combs, Benjamin F. - Esther Arrant.......... 3-10-1825
Combs, Elijah - Rebecca Reed................ 8-16-1797
Combs, Ezekiel - Elizabeth Shatterthite..... 3-03-1802
Combs, George H. - Sarah Johnstone.......... 4-11-1842
Combs, Joel H. - Pheobe Williams............ 2-22-1827
Combs, Jonathan - Rebecca Clayton........... 3-10-1818
Combs, Joseph - Catherine Schenck........... 9-23-1816
Combs, Joseph - Lydia Gorden................ 1-07-1823
Combs, Joseph - Mary Patterson.............. 1-03-1818
Combs, Joseph - Matildah Woodhull........... 9-21-1836
Combs, Lewis - Rebeccah Sylcox.............. 2-04-1802
Combs, Robert - Lydia Curtice............... 1-13-1816
Combs, Solomon - Catherine Conover.......... 11-08-1797
Combs, Stephen - Deborah Herbert............ 10-01-1814
Combs, Thomas - Jerusah Wainwright.......... 12-31-1801
Comley, John - Mary Patterson............... 4-14-1821
Compton, David - Mary A Dewit............... 4-13-1830
Compton, James - Rebeca Hankins............. 1-14-1830
Compton, John - Eliza Davis................. 2-19-1823
Compton, Joseph - Patience Garrison......... 10-01-1811
Compton, Joseph - Sarah Davis............... 2-19-1823
Compton, William - Rebecca Primmer.......... 4-01-1807
Conaro, Joseph - Sarah Newman............... 3-10-1829
Conck, Anthony - Margaret Johnson........... 3-03-1807
Conck, John - Sarah Richmond................ 9-19-1800
Conck, Stephen - Hannah Pearce.............. 3-28-1818
Conck, William - Ann Stricklin.............. 1-08-1813
Congo, Samuel - Hannah Nixon................ 10-20-1821
Conine, Henry - Sarah Combs................. 3-09-1814
Conine, John - Elizabeth Bennet............. 12-22-1824
Conine, John - Rachel Bennet................ 12-11-1816
Conk, A. - Adelaid Miller................... 8-30-1837
Conk, Daniel - Phebe Cottrell............... 6-27-1835
```

```
Conk, John - Merriby Heirs................... 12-07-1832
Conk, Johnathan - Adaline Morris............. 8-04-1839
Conk, Thomas - Willampe Emens................ 7-23-1808
Conklin, John - Mary Fielder................. 8-26-1841
Conklin, Peter - Levina Soper................ 7-07-1808
Conkling, Benjamin - Mary Inman.............. 3-24-1825
Conkling, Benjamin - Sarah Inmen............. 2-20-1821
Conkling, Caleb - Elizabeth Predmore......... 6-27-1801
Conkling, John Jr. - Elizabeth Cramer........ 4-15-1802
Connely, Patrick - Sarah Foster.............. 10-02-1797
Connett, Matthew - Mary Gifford.............. 2-01-1810
Connroe, Jacob - Mary Bruere................. 1-08-1829
Conover, Aaron - Frenchy Conover............. 12-28-1826
Conover, Aron - Susan Bray................... 11-08-1814
Conover, Arthur - Eliza Ann Vanderveer....... 10-06-1831
Conover, Barnes - Amelia Kelehan............. 8-21-1830
Conover, Benjamin - Allas Buckalew........... 7-04-1801
Conover, Benjamin - Ellen Herbert............ 2-06-1809
Conover, Benjamin - Margaret Forman.......... 1-09-1806
Conover, Cornelius - Debrough Morris......... 1-28-1835
Conover, Cornelius - Joannah Rogers.......... 11-08-1826
Conover, Daniel - Mary M.Smith............... 8-06-1833
Conover, Daniel G. - Ann Fields.............. 5-20-1832
Conover, David C. - Lois Errickson........... 3-25-1830
Conover, David G. - Ann Mount................ 8-11-1816
Conover, Elias - Ann Schenck (both black).... 8-16-1834
Conover, G. H. - Gertrude Vanderbilt......... 1821
Conover, Garret - Tenssq Reed................ 9-27-1836
Conover, Garret H. - Sarah Gordon............ 6-25-1810
Conover, Hendrick - Ann Crawford............. 3-21-1805
Conover, Hendrick - Mary Barcalow............ 12-23-1834
Conover, Hendrick - Mary Holmes.............. 1-25-1821
Conover, Holmes - Caroline Crawford.......... 3-03-1841
Conover, Isaac - Elletter Bennet............. 3-20-1828
Conover, Jacob - Eleanor Smock............... 11-13-1816
Conover, Jacob - Elener Van Deveer........... 6-15-1836
Conover, Jacob - Elizabeth Stout............. 1- 1828
Conover, Jacob - Rebecca Hopping............. 3-24-1823
Conover, James - Sarah Hopping............... 3-14-1833
Conover, John - Ann Magill................... 3-03-1842
Conover, John - Elizabeth Emmons............. 9-16-1814
Conover, John - Ellen Peacock................ 3-17-1821
Conover, John - Mary A. Haight............... 12-19-1815
Conover, John B. - Eliza Baird............... 6-07-1810
Conover, John C. - Elizabeth Veenderbelt..... 12-03-1821
Conover, John W. - Anna Walk................. 11-05-1821
Conover, John W. - Rebecca M. Ely............ 12-12-1827
Conover, Joseph - Ellie Laird................ 11-29-1808
Conover, Joseph - Marian Taylor
    (both black)............................. 12-24-1833
Conover, Joseph - Ruth Jaques................ 2-02-1809
Conover, Cornelius L. - Phebe Winter......... 9-06-1835
Conover, Levi - Deborah Conover.............. 3-20-1807
Conover, Martinus - Jane Covenhoven.......... 1-10-1804
Conover, Mathais - Ann Schenck............... 4-18-1821
```

```
Conover, Peter - Delilah Hulett..............  6-24-1826
Conover, Peter - Mary Parent.................  4-20-1837
Conover, Peter - Rebecca Conover.............  11-15-1832
Conover, Peter H. - Mary Rue.................  2-17-1799
Conover, Peter H. (wid'r) - Patience Scott...  5-19-1816
Conover, James R. - Hannah Shepherd..........  1-27-1823
Conover, Rulif - Elenor Vancleaf.............  12-01-1822
Conover, Ruliff - Maria Van Cleave...........  4-21-1814
Conover, Ruliff G. - Jane Drummond...........  1-17-1828
Conover, Ruloff - Maria Van Cleve............  4-21-1814
Conover, Samuel - Mary Platt.................  1-23-1830
Conover, Tunis M. - Rebecca Conover..........  5-19-1830
Conover, Wikoff - Ely Craig..................  10-27-1812
Conover, William - Ann Clayton...............  4-11-1842
Conover, William - Arintha Schenck...........  2-05-1817
Conover, William - Charlotte Baker...........  2-08-1839
Conover, William - Deborah Mater.............  1-13-1831
Conover, William of New York City -
    Elizabeth Vallentine.....................  1-31-1838
Conover, William - Hannah Chambers...........  2-16-1803
Conover, William - Margaret Vorhees..........  1-05-1832
Conover, William - Mary E. Reed..............  9-27-1838
Conover, William - Sarah Lemman..............  12-15-1840
Conroe, Darlies - Susannah Hurley............  6-15-1807
Conrow, Charles - Maria Sutphen..............  2-27-1834
Conrow, Clayton - Eliza I. Vanarsdale........  2-29-1840
Conrow, Darnling - Abiel Morton..............  8-19-1802
Conrow, John - Mary Vannote..................  3-25-1830
Conrow, John D. Sarah Stillwell..............  5-24-1829
Conrow, Levi - Ann Cook......................  10-05-1833
Conrow, Thomas - Amelia McQueen..............  12-29-1831
Conrow, William - Sarah Covert...............  1-07-1829
Cook, Aaron Sr. - Sarah Gordon...............  4-27-1811
Cook, Benjamin - Margaret Buckalew...........  8-10-1796
Cook, Edward - Elizabeth Rively..............  1-22-1816
Cook, Edward - Sarah Jones...................  10-14-1804
Cook, Enoch - Prudence Chadwick..............  8-26-1840
Cook, Fennel - Susannah Patterson............  10-24-1827
Cook, George - Ann Runyan....................  1-18-1823
Cook, George - Mary Davis....................  11-15-1828
Cook, James - Hannah Wardell.................  11-02-1831
Cook, James - Mary Newbury...................  4-12-1810
Cook, James - Mary Williamson................  6-14-1817
Cook, Jessee - Deborah West..................  11-02-1839
Cook, Jessee - Elizabeth Harris..............  1-07-1810
Cook, John - Ann Heuston.....................  5-22-1813
Cook, John - Catherine Gaston................  12-04-1811
Cook, John - Eliza Jones.....................  1-16-1828
Cook, John - Esther Brand....................  2-23-1809
Cook, John - Mrs. Molly Morris...............  3-21-1812
Cook, John D. - Maria Flinn..................  8-10-1836
Cook, Joseph - Anny Frazee...................  11-25-1820
Cook, Joseph - Elizabeth Applegate...........  10-18-1825
Cook, Joseph - Fanny White...................  10-14-1834
Cook, Joseph - Jane Cook.....................  4-19-1815
```

```
Cook, Joseph - Lydia Maxson.................  2-14-1835
Cook, Morris - Ann I. Herbert...............  2-18-1838
Cook, Nathaniel - Miraba Jackson............  3-02-1797
Cook, Nicholas - Rebeca Thompson............  9-25-1823
Cook, Peter - Catherine Stilwell............ 12-28-1797
Cook, Peter of N. Y. - Polly Dennis.........  3-08-1797
Cook, Peter - Theresa Hagerty...............  8-02-1837
Cook, Samuel - Mary Britton................. 10-09-1815
Cook, Silas - Susannah Austin...............  3-17-1805
Cook, Simeon - Beule Taber..................  2-03-1803
Cook, Stephen - Deborah Woordell............  2-05-1825
Cook, Thomas - Contented John...............  9-15-1799
Cook, Thomas - Lydia Longstreet.............  2-13-1820
Cook, Tucker - Nancy Edward.................  2-27-1817
Cook, William - Abigail Edwards.............  5-09-1805
Cook, William - Gemima Seaman............... 12-08-1811
Cook, William - Mary Chadwick...............  3-20-1800
Cook, William - Rebecca Wardell............. 12-22-1841
Cool, Allen - Deborah Woolley...............  3-28-1842
Cool, David - Margaret Noble................  3-18-1835
Cool, Edward of N. Y. - Mary Reboll......... 11-28-1842
Cool, John - Hannah Reynold.................  3-05-1836
Cool, Joseph - Susanna Prise................  4-21-1834
Cool, Thomas - Alphia Longstreet............  2-06-1840
Cool, Thomas - Jane Robinson................ 10-  -1817
Cool, William of Trenton, N. J. -
    Elizabeth Warrell......................  1-04-1834
Cooley, Ely (Rev.) - Catherine B. Henderson..  9-03-1818
Cooper, Benjamin - Hannah Woolley...........  9-21-1833
Cooper, Benjamin - Rebecca Tilton...........  9-25-1816
Cooper, Benjamin B. - Sarah Vanmater........  9-26-1811
Cooper, David - Elizabeth Wilber............  3-02-1821
Cooper, David - Sarah Ketchem...............  6-22-1799
Cooper, Francis - Catherine Layton.......... 12-18-1803
Cooper, Francis - Elizabeth Borden..........  5-05-1821
Cooper, George - Maria Michean..............  5-26-1816
Cooper, George - Sarah Herbert..............  9-02-1832
Cooper, Granding - Ellen Francis............  2-20-1830
Cooper, Jacob - Hannah Davis................  4-03-1821
Cooper, Jacob - Mary Gifford................ 11-01-1832
Cooper, James - Mary Reynolds............... 12-13-1834
Cooper, James - Rebecca Paterson............  3-17-1829
Cooper, John - Ida Taylor................... 12-20-1810
Cooper, John - Mary Parker.................. 12-26-1812
Cooper, Jonathan - Sarah Morris.............  2-22-1810
Cooper, Joseph - Anna Leonard...............  7-11-1798
Cooper, Joseph - Martha Stillwell...........  2-05-1815
Cooper, Joseph - Prudence Lewis.............  1-11-1807
Cooper, Lloyd - Mary Ann Lewis..............  5-20-1832
Cooper, Obed - Letty Vanpelt................  4-27-1827
Cooper, Peter - Amie Conke..................  9-05-1801
Cooper, Phillip - Eliza Riddle..............  8-18-1821
Cooper, Samuel - Elizabeth Stillwell........  8-18-1801
Cooper, Samuel - Rachel Woolley.............  4-10-1828
Cooper, Thomas - Rebecca Ackenson........... 12-29-1825
```

```
Cooper, William - Lucy White................. 12-20-1834
Cooper, William - Mary Ann Woolley........... 3-14-1832
Coovert, David - Catherine Yetman............ 7-30-1838
Coovert, Ebenezer Albert -
    Gitty Ann Roberts....................... 5-22-1840
Cord, John Jurden - Elizabeth Davison........ 11-20-1810
Corlies, Benjamin A. - Caroline White........ 12-23-1825
Corlies, Jacob - Elizabeth Corlies........... 2-14-1801
Corlies, Jacob Jr. - Hannah Usteck........... 5-20-1824
Corlies, John - Caroline Conover............. 1-02-1842
Corlies, John - Charlotte Bogart............. 3-09-1830
Corlies, John - Deborah Cook................. 6-14-1840
Corlies, Joseph - Gertrude A. Hampton........ 7-30-1834
Corlies, William - Nancy Corlies............. 11-20-1802
Corlis, Jacob - Prudence Pearce.............. 2-06-1825
Corlis, James - Mary Remer................... 11-12-1835
Corlis, Joseph - Mary Cramer................. 12-01-1815
Corlis, Seth - Elizabeth Ginnings............ 1-02-1822
Corlis, Stacy - Blumer Headley............... 12-26-1819
Corlis, Uriah - Elizabeth Huett.............. 11-05-1801
Corlius, Samuel - Letty Labour............... 8-16-1817
Cornelius, Frances - M. Leming............... 7-15-1825
Cornelius, George - Lydia Jefery............. 1-20-1821
Cornelius, John - Harriet Hutchinor.......... 2-20-1840
Cornelius, John Jr. - Sarah Bower............ 1-20-1827
Corsart, Abner of Essex Co., N. J. -
    Catherine Stout......................... 4-23-1832
Cortis, John - Nancy Corlies................. 12-20-1801
Coster, James - Catherine Applegate.......... 5-12-1827
Cotrel, Gersham - Sarah Layton............... 1-04-1822
Cotrell, Richard - Anne Hankins.............. 9-25-1803
Cotrell, William - Elizabeth McGee........... 6-16-1802
Cottale, William - Lucy Woodward............. 10-16-1828
Cottel, Samuel - Deliverance Rogers.......... 10-01-1834
Cottell, Garret - Rachel Lewis............... 12-25-1832
Cotter, Andrew - Sarah Worth................. 3-21-1832
Cotteral, Abraham - Sarah Vanderhoff......... 4-06-1807
Cotteral, John T. - Ann Cook................. 4-17-1817
Cotteral, Joseph - Ann Stillwell............. 11-06-1830
Cotteral, Reuben - Martha Hall............... 1-17-1806
Cotterall, John I. - Mary Bennet............. 1-17-1826
Cotterall, John F. - Mary Cook............... 1-17-1826
Cotterall, Nimrod - Rebeh Anderson........... 10-26-1822
Cotterell, Joseph son of George Jr. -
    Catherine Hendrickson dg. of Joseph dec'd 12-08-1824
Cottrel, Gesham - June Emmos................. 5-17-1796
Cottrel, James - Ann Van Pelt................ 2-10-1800
Cottrel, Samuel - Abigail Buckelew........... 1-25-1794
Cottrell, David - Alice Anderson............. 12-30-1835
Cottrell, David - Martha Myres............... 4-30-1840
Cottrell, Enoch - Catherine Campbell......... 4-26-1836
Cottrell, George - Elizabeth Anderson........ 10-06-1811
Cottrell, George - Mary Gaston............... 5-25-1835
Cottrell, James - Catherine Layton........... 1-30-1814
Cottrell, James - Ellis Hance................ 6-01-1824
```

```
Cottrell, Job - Hannah Harris...............     5-20-1812
Cottrell, William - Hellen Yetman...........     4-09-1836
Countrey, John - Hannah Elberson............     5-01-1819
Couser, Theodore - Sarah Minna..............     1-28-1841
Covenhoven, Albert - Elizabeth Shepherd......   12-27-1796
Covenhoven, Cornelius - Margaret Hans........   11-26-1797
Covenhoven, Cornelius - Mary Stoutenborough..    3-09-1807
Covenhoven, David - Sarah Ann Cooper.........   12-16-1818
Covenhoven, Ebenezer - Mary Jefferson........   12-17-1807
Covenhoven, Elias - Mary Schenck.............    7-01-1798
Covenhoven, Garret - Maria Schenck...........   12-14-1814
Covenhoven, Garret - Ruth Stout..............    1-31-1796
Covenhoven, Garret - Sarah Covenhoven........    5-13-1798
Covenhoven, Garret - Sarah Schenck...........    1-06-1807
Covenhoven, George - Mary Du Bois............    6-19-1815
Covenhoven, Jacob - Catherine Schenck........    9-26-1799
Covenhoven, Jacob - Mary Horsefield..........   11-29-1818
Covenhoven, Jacob - Polly Dorsett............    1-20-1796
Covenhoven, John - Ann Smock.................    2-08-1814
Covenhoven, John I. - Lydia Johnson..........   12-16-1807
Covenhoven, Joseph - Gertrude Conover........    3-03-1807
Covenhoven, Lewis - Catherin Denise..........    1-28-1806
Covenhoven, Peter - Mary Rue.................    2-17-1799
Covenhoven, Peter - Sophia Bois..............    3-19-1797
Covenhoven, Peter Forman - Jane Denise.......   11-27-1799
Covenhoven, Robert - Getty Sutfin............   11-26-1812
Covenhoven, Ruliff - Pamela Wallen...........    7-17-1809
Covenhoven, Theodorus - Rachel Webb..........   12-14-1805
Covenhoven, Timothy - Mary Woolley...........    2-28-1812
Covenhoven, Toiley - Maria Schenck...........   12-09-1812
Covenhoven, William - Catherine Zutphin......    1-18-1805
Covenhoven, William - Elizabeth Covenhoven...    9-15-1819
Covenhoven, William - Jane Davis.............   12-07-1805
Covenhoven, William - Jane Vanderveer........    2-19-1801
Covert, Daniel - Lydia Brinley...............   11-22-1804
Covert, Ebenezer - Sarah Haines..............    2-23-1803
Covert, James - Elizabeth Robert.............    8-05-1841
Covert, James - Mary Roats...................   11-13-1815
Covert, John - Elizabeth Johnston............    2-26-1823
Covert, Joseph - Catherine Lambertson........    2-19-1817
Covert, Peter - Emeline LLoyd................    4-11-1829
Covert, Richard - Charlotte Tallman..........   11-21-1815
Covert, Richard - Mary Lemmon................    5-25-1810
Covert, Richard - Mrs. Amy Rively............   12-05-1812
Covert, Thomas - Rhoda Wilson................    5-10-1842
Covert, William - Ann Eliza Compton..........   11-06-1842
Coverwand, William - Deborah Wooley..........    1-04-1800
Coward, Alexander - Jane A. Smires...........    9-06-1830
Coward, Clayton - Rebecca Hendrickson........   11-03-1807
Coward, Daniel - Betsey Rouse................   10-10-1799
Coward, Enoch - Ann Mariah Bowne.............    6-14-1836
Coward, Enoch - Elenor Dubois................    3-09-1806
Coward, Jacob - Sarah Thompson...............   10-31-1802
Coward, John - Eufame Lyell (both black).....    1-02-1814
Coward, Samuel - Elizabeth Taylor............    3-01-1821
```

```
Coward, Samuel - Elizabeth Walton............  1-03-1798
Coward, Thomas - Hannah Stout................ 10-20-1832
Coward, William - Isabel Knott............... 11-17-1811
Cowdrick, Alton - Ann Johnson................ 12-30-1820
Cowdrick, John S. - Jane Barcalow............  5-07-1825
Cowens, Joel - Elizabeth Reed................  3-22-1836
Cox, George - Francineka Hendrickson.........  3-04-1840
Cox, James - Elisa Robins.................... 12-27-1812
Cox, Jonathan - Rebeccah Burr................  5-01-1819
Cox, Joseph - Abigail Parker.................  3-15-1797
Cox, Oliver - Sarah Boice.................... 12-17-1832
Cox, Peter - Septima Calvin..................  2-17-1816
Cox, Sylvanus - Jemima Burr..................  3-24-1824
Cox, William - Mary Brown.................... 12-02-1812
Cox, William - Mary Wilcox...................  8-05-1824
Cox, William - Sarah Potts...................  9-11-1832
Coxtun, Joseph B. - Elizabeth Leaman.........  1-26-1837
Coye, William - Phebe Van Mater..............  9-29-1831
Crafford, John - Elizabeth Cramer............  2-07-1837
Craft, James - Susanna Moore.................  4-19-1797
Craft, Job - Ann Cox.........................  6-15-1810
Craig, Charles - Margaret Perrine............  9-08-1818
Craig, David - Elinor Conover................ 11-12-1804
Craig, David (Cap't.) - Margaret Wood........  9-19-1804
Craig, James - Lydia Conover.................  1-29-1821
Craig, Robert - Ann Perrine dg. of John......  7-29-1819
Craig, William - Eleaner Bishop
    both of Burlington Co., N.J..............  3-01-1838
Craig, William - Mary Walton.................  5-17-1808
Craige, William - Elizabeth Havens...........  4-25-1834
Cramer, Jesse of Burlington, Co. N. J. -
    Rebecca Lets.............................  8-11-1795
Cramer, Joseph - Emaline Jones...............  7-19-1828
Cramer, Isaiah - Hannah Whight...............  9-15-1811
Cramer, Richard - Elizabeth Frelon...........  5-17-1815
Cramer, Semer - Mary Goldsmith...............  3-26-1795
Cramer, Wilkison - Susan Gaskill............. 11-04-1803
Crammel, William - Yanne Bolling
    (both black).............................  5-29-1813
Crammell, Obediah - Sary King (both black)...  4-28-1821
Crammer, Abraham - Elizabeth Bowker..........  1-12-1815
Crammer, Alexander - Mary Salmons............ 10-06-1811
Crammer, Barzillah - Charity Alexander....... 12-14-1817
Crammer, Elias - Hannah Spragg...............  3-22-1821
Crammer, Isaiah - Rachall Randolph...........  8-17-1813
Crammer, James - Patty Woodmansee............  2-21-1822
Crammer, John - Jane Chamberlain.............  9-03-1797
Crammer, John - Malinda Price................  7-27-1842
Crammer, Joseph - Hannah Lamson.............. 10-08-1809
Crammer, Timothy - Julian Crammer............ 11-05-1809
Crammer, William - Elizabeth Weeb............  6-19-1819
Cramner, Elias - Hannah Sprag................  3-22-1821
Crane, Alvah of New York -
    Mrs. Rachel Willing...................... 10-23-1837
Crane, Henry Gardner - Hannah Kilpatrick.....  3-23-1807
```

```
Crane, Jesse - Keziah Letts..................  1-27-1816
Crane, John - Elizabeth Brown...............   3-23-1811
Crane, Nathan - Mary Brown..................   1-12-1795
Crane, Silas - Catherine Brower.............   9-08-1833
Crane, Silas - Eliza Stillwell..............   1-12-1823
Crane, William - Ann Salmer.................   6-06-1842
Crane, William - Sarah Greary...............   2-09-1815
Crane, William - Sarah Green................   2-  -1815
Cranmer, Clayton - Lois Southard............   1-08-1819
Cranmer, James - Elizabeth Nale.............   2-09-1843
Cranmer, John - Emma Giberson...............   1-13-1820
Cranmer, Isaiah - Amelia Willits............  10-05-1841
Cranmer, Presgrove - Charity Cranmer........   2-14-1842
Cranmer, Reuben - Rachel Willgas............   7-12-1818
Cranmer, Stacy - Massy Ware.................   9-18-1814
Cranmer, William - Ann Thorp................   4-15-1820
Cranmore, Richard - Mary Bowker.............   5-06-1818
Crawford, Andrew - Deborah Posty (wid.).....   9-11-1798
Crawford, David - Margaret Matthews.........   5-11-1822
Crawford, George - Elenor Schenck...........   1-27-1798
Crawford, Gigion - Sarah Burnett............  11-05-1797
Crawford, Gilbert - Amey Van Cleaf..........   8-25-1801
Crawford, John - Elizabeth Laten............   8-31-1820
Crawford, John B. - Katherine Crawford......   2-03-1825
Crawford, Joseph - Catherine Helsey.........  11-02-1812
Crawford, Richard - Elizabeth Wilbur........  12-21-1825
Crawford, Samuel - Rachel Thomson...........  12-02-1802
Crawford, Stephen - Ann Stout...............   4-18-1838
Crawford, William - Catherine Leighton......   2-03-1798
Crawford, William - Elizabeth Fields........   1-20-1833
Crawford, William - Leah Conover............   1-08-1834
Crawford, William - Zilpha Perrine..........   1-23-1841
Creeley, Jacob - Amy Soper..................   7-23-1832
Crocheron, Henry - Leah Stoutenborough......   6-27-1807
Crockerson, John S. of Alabama -
    Catherine Longstreet dg. of John........  11-16-1836
Croes, John J. (Rev.) - Eleanor Vanmater....  10-13-1812
Crofford, William - Catherine Leighton......   2-03-1798
Crofford, William - Mary Rouze..............  10-14-1815
Cromwell, Aaron - Rhoda Longstreet..........  11-28-1809
Cromwell, Amos - Delia Richardson
    (both black)............................   3-07-1831
Cromwell, Isaac of Burlington Co., N. J. -
    Harriet Minna...........................   9-25-1842
Cromwell, Juba - Sarah Quere (both black)...   7-31-1838
Cromwell, Oliver - Ann Pearce...............   9-20-1823
Cromwell, William - Parker Jude
    (both black)............................   4-18-1802
Cross, Caleb - Sarah Woolston...............   4-11-1833
Cross, Charles - Mary Ann Lewis.............  11-14-1840
Cross, Poinsett - Sarah Johnson.............  11-13-1796
Crossbey, George - Susan Ashley.............  12-28-1820
Crossman, Thomas - Ann Bucklew..............   6-27-1807
Crow, Thomas - Catherine Hopping............   1-25-1842
Crowther, Thomas - Catherine Price..........   3-28-1829
```

```
Croxen, William - Allice Corlies.............  1-27-1841
Croxon, Jonathan - Margaret Harent...........  2-09-1837
Croxon, Samuel - Elizabeth Forsyth........... 10-04-1834
Croxon, Thomas - Mrs. Susan Francis.........  4-04-1826
Croxon, William - Sarah Clayton..............  1-27-1801
Croyen, James - Phebe Casher.................  5-01-1833
Crucherson, Asberry - Jane Stotenborough..... 12-30-1821
Crum, Richard - Elizabeth Emmons.............  5-28-1823
Crumb, John - Mary Taylor....................  5-21-1812
Crumell, Jacob - Eliza Richardson............  5-24-1817
Crumin, Richard - Mary Brooks................  7-28-1831
Crummele, Isek - Patience Sullivan...........  2-08-1817
Crummell, Edward - Leah Stone................  2-04-1830
Crummell, Jacob - Friza Richardson..........  5-24-1817
Crune, John - Mary Taylor....................  5-21-1812
Cubberly, Ezekiel - Julia Ann Hughs.........  2-14-1828
Cubberly, James - Lucy Dancer................ 10-15-1829
Cubberly, John C. - Sarah Vannote............  2-15-1827
Cubberly, Samuel - Angelina Bailou........... 12-19-1839
Cubberly, Stephen - Elizabeth Ivers......... 10-10-1832
Cullin, Richard - Sarah Joseph...............  7-24-1832
Cummings, Joseph - Elizabeth Jones...........  3-12-1842
Cummings, Patrick - Hannah Morris (wid.).....  7-31-1829
Cummings, Robert - Emma Fresty Forman........  5-13-1808
Curtice, Thomas - Ann Oatman.................  4-24-1824
Curtis, David - Content Truax................  3-31-1831
Curtis, James - Sarah Chapman................  6-01-1816
Curtis, John - Catherine Johnson............. 10-31-1839
Curtis, John - Lydia Pearce..................  1-20-1817
Curtis, John C. - Jane Pearce................ 12-19-1839
Curtis, Samuel - Clarey Chadwick.............  6-04-1808
Curtis, Samuel - Margaret Britton...........  7-09-1810
Curtis, Thomas - Elizabeth Longstreet........  3-03-1831
Curtis, Thomas - Leadya Brand................ 11-24-1799
Curtis, Timothy - Rebecca Conrow.............  1-07-1831
Curtis, Walter - Ann Fowler................. 12-01-1825
Cuttrell, Enoch - Hannah -----...............  4-22-1819
Dailey, Patrick - Rebecca Mason.............. 11-12-1797
Dailey, Thomas C. - Fanny Hankins...........  9-04-1828
Dancer, Nathan - Elizabeth Radford..........  3-13-1827
Dancer, Ralph - Mary Hulett.................  3-16-1836
Dangler, Daniel - Mrs. Elizabeth Layton......  1-30-1813
Dangler, Garret - Catherine Layton.......... 12-27-1817
Dangler, Henry - Julian Covert..............  9-25-1824
Dangler, James - Lydia A. Jackson...........  8-03-1828
Dangler, John - Martha Saxton...............  6-09-1839
Dangler, John - Mary Luire.................. 11-26-1804
Dangler, John - Sarah Talman................  3-25-1810
Dangler, Leonard - Deborah Aumack............ 10-01-1828
Dangler, William - Deborah Lippencott........  1-10-1805
Dangler, William - Emilee Jackson........... 12-22-1842
Daniel, George M. - Rachel Challender of
     Burlington  Co., N. J...................  6-04-1826
Danile, John - Abigail Mires................  5-15-1795
```

```
Danley, John of Burlington Co. N. J. -
   Martha Reynold.......................... 6-27-1839
Dansburg, Samuel - Mary Ackel.............. 10-20-1811
Danser, Zachariah - Elizabeth Bucklew........ 2-19-1820
Dantassel, Barney - Deborah Morris........... 8-24-1816
Date, Daniel - Mary Ann Patterson............ 4-28-1833
Daubley, Charles - Sarah Camps............... 7-19-1812
Davidson, John - Mary Perrine................ 11-10-1842
Davis, Aaron - Margaret Mason................ 3-10-1824
Davis, Benjamin - Charity Burge.............. 7-24-1816
Davis, Edward T. - Elijah Saxton............. 2-24-1831
Davis, Isaac - Eleanor Laird................. 4-27-1820
Davis, Ivins - Mrs. Sarah Fiffer............. 12-13-1835
Davis, Jacob of Burlington County, N. J. -
   Ann Wilbur.............................. 4-29-1837
Davis, James - Eleanor Rap................... 12-07-1839
Davis, John - Lidia Morris................... 4-13-1826
Davis, John D. - Dounder Forman.............. 3-12-1823
Davis, Louis - Hannah Hardy.................. 7-14-1841
Davis, Obediah - Mary Morris................. 5-15-1833
Davis, Richard - Lydia Johnson............... 3-13-1839
Davis, Thomas - Phebe Forman................. 1-04-1819
Davis, Tunis - Sarah Fiffer.................. 12-13-1835
Davis, William - Catherine Combs............. 2-06-1808
Davis, William - Elizabeth Jeffery........... 12-12-1801
Davis, William - Phebe Duell................. 2-28-1837
Davison, Daniel - Mary Maxon................. 7-31-1811
Davison, Daniel - Susanna Sherp.............. 11-07-1811
Davison, Garret - Anna Lloyd................. 5-09-1810
Davison, George - Mary Goodenough............ 12-08-1841
Davison, George - Rebecca Kerly.............. 9-28-1836
Davison, James - Jane Gaston................. 2-12-1818
Davison, James - Lecretia Johnson............ 2-12-1812
Davison, John - Jane Davison................. 2-23-1826
Davison, John - Rafe Snediker................ 2-28-1797
Davison, John - Susannah Forman.............. 4-15-1814
Davison, Joseph - Moicah Reed................ 1-08-1806
Davison, Lewis - Mary Conk................... 12-02-1837
Davison, Peter - Elizabeth Jackson........... 11-25-1825
Davison, Richard - Rebecah Jackson........... 5-20-1819
Davison, William - Amelia Lennon............. 10-17-1839
Davison, William - Ann Herbert............... 2-27-1840
Davison, William - Elizabeth Vancleve........ 6-13-1802
Davison, William - Margaret Miller........... 8-29-1825
Davey, James - Nancy Taylor.................. 4-23-1803
Dawdney, Wilbur - Ann Woolley................ 3-22-1832
Day, William son of William -
   Jane Perine dg. of Peter................ 10-05-1796
Dayton, Nathaniel - Charlott Smith of
   Middlesex Co., N. J..................... 4-21-1839
Deacon, Job - Rebecca Wolston................ 5-29-1810
Dearce, David - Rhoda Bray................... 12-30-1824
Debow, John - Ann Dey....................... 1-25-1820
Debow, John - Ann Laird..................... 12-10-1811
Debow, John - Lydia Morse................... 8-06-1838
```

```
Debrough, William - Hannah Hunter...........    3-04-1839
De Camp, James - Susan Grant................    1-01-1831
De Camp, John - Martha Shinn................    8-15-1824
Decampt, Job - Mary Horner..................    4-04-1813
Decannon, Robert L. - Sarah Richardson
   (both black)............................    9-08-1822
Deen, James - Mary Dunnison.................    8-12-1809
De Grant, Alfred - Amelia Manuel
   (both black)............................    9-04-1840
Degrout, John - Margaret Harvey.............    4-14-1829
De Hart, Lewis - Ann Williams (both black)...   6-25-1821
Delatush, John - Martha Sutkins.............   10-31-1833
Delavan, Hiram - Lydia Maxon................   10-17-1807
Dellevan, Asa - Sarah Leonarde..............    7-29-1827
Demerest, John - Rebecca Horner.............    2-15-1826
Demmehay, Thomas - Abigail Lewis............    4-22-1809
Denice, John - Catherine Thompson...........    2-03-1819
Denice, Samuel - Jane Brown.................    3-08-1815
Denise, Sidney - Anne Covenhoven............   11-18-1806
Denise, Teunis - Elizabeth Diddle...........   11-30-1799
Denise, William - Eleanor Tennent Schenck....  11-23-1802
Dennaker, Joseph - Lavinea Heaveland........   11-06-1830
Dennis, Anthony - Elizabeth Huston..........    5-14-1828
Denise, Daniel - Ann Wikoff.................    2-27-1816
Denise, Daniel - Mary Stilwell..............    3-15-1806
Denise, Denise - Aaltie Hulse...............    9-28-1818
Dennise, Edward - Mary Dunsee...............   11-12-1814
Dennis, Isaac - Zelpha Dangler..............    1-22-1829
Dennis, Jacob - Catherine Jackson...........    9-30-1822
Dennis, Jacob - Esther Borden...............    3-29-1835
Dennis, Jacob - Mary Borden.................   12-23-1797
Dennis, Jacob - Rebecca Williamson..........    9-04-1796
Dennis, John - Lydia Esla...................   11-03-1795
Dennis, Joseph - Ellen West.................   10-02-1824
Dennis, Peter C. - Esther Truax.............   11-16-1825
Dennis, Philip - Lydia King.................    5-27-1841
Dennis, Phillip - Charity Cook..............    5-14-1810
Dennis, Samuel - Lydia Chamberlin...........    3-02-1820
Dennis, Samuel of Burlington Co., N. J. -
   Martha Cook.............................    5-07-1831
Dennis, William - Mary Patterson............   12-30-1827
Dennis, William - Nancy Taylor..............    4-21-1799
Denton, George - Rachel Brown...............    1-01-1811
Denyse, Garret - Elizabeth Vanderhaige......   12-25-1841
Deremus, Francis - Phebe Smith..............   12-24-1808
Dern, John - Sarah Hoffman..................    8-15-1796
Derrick, Andrew - Elenor McDee..............    8-18-1842
Dervies, Seloester V. - Catherine Van Derveer  2-10-1799
Despreaux, Lewis - Charlotte Leonard........    7-31-1827
Despreaux, Michael - Mary Eldridge..........    8-01-1813
Devenne, Ephraim - Elizabeth Mick...........   11-22-1808
Devine, Samuel - Catherine Harvey...........    2-16-1818
Devinne, Richard - Elizabeth Burdon.........    1-27-1800
Devinney, Daniel - Phebe Taylor.............    2-02-1843
Devinney, Isaac - Mary Starkey..............    1-25-1797
```

```
Dewert, Joseph - Mary Carson................  4-22-1836
Dexter, Newton Of New York - Lydia Cool......  11-15-1840
Dey, Benjamin - Ann Walton...................  2-25-1819
Dey, Charles B. - Sarah Fleming..............  2-17-1836
Dey, Daniel - Lydia Perine...................  1-11-1802
Dey, Frederick - Sarah Voorheez..............  2-  -1840
Dey, Jacobs - Poline Peron...................  8-27-1826
Dey, James - Catherine Whitlock..............  1-12-1822
Dey, John - Lydia Bailey.....................  1-03-1822
Dey, John L. - Sarah Freehern (wid.).........  1-28-1818
Dey, Joseph - Ann Huley......................  3-01-1817
Dey, Joseph - Elizabeth -----................  12-12-1811
Dey, Lewis - Catherine Stilewell.............  9-10-1806
Dey, Matthew R. - Achsah Herbert.............  1-24-1822
Dey, Peter - Sally Rue.......................  2-03-1843
Dey, William - Jane Laird....................  3-24-1810
Dey, William - Nancy Bucklew.................  6-02-1814
Dickeson, Nathaniel - Sarah Burdge...........  5-14-1797
Dillen, Charles - Ann Cole...................  10-05-1833
Dillin, John - Keturah Cale..................  9-03-1820
Dillon, Randalph - Priscilla South...........  5-23-1829
Disbrow, John - Elizabeth Applegate..........  7-08-1802
Disbury, Joseph - Susannah Brown.............  10-23-1819
Divine, John - Jane Harvey...................  9-27-1803
Dodge, Samuel - Lydia Lowden.................  6-24-1804
Donaldson, William - Eliza Bills.............  12-01-1832
Donelly, Benjamin - Rebecca Smith............  1809-1811
Donelly, William - Ellenor Wert..............  1-24-1811
Dorset, Joseph - Maria Schenck...............  10-27-1805
Dorset, Joseph - Sarah Ogborn................  4-09-1805
Dorsett, Benjamin - Cornelia Dennis..........  3-19-1811
Doty, John - Eliza Bennet....................  11-09-1841
Doughty, Christopher - Delean Herbert........  3-12-1829
Doughty, Christopher - Elizabeth Smith.......  1-16-1824
Doughty, John - Fanny Chamberlin.............  7-11-1806
Doughty, John - Mrs. Huldah Louise Chandler..
   recorded..................................  11-08-1832
Dover, Edward Feeney - Hannah Applegate......  8-28-1808
Down, Ephraim - Elizabeth Burk...............  2-25-1842
Down, James - Ann Anderson...................  11-17-1810
Downs, Charles (Rev.) - Mary M. Simpson......  7-22-1842
Drake, Charles - Lucy Clayton................  11-29-1828
Driskey, Samuel - Mary Algor.................  8-04-1813
Drum, William - Nancy Aumack.................  4-10-1808
Drummond, Benjamin - Mrs. Mary Tallman.......  5-04-1829
Drummond, John - Hannah Williams.............  11-26-1802
Drummond, John C. - Harriet Brindley.........  3-01-1821
DuBois, Benjamin - Willampe Vandorn..........  2-16-1803
DuBois, Charles - Elenore Vandeveer..........  3-02-1803
DuBois, Daniel - Elizabeth Cowenhoven........  2-09-1803
DuBois, David - Rachel Rue...................  1-29-1834
DuBois, Tunis of Ohio - Elizabeth Smock
   dg. of Aaron..............................  4-09-1831
DuBois, Tunis D. - Sarah Vanderveer..........  12-22-1796
DuBois, Teunis D. - Sarah Smock..............  3-07-1807
```

```
Dull, Isaac - Ann Moore...................... 10-11-1834
Dunahey, Thomas - Phebe Patterson............ 9-17-1842
Duncan, Frances W. - Margaret Hernahan....... 5-05-1833
Duncan, William - Mrs. Jane Estory of
    Newburgh, N. Y........................... 8-21-1825
Dunfee, John Jr. - Pemelia Lee............... 11-27-1828
Dunfey, Charles - Ann Forman................. 2-09-1833
Dunhun, Samuel - Angeline Rabin.............. 7-03-1840
Dunkin, George - Jane Stilwell............... 10-01-1815
Dunlope, Joseph - Margaret Little............ 6-17-1827
Dunphey, John - Ann Groff.................... 10-23-1841
Dunphy, Robert - Mary Ann Norman............. 1-19-1843
Dunston, James - Amanda Burr................. 10-07-1829
Duright, Samuel - Abigail Revy (both black).. 10-15-1798
Dushey, Stephen - Mary Lukne................. 2-11-1826
Duty, Joseph - Lydia Little.................. 12-01-1817
Dwight, Samuel - Abigail Revy................ 12-16-1826
Dye, David - Mary Bennet..................... 11-21-1798
Dye, Eli - Eliza Hughes...................... 1-08-1824
Dye, Eli - Lucy Rogers...................... 7-13-1826
Dye, Henry - Winchy Updyke.................. 12-31-1826
Dykeman, Robert - Susan Wooley.............. 10-26-1815
Ealey, John - Deborah Shibla................ 2-11-1830
Ealy, William - Abagael Van Hese............ 1-26-1829
Earl, Thomas T. - Abigail B. Holmes......... 11-28-1816
Eastborn, Thomas - Ann White................ 1805
Easton, Isaac - Peace Chadwick.............. 2-18-1798
Eastwood, Enos - Louisa Renthaw............. 9-15-1831
Eastwood, Lewis - Emeline Wykoff............ 1-30-1836
Eastwood, Nathaniel - Mrs. Phebe A. Shearman. 11-04-1826
Ebertson, Thomas - Levina Wells............. 4-19-1817
Edmond, John - Elizabeth Applegate.......... 3-30-1834
Edmond, Tyler - Charlotte William........... 10-23-1838
Edmond, William - Nancy Taylor.............. 11-06-1819
Edwards, Benjamin - Juliann Bailey.......... 2-27-1822
Edwards, Brittain - Margaret West........... 1-26-1798
Edwards, Daniel - Aneliza Iseble............ 9-02-1833
Edwards, Daniel - Dinah Sutphin............. 9-07-1831
Edwards, Daniel - Nancy Wardell............. 5-12-1800
Edwards, George - Hannah Wills.............. 2-13-1826
Edwards, Henry - Phebe Jolene............... 12-25-1833
Edwards, Hyers - Ann Barnes................. 5-03-1806
Edwards, James - Elizabeth Parker........... 3-23-1836
Edwards, James - Sarah Morris............... 1-01-1811
Edwards, Job - Nancy Slaught................ 4-23-1825
Edwards, John - Amy Jermison................ 9-05-1835
Edwards, Joseph - Amy Johnson............... 1-18-1825
Edwards, Joseph - Harriet Dye............... 4-01-1806
Edwards, Taylor - Margaret Brinley.......... 1-03-1824
Edwards, Thomas - Easter Clayton............ 9-23-1829
Edwards, Webley - Idea Brown................ 11-19-1836
Edwards, William - Margaret Bowers.......... 3-08-1802
Egbert, James - Eliza Edwards............... 6-30-1830
Egbert, James - Mrs. Sarah Schooley......... 6-15-1834
Egbert, William - Hannah Abraham............ 6-14-1798
```

Eggbert, Owen J. - Lois Hill................. 9-08-1825
Eggbert, William - Mary Herbert.............. 5-08-1829
Eire, W. Abram - Mary Irons.................. 2-04-1811
Elberson, Joseph - Rachel Lett.............. 4-15-1820
Eldridge, Abraham - Theodocia Neelson........ 3-01-1838
Eldridge, Ely - Rebecca Potter.............. 12-12-1827
Eley, James of Trenton, N. J. -
    Rebecca Wells........................... 1-31-1807
Eley, William - Rebecca VanMatter............ 1-02-1822
Elley, Joseph - Catherine Tapscott........... 12-13-1798
Elliot, Thomas - Elizabeth Coward............ 5-03-1807
Elliot, William - MaryAnn Wikoff............. 8-27-1846
Ellis, James - Eleanor Clayton.............. 7-14-1833
Ellis, John Jr. - Elizabeth Tilton........... 2-05-1810
Ellis, Rollen - Catherine Vanderveer......... 10- -1831
Ellison, David - Rebecca Snyder.............. 10-25-1804
Ellison, Jackson - Elizabeth Craver.......... 3-02-1842
Ellison, James - Hannah Pearce.............. 2-27-1798
Elmer, Isaac - Getty Wooley................. 2-05-1827
Elmer, Isaac - Sarah Robinson.............. 1-27-1816
Elmer, John - Sarah Jones................... 12-31-1823
Elmer, Ryley - Lydia Pearce................. 2-27-1841
Ely, Allison - Lydia E. Thompson............ 5-17-1823
Ely, David - Anne Gravatt................... 7-29-1840
Ely, George - Jane T. Thompson.............. 1-10-1833
Ely, Horatio - Helen Conover................ 12-03-1834
Ely, James - Marie Hoffere.................. 12-12-1821
Ely, James - Mary McKay..................... 10-14-1838
Ely, John - Ann L. Clayton.................. 2-04-1823
Ely, John - Elizabeth Baird................. 6-07-1837
Ely, John - Mary Perrine.................... 6-01-1814
Ely, John - Rebeckah Fleming................ 2-20-1808
Ely, Joseph - Achsa Rue..................... 12-16-1835
Ely, Joseph - Margaret Duncan............... 8-18-1837
Ely, Joseph - Sarah James................... 3-10-1842
Ely, Joseph - Sarah Perrine................. 12-16-1820
Ely, Joshua - Ann Mariah Garritson.......... 3-24-1831
Ely, Joshua - Elizabeth Dey................. 3-12-1817
Ely, William - Ann Conover.................. 11-07-1832
Ely, William of Pa. - Lydia Hulse........... 1-07-1836
Ely, William L. - Sarah Ann Hendrickson..... 6-06-1834
Emans, Cornelius - Catherine Thompson........ 10-18-1805
Emans, Daniel - Rachel Tyson................ 8-30-1809
Embley, John - Bulah Warren................. 1-13-1810
Embley, Joshua - Elizabeth Kelly............ 6-05-1826
Embley, Thomas - Margaret Errickson......... 3-07-1814
Emens, Ezekiel - Rebecca Tilton............. 4-15-1803
Emens, Francis - Hannah West................ 5-29-1802
Emens, John - Mary Clayton.................. 6-06-1805
Emens, Nathan - Phebe Pitenger.............. 3-07-1805
Emens, Peter - Ann Tison.................... 1-15-1807
Emley, Antony - Hannah Ware................. 3-25-1815
Emley, David - Elizabeth Messler............ 4-27-1837
Emley, John - Rebecca Havens................ 12-20-1811
Emley, John - Susannah Oatman............... 3-01-1797

MARRIAGES OF MONMOUTH COUNTY, NEW JERSEY

Emley, Joseph - Elizabeth Van Horn........... 10-14-1839
Emley, Joshua - Elizabeth Kerby.............. 6-05-1826
Emley, Robert - Nancy Garrison.............. 4-15-1801
Emley, Samuel E. - Alice Sill............... 12-24-1812
Emley, Stratten - Harriet Cooke............. 9-07-1817
Emley, Thomas - Mary DeCamp
  of Burlington Co., N. J................. 3-01-1831
Emmans, William - Catherine Vanmeter......... 1-15-1801
Emmens, Jonathan - Ann Thorp................. 1-20-1814
Emmens, Joseph - Elizabeth Irons............. 10-21-1842
Emmens, Peter - Mary Matchet................. 1-30-1815
Emmens, Tylee - Jerutioy Giberson............ 6-15-1822
Emmins, Richard - Sarah Homer................ 1-03-1808
Emmon, Daniel Jr. - Esther Hulshart.......... 1-28-1813
Emmons, Andrew - Leah Bowls.................. 3-03-1841
Emmons, Benjamin - Sarah Cotrell............. 2-15-1816
Emmons, Charles - Catherine Emmons........... 3-12-1837
Emmons, Corlis - Lucy King................... 5-03-1837
Emmons, David - Mrs. Esther Hulshart........ 1-28-1813
Emmons, David - Rosannah Morris.............. 2-14-1808
Emmons, Elias - Nancy Covener............... 4-21-1796
Emmons, Ezekiel - Deborah Shepperd.......... 4-24-1820
Emmons, Hyler - Elizabeth Plat.............. 12-06-1816
Emmons, Isaac - Rebecca Crum................ 11-15-1829
Emmons, James - Eliza Ann Sickels........... 8-24-1840
Emmons, Jesse of Burlington Co., N. J. -
  Lydia M. Daniel........................ 8-08-1841
Emmons, John son of John - Catherine Sickle
  dg. of William (sailor)................ 10-13-1822
Emmons, John Jr. - Elsie Gulick............. 8-26-1824
Emmons, Joseph - Jane Emmons................ 3-06-1839
Emmons, Joshua - Ann Archer................. 6-08-1833
Emmons, Longstreet - Adry Bennet............ 11-02-1837
Emmons, Robert (carpenter) -
  Hetty Anderson (spinster).............. 3-07-1809
Emmons, Tunas - Elizabeth Lewis............. 1-02-1828
Emmons, Tyle - Jerusha Giberson............. 6-15-1822
Emmons, William - Mary Van Kirk............. 7-30-1839
Emmott, James - Hulel Compton............... 1-24-1825
Emons, Asa - Eliza Ryon..................... 3-18-1816
Emson, Christian D. - Lydia Potter.......... 10-07-1826
England, Thomas - Clamens Lloyd............. 2-14-1833
English, Amos - Elizabeth Bennett........... 5-27-1834
English, William - Lydia Ann English........ 12-25-1828
English, William - Merebah Chandler......... 3-03-1824
Erickson, John - Nelly Schenck dg. of
  William................................ 8-24-1797
Erickson, Joseph - Elizabeth Wilson......... 8-24-1841
Errickson, Adonijah Jr. - Eliza Hankins...... 10-20-1832
Errickson, Charles - Lydia Ann Clayton....... 2-11-1836
Errickson, Daniel - Hannah Conover.......... 1-09-1809
Errickson, James - Rachel Karr.............. 1-24-1821
Errickson, John - Allice Mathias............ 2-08-1817
Errickson, John - Sarah Ann Young........... 3-26-1835
Errickson, Jonathan - Juliann Rogers........ 4-09-1821

```
Errickson, Joseph - Ann Stillwell...........    4-14-1836
Errickson, Michael - Elizabeth Reynolds......   6-10-1815
Errikson, James - Abigail Taylor.............   3-26-1797
Errikson, Thomas - Hester Patterson..........   4-26-1795
Erwin, William B. - Ann Reed.................  11-18-1823
Eslick, Alexander - Hannah Walman............   9-08-1827
Estal, James - Deborah Pearce................   3-26-1804
Estel, David - Mary Sharp....................   2-24-1805
Estell, David Lewis - Phebe Hankins..........   3-15-1834
Estell, James - Sarah Truax..................   2-01-1840
Estell, Robert - Joan Johnson................  11-10-1835
Estill, Benjamin - Mary Vanck................   5-29-1832
Estle, John - Catherine Matthews.............   3-21-1813
Estle, Samuel - Matilda Morris...............  12-15-1820
Estle, William - Abigail Little..............  11-16-1813
Estoll, James - Mary Skidmore................  12-23-1815
Eveleth, John H. of N. Y. - Mary White.......  12-22-1831
Evelett, John of New York City - Mary White..  12-22-1831
Evelmem, Luis - Elizabeth Dillen.............  10-20-1820
Evenham, Asa - Altea Hendrickson.............  10-16-1828
Evens, John - Charity Cranmer................  11-12-1842
Everingham, Elime - Martha Smith.............   9-06-1818
Everingham, John - Sarah Bennet..............  11-24-1810
Everingham, Joseph - Louisa Cornelia Leek
  both of Burlington County, N. J...........    1-10-1837
Everingham, William - Hester McKinney........   7-06-1837
Everitt, Joseph - Rachel Combs...............   9-23-1835
Evernham, Aaron - Margaret Schenck...........   5-16-1838
Evernham, Ezekiel - Anne Journee.............   3-07-1821
Evernham, George E. - Lucy Evernham..........  11-15-1834
Evernham, William of Middlesex County, N. J.
  - Merriah Thompson.........................   4-16-1827
Ewin, Cornelius - Ann Applegate..............  12-16-1805
Fagen, Abel - Lydia Bowne....................  12-13-1795
Falkenburg, John - Susannah Chadwick.........   8-02-1816
Falkenburg, Samuel - Massey Cramer...........   1-01-1807
Falkenburg, William C. - Permeliah H. Mount..   2-03-1838
Falkinburg, John - Sussannah Chadwick........   8-02-1816
Falkinburg, Lawrence - Abigail Ginings.......  10-24-1822
Fallen, Samuel - Phebe Goble.................   2-10-1829
Fane, Michael - Lidia Fane...................   1-14-1827
Fardun, Thomas - Eliza Katcham...............   6-26-1823
Faris, James - Elizabeth Hutchinson..........   1-10-1796
Farris, Josiah - Jane Vanhart................   5-29-1796
Fargason, James - Mary Dunkin................   1-15-1834
Farmer, Jacob - Anne Clark...................  10-07-1801
Feild, Ezekiel Jr. - Joanna Runnely..........  10-25-1817
Feilder, Francis - Catherine Pattison........   6-21-1817
Fell, James - Mary Foster....................   8-25-1796
Fenex, John - Mary Woodruff (both black).....   6-14-1834
Fennimore, Elisha - Hannah Applegate.........   8-13-1842
Fenton, James - Hope Rockhill................   6-11-1839
Fenton, John - Sarah Van Brunt...............  12-21-1816
Fenton, Samuel - Harriet Mount...............   4-07-1836
Fenton, Thomas - Eliza Jackway...............   6-02-1805
```

```
Fenton, Thomas - Phebe Gibbons..............  3-13-1841
Fenton, William - Rachel Emmons.............  3-25-1815
Fenton, William Jr. - Edy Webb..............  4-01-1800
Ferry, Sylvester of Ireland - Lydia Hurley...  8-09-1819
Fews, Sirow - Sarah McChesnee............... 11-16-1827
Fidler, Samuel W. - Elizabeth Imlay......... 12-23-1841
Fidler, Thomas B. - Hellena Holcomb.........  8-05-1834
Field, Benjamin - Rebekah Novlan............  2-22-1820
Field, Elijah Jr. - Lydia Hendrickson....... 11-07-1821
Field, Elnathan - Margaret Conover..........  3-25-1830
Fielder, Benjamin (Capt.) - Hannah Gifford... 12-31-1832
Fielder, Issac - Eliza Patterson............  9-03-1830
Fielder, Isaac - Sarah White................  3-13-1812
Fielder, John - Phebe Vannote............... 10-29-1828
Fielder, Robert - Hannah Brown..............  3-20-1819
Fields, David - Ann Woolley.................  5-23-1831
Fields, Elnathan - Mary Braeims.............  7-07-1799
Fields, Elnathan - Rebecca Fields........... 11-24-1838
Fields, John - Margaret Britton.............  4-17-1802
Fields, Stephen - Adelaide Shephard.........  2-10-1835
Fields, Thomas - Martha Taylor..............  5-12-1835
File, David of New York City -
    Rebecca Smith...........................  9-10-1820
Fish, Benjamin - Ann Young..................  4-19-1817
Fish, Samuel - Julia Applegate.............. 11-07-1812
Fisher, Benjamin - Martha Hinds.............  8-03-1813
Fisher, Charles - Hannah Stout..............  6-26-1823
Fisher, David - Anner Rodgers...............  2-16-1804
Fisher, David - Elizabeth Clayton........... 12-28-1814
Fisher, David - Sarah Phillips..............  5-23-1811
Fisher, Henry - Mary Derry..................  5-01-1841
Fisher, Jacob - Rebecca Die.................  1-31-1839
Fisher, James - Ann Mount...................  4-28-1840
Fisher, Jesse - Sarah Philips...............  3-04-1828
Fisher, Thomas of Burlington County, N.J. -
    Sarah Fewts............................. 12-07-1820
Fisk, Jonathan - Mary A. Imlay..............  1-14-1834
Fleming, Jacob - Mary Pearce................  1-10-1828
Fleming, James - Elizabeth Bennett..........  3-30-1811
Fleming, John - Jane Thompson...............  2-17-1810
Fleming, Joseph - Lydia White...............  6-21-1806
Fleming, Richard - Margaret Young...........  4-16-1840
Flen, John - Jane Emons..................... 10-03-1812
Flinn, John - Harriet Wardell...............  3-01-1841
Flinn, William - Elizabeth Wardell.......... 10-05-1836
Fokinbury, Charles - Sarah Brindly.......... 11-08-1795
Folwell, James - Eliza Davenport............  4-20-1806
Foolcott, Job - Mrs. Margaret Emmons........  9-06-1821
Forbes, Alexander - Deborah Morton.......... 10-18-1837
Ford, David - Elizabeth Robins..............  6-04-1837
Ford, Isaac - Mrs. Sarah Neal...............  2-04-1819
Ford, Jacob - Elizabeth Robbins............. 11-17-1825
Ford, James - Mary Bowers................... 10-27-1796
Ford, Jeremiah - Catherine Perrine..........  5-20-1835
Ford, John - Martha Radford (both black).....  4-03-1841
```

Ford, Nathaniel - Elizabeth Brown............ 3-25-1830
Ford, Robert - Sarah Dye.................... 10-13-1825
Ford, Solomon - Catherine Loiman............ 11-29-1808
Ford, Wiliam - Achsah Hutchinson of
   Hunterdon County, N. J.................. 2-06-1835
Ford, William - Mary Hutchinson............. 3-20-1796
Fordy, Jacob D. (Rev.) - Cornelia Scudder.... 7-23-1821
Forehead, Ephraim of N. Y. - Nancy Willson... 1822
Forgeson, Joshua - Sarah Cornelius.......... 5-06-1807
Forguson, William - Isabella Newell......... 1-29-1808
Forman, David - Nelly Van Brunt............. 12-04-1799
Forman, Denice - Elizabeth Laird............ 1-13-1801
Forman, Ebenezer - Nancy Gaston............. 3-20-1842
Forman, Ezekiel - Phebe Sutfin.............. 4- -1817
Forman, Garret - Ann Ker.................... 2-11-1800
Forman, Isaac - Clarissa Crawford
   (both black)............................ 2-23-1842
Forman, Isaac - Elizabeth Ely............... 2-16-1836
Forman, John - Lydia Preston................ 10-21-1809
Forman, John - Sarah Gifford................ 12-30-1819
Forman, John B. - Hope B. Henderson......... 1-30-1811
Forman, John (Esq.) - Sarah Antonidis (wid.). 9-28-1800
Forman, Jonathan - Matilda Scudder.......... 1-02-1828
Forman, Joseph - Hetty Holmes............... 4-26-1803
Forman, Samuel - Gertrude Applegate......... 1-29-1840
Forman, Samuel - Mary Clayton............... 3-16-1818
Forman, Stephen - Hannah Wardell............ 6-03-1795
Forman, Tunis - Elinor Remson............... 11-27-1799
Forman, William - Gitty Gravat.............. 11-28-1822
Forman, William Gordon - Sarah Woodhull...... 9-02-1806
Fornica, John - Mary Emmons................. 12-12-1819
Forsythe, Thomas - Mary Eldridge............ 3-01-1838
Fort, William - Sarah Creed................. 6-03-1841
Fortenborg, David - Hannah Brewer........... 7-13-1809
Fortin, ----- - Mary Comel (both black)...... 12-02-1797
Foster, Altanson - Mary Huggins............. 11-09-1811
Foster, Ephraim - Sarah Chamberlain......... 11-15-1832
Foster, Jacob - Sarah Jeming................ 10-05-1833
Foster, John - Ann Reed..................... 2-25-1826
Foster, John - Mary Cox..................... 12-24-1829
Foster, Joshua - Susan Douglass............. 11-13-1828
Foster, William - Elizabeth Reynolds......... 2-22-1823
Foster, William of Burlington County, N. J.
   - Eunity Ramer.......................... 11-10-1835
Foster, William - Nancy Imley............... 12-01-1830
Foulks, John - Mary Imlay................... 1-08-1809
Fourd, Ephraim - Rachel Collins............. 4-24-1803
Fow, Asa. - Vermelia Huggins................ 1-13-1835
Fowler, Benjamin - Mary Forsyth............. 1-05-1825
Fowler, Charles - Mary Buckelew............. 1-06-1819
Fowler, Charles of Burlington County, N. J.
   - Zilpha Horner......................... 7-18-1839
Fowler, David - Catherine Hyer.............. 11-21-1802
Fowler, Elijah Jr. - Hannah Bennet.......... 8-06-1832
Fowler, Frederick - Sarah Skidmore.......... 2-12-1842

```
Fowler, James - Susan Lippincott.............  3-19-1836
Fowler, John - Elizabeth Buckalew............ 11-14-1812
Fowler, John L. - Amy Still.................. 11-25-1832
Fowler, Joseph - Elizabeth Reynolds..........  5-09-1806
Fowler, Joseph - Sarah Garwood...............  9-20-1828
Fowler, Rheuben - Catherine Gaskins.......... 12-10-1818
Foster, William of Burlington County, N. J.
    - Emily Remer............................ 11-10-1835
Fox, John - Chalotee Gilchrist............... 10-14-1798
Fragen, William B. - Catherine Reingold......  2-16-1826
Frake, Samuel - Elizabeth Reaves.............  8-15-1829
Francis, Aaron (Capt.) - Ann Erickson........  2-04-1807
Francis, John - Margaret Kilpatrick..........  9-03-1797
Francis, John - Mary Reynolds................  5-08-1818
Francis, Nathan - Mary Errickson.............  4-11-1805
Francis, Nehemiah - Anni Stricklou...........  8-31-1805
Francis, Richard - Susan Mary Fenton......... 11-03-1836
Francis, William - Nancy Garrison............  7-08-1838
Francis, William - Sarah Vorhees.............  1-07-1837
Franklin, John of N. Y. - Charity Cornell....  9-25-1795
Franus, John - Ann Morris.................... 10-21-1801
Fraser, Stephen - Mary Havens................ 10-13-1830
Frazer, Alexander Granfield -
    Deborah Herbert..........................  2-11-1818
Free, Cato - Lydia ----......................  9-01-1800
Freeland, Richard - Lavinia Ridgeway.........  7-13-1816
Freeman, Benjamin - Mary Biddle..............  5-12-1818
Freeman, Daniel - Mrs. Hannah Harvey.........  5-16-1813
Freeman, Henry - Eliza Vanbrunt.............. 12-08-1808
Freeman, Isaac - Mary Melet..................  5-19-1805
Freeman, James - Hannah Clayton..............  2-03-1803
Freeman, James - Margaret Boice..............  9-14-1837
Freeman, Morris - Mary Brown................. 12-30-1812
French, Ensign - Mary Smith..................  5-25-1823
French, Insine - Mary Smith..................  8-08-1824
Fricker, James - Mary Gregory................  6-08-1806
Frost, Jessie - Celia Maguire (both black)...  8-20-1841
Frost, John - Catherine Conover..............  1-12-1818
Frost, Shores - Mary Jane West...............  5-07-1834
Fry, William of Salem County, N. J. -
    Rosetta Fanny............................  7-17-1827
Furry, John - Mariah Leonard.................  4-23-1827
Cable, James - Jane Chadwick.................  8-10-1831
Gable, Jonathan - Rebecca Johnston...........  6-08-1825
Gamble, John - Patience Bird.................  3-21-1807
Gandy, Webster of Cumberland County, N. J.
    - Huldy Tice.............................  8-22-1835
Gant, Charles - Margaret Thompson............  7-31-1839
Gant, Ezieck - Deborah Ann Clayton...........       1833
Gant, Israel - Ann Hulse.....................  3-20-1840
Gant, Israel - Deborah Hules................. 12-24-1831
Gant, Jonathan - Martha Howell...............  7-10-1824
Gant, Robert - Hannah Estel.................. 11-21-1833
Gant, Zachariah - Hannah Billsborth..........  9-30-1823
Gant, Zachariah - Margaret Emmons............       1834
```

```
Gardener, Jmaes - Isabel Hannah..............  8-18-1813
Gardener, John - Hannah Boud.................  1808-1809
Gardiner, Calvin H. of N. Y. - Content Bills. 10-19-1834
Gardiner, John Jr. - Hester Newman..........  3-04-1840
Gardiner, Richard - Elenor Pott..............  5-05-1831
Gardner, John - Hannah Boud.................. 10-27-1808
Garniel, Francis - Caroline Cook.............  1-05-1841
Garrabrunt, Jeremiah - Ellen Laen............  2-11-1830
Garret, George - Mary Nutt...................  9-14-1826
Garret, John - Mary Nutt.....................  9-14-1826
Garretson, Peter - Jane Conover.............. 10-18-1819
Garretson, Samuel - Martha Anderson..........  2-01-1806
Garretson, Stephen - Marthy Van Note.........  8-22-1839
Garrison, Smith - Elizabeth Hur..............  8-21-1817
Garwood, Jacob - Rachel Nut.................. 11-10-1798
Garwood, John - Lucy Dennis..................  2-24-1821
Garwood, Joseph - Lavinia Dunkay.............  4-21-1838
Gaskile, Samuel - Deborah Singleton..........  4-05-1804
Gaskill, Asa - Rebeccah Lamb.................  8-04-1799
Gaskill, Hudson - Sarah Kemmy...............  4-08-1816
Gaskill, James - Elizabeth Tharrow...........  1-25-1834
Gaskill, John - Mercy Heywood................  2-26-1839
Gaskill, Moses - Rachel Sprag............... 11-22-1808
Gaskill, William - Eleanor, Cranmer..........  6-07-1828
Gaskill, William - Sarah Cranes..............  5-31-1800
Gaskin, John - Jemima Woolley................  8-02-1838
Gaskin, Thomas - Mary Gifford...............  4-11-1816
Gaston, Aaron - Deborah Hepburn..............  9-26-1822
Gate, Samuel - Thena Brown of
    Burlington County, N. J..................  3-14-1835
Gates, Isaac - Sarah Meligan.................  3-30-1833
Gatman, Jeremiah - Mary Magahan..............  7-31-1808
Gaunt, Richard - Jemima Vannote..............  1-12-1822
Gelany, James - Phebe Slocum................. 12-19-1798
Geline, James - Sally Williamson............. 10-21-1832
Gennings, Edward Jr. - Mercey Smith.........  6-28-1828
Gent, John - Jane Miller.....................  1-01-1800
George, David - Catherine Painter........... 11-15-1814
Gerton, Thomas - Ann Armstrong..............  9-21-1822
Giberson, Abel - Ann Munsall.................  4-13-1842
Giberson, Abel - Jane Archer................. 11-12-1837
Giberson, Benjamin Jr. - Hannah Henderson....  3-01-1804
Giberson, Enoch - Phebe Anderson............  9-03-1809
Giberson, George - Charity Jeffery..........  2-13-1840
Giberson, Harmen Jr. - Betsy Preston.........  1-23-1806
Giberson, Israel - Margaret Throckmorton..... 11-29-1822
Giberson, James - Sarah Wisner............... 10-12-1831
Giberson, John - Sarah Wilber............... 11-18-1820
Giberson, Joseph - Hope Taylor.............. 10-04-1816
Giberson, Samuel - Ann Wisner...............  9-23-1832
Giberson, Samuel - Elizabeth Warner.........  6-21-1807
Giberson, Samuel - Mary Hendrickson......... 12-09-1810
Giberson, Samuel - Saryann Perry............ 12-29-1830
Giberson, William - Catherine Fielder........ 12-31-1811
Giberson, William - Ellen Estill.............      1833
```

```
Giberson, William - Rachel Flinn.............  8-13-1803
Gibeson, John - Rebecca Flat................  1-26-1841
Gifford, Amos - Mary Johnson................  5-28-1823
Gifford, Amos - Mercy Cook..................  6-03-1818
Gifford, Annaniah - Elizabeth Brewer........  7-13-1809
Gifford, Asel - Mary Bailey.................  2-03-1814
Gifford, Asil - Susan Shafto................  1-07-1816
Gifford, Benjamin - Prudence Morton......... 11-08-1807
Gifford, Freeman - Cornelia Fieldley........ 10-15-1828
Gifford, Job - Elizabeth Morton.............  3-25-1830
Gifford, Job - Emma Morton..................  9-21-1841
Gifford, John - Anna Morton.................  6-08-1807
Gifford, John - Louisa Emmons............... 10-24-1835
Gifford, Joseph - Mary Brewster.............  7-05-1797
Gifford, Joshua - Leah Jackson..............  1-17-1807
Gifford, Joshua - Mary Jeffree..............  5-18-1802
Gifford, Richard - Hannah Brown............. 10-01-1840
Gifford, Samuel - Eleanor Osborn............  3-24-1836
Gifford, William - Abigail Vannote..........  7-18-1834
Gifford, William - Edith Carmer.............  5-18-1805
Gilbert, Charles - Phebe Cathcart...........  2-29-1840
Ginglen, David - Rebecca Runnels............ 11-09-1802
Ginnings, Stacy - Pheby Inman............... 11-05-1818
Ginnings, Stacy - Sarah Hazelton............  3-22-1825
Githens, John - Caroline Little.............  3-13-1831
Glanson, Nichlas - Mary Hyers...............  1-02-1815
Glen, John - Achsah Cook....................  4-30-1804
Glesson, Morris - Lydia Morton..............  4-24-1815
Glifsen, James - Charity Bennet.............  2-20-1817
Goble, Isaac - Rebecca Curtis...............  8-21-1832
Golden, Abraham - Allice Woolley............  1-11-1832
Golden, Ellias - Catherine Stillwell........ 12-03-1797
Golden, Jasper of Philadelphia, Pa. -
    Phebe Southard..........................  7-  -1820
Golden, John - Catherine Schenck............  1-20-1822
Golden, Mathias A. - Catherine Van Mater.....  6-24-1802
Goodenough, Abraham - Mary Brown............ 11-29-1819
Goodenough, Joseph - Jane Golden............ 11-19-1797
Goodenough, William H. - Mary Patterson......  4-08-1826
Goodman, William - Elizabeth Lesslis of
    New York................................  7-27-1830
Goodnough, Joseph - Elizabeth Glisson........  6-26-1809
Goodrich, John D. - Sarah White.............  8-22-1809
Goodrich, Leonard of New York City -
    Mary Rowland............................ 10-25-1837
Goodrich, Morris - Ann Eliza Matthews........ 12-25-1839
Goodwin, John of New York - Ann Wooley.......  2-08-1827
Gorden, David - Gesha Covenhoven............  8-20-1801
Gorden, James - Jane Jewel..................  2-10-1810
Gorden, John L. - Rebecka Clayton...........  3-25-1810
Gorden, Jonathan R. - Jane Covenhoven........ 10-23-1805
Gorden, Joseph - Mary Hampton...............  4-27-1815
Gorden, Joseph - Sarah Barge................  2-04-1801
Gorden, Samuel - Abigail Barkalow...........  5-24-1824
Gordon, David - Mariah Ashley...............  5-31-1795
```

```
Gordon, David - Rachel Patterson.............  2-14-1798
Gordon, Elias - Lettis Aker.................  1-06-1828
Gordon, Elisha (Esq.) - Elizabeth Elliot.....  2-04-1830
Gordon, Joseph - Ruth Van Scholck............ 12-30-1813
Gordon, William - Rebecca Mount..............  1-16-1817
Goshen, Aaron - Mary Parker..................  4-09-1831
Graham, George - Lucy Woolley (both black)...  5-18-1837
Graham, John - Jemima Swart..................  3-04-1811
Grant, Asa - Nancy Wells.................... 12-10-1821
Grant, Harris - Abigail Moore................  3-02-1834
Grant, Irons - Susan Horner..................  4-12-1828
Grant, Israel - Durutha Hynes................ 12-14-1820
Grant, James - Margaret Hilyer...............  9-23-1820
Grant, Joel - Amy Harres....................  5-25-1812
Grant, John - Ann Hance..................... 10-11-1807
Grant, John - Catherine Pearce............... 10-11-1834
Grant, Joseph - Elizabeth Hall...............  9-11-1819
Grant, Miles - Elizabeth Lewker.............. 10-28-1819
Grant, Thomas - Elizabeth Grover............. 12-24-1823
Grant, William - Mariah Lippincott...........  1-24-1829
Gravat, Peter - Hannah Van Cleaf.............  4-02-1814
Gravatt, Joseph - Sarah Castler..............  1-25-1819
Gravatt, Peter - Lydia Ann Lippincott........  9-07-1833
Gray, Andrew - Catherine Simmons.............  8-05-1800
Gray, John - Mary Walling...................  7-02-1837
Gray, Levy - Catherine Rogers................  1-03-1799
Gray, William - Hannah Johnson...............  1-30-1828
Green, Anthony - Constant Woolley............  1-01-1832
Green, Armitage - Ann Maria Williams.........  3-  -1818
Green, George - Elizabeth Kittle.............  6-06-1825
Green, George - Hannah Moses.................  7-29-1834
Green, Henry - Mary Stillwell................  1-27-1807
Green, Henry - Phebe Tucker.................. 11-21-1833
Green, Henry - Sally Forman.................. 10-25-1809
Green, Henry - Susan Brinley.................  2-09-1820
Green, James - Elizabeth Murphy of
     Philadelphia, PA....................... 10-24-1829
Green, James H. - Jane Goodman Lisby.........  1-06-1829
Green, Joel - Rebecca Jeffrey................  1-29-1824
Green, John - Anne Brown....................  2-13-1816
Green, John - Elizabeth Morris...............  3-28-1801
Green, John - Maria Bedle................... 10-15-1823
Green, John - Olley Vankirk.................. 12-23-1820
Green, John - Sarah Errickson................  1-11-1841
Green, John Jr. - Deborah Lewis..............  1-06-1827
Green, Richard Montgomery - Mary Henderson...  5-06-1806
Green, Samuel - Theodocia Brown..............  9-16-1835
Green, Sylvanus - Mary Shewmard..............  5-04-1819
Green, Thomas - Elizabeth Sexton.............  1-10-1829
Green, William of Burlington Co., N. J. -
     Mary Emmons............................  9-19-1829
Greenwood, Henry - Mary Ann Clayton..........  3-03-1841
Greenwood, John - Elizabeth Conover.......... 12-27-1838
Greenwood, Thomas - Catherine Van Brakel..... 12-06-1804
Gregory, John Jr. - Edith Chamberlain........ 10-06-1814
```

```
Griffin, Benjamin - Frances Lucretia Hanes...    5-20-1840
Griffith, James - Sarah Woolley..............    5-19-1839
Griggs, Benjamin - Mary Witlock..............    4-09-1799
Griggs, Charles - Elizabeth Longstreet.......    9-13-1840
Griggs, Edmund - Emmaline Johnson............    9-22-1835
Griggs, William - Lydia Ann Holdman..........    9-11-1832
Grishey, Samuel - Rebecca Emley..............   12-26-1824
Griskey, Samuel - Ann Hers...................   11-05-1800
Griswold, Calvin - Sarah Lippincott..........    6-29-1805
Groom, Harmon - Porthena Buckaloo............   12-08-1810
Groom, Samuel - Beulah Valentine.............    2-26-1829
Groome, Stacy - Ann Hughes...................    1-16-1826
Grover, Brazilla - Sophia White..............   11-14-1835
Grover, James - Rachel Smith.................   10-25-1842
Grover, John - Catherine Wilgus..............   10-25-1812
Grover, John - Eliza Perrine.................   11-03-1833
Grover, Joseph - Elizabeth Luker.............    3-20-1797
Grover, Joseph - Lucy Ann Hilyer.............    2-04-1837
Grover, Joseph Jr. - Sarah Webb..............    8-18-1835
Grover, Samuel - Sarah Anderson..............    2-17-1808
Groves, Ruben - Catherine Holeman............   12-29-1828
Guggs, John W. - Hannah A. Hankinson.........    2-02-1829
Guidley, Jesse of Philadelphia, Pa.-
    Frances Throckmorton dg. of Thomas.......   12-11-1841
Gulic, Nimrod - Ruth Wooley..................    8-02-1826
Gulich, Abner - Elizabeth Ford...............   10-17-1835
Gulick, Abner - Hannah Applegate.............   10-28-1820
Gulick, James - Ann Herbert..................    1-13-1821
Gulick, William - Phebe Falkenburg...........    1-03-1824
Hadsall, Rice of Conn. - Rebekah Robbins.....    5-05-1822
Hagan, John - Catherine Applegate............    7-27-1816
Hagarman, Barnett - Jane White...............    3-20-1833
Hagerman, Barrance - Marcy Pettenger.........    9-19-1795
Hagerman, Charles - Sarah A. Heaviland.......    9-15-1827
Hagerman, Daniel - ---- Van Hise.............   11-18-1835
Hagerman, Jacob - Lydia Haviland.............    6-02-1827
Hagerman, James - Catherine Herbert..........    7-12-1834
Hagerman, John - Hannah Gifford..............    2-15-1801
Hagerman, Richard - Mrs. Mariah Haviland.....    3-03-1827
Hagerty, Asher - Susannah Howland............    2-20-1812
Hagerty, Taylor - Clemence Holmes............   11-28-1811
Haggarty, John - Susan Hardy.................    8-07-1836
Haight, Elias - Matilda Auger................    2-14-1829
Haight, William - Mary Tilton................    5-23-1839
Haines, Stacy - Eliza Potts both of
    Burlington Co., N. J.....................    1-03-1833
Hains, Elia of Burlington Co., N. J. -
    Euphamy Holeman..........................    2-05-1824
Haldman, William - Mary Wells................    8-24-1835
Haley, Charles - Ann Haveland................    2-28-1818
Haley, George - Clemence Bruere..............   11-12-1834
Haley, John - Elizabeth Ellison..............    5-23-1832
Haley, John - Mary Tomson....................    3-19-1814
Haley, William - Coziah Hendrickson..........   10-19-1835
Halkinburgh, Samuel - Elizabeth Platt........   11-23-1819
```

Hall, John - Alice Gordon.................... 12-07-1805
Hall, John - Rebecca Knott................... 1-16-1826
Hall, John T. - Rebecca Patterson........... 2-23-1828
Hall, Samuel - Marget Newberry.............. 3-08-1798
Halloway, James M. - Elizabeth Lafetra...... 5-13-1835
Halsey, Samuel - Lydia Pierce............... 12-16-1837
Halsy, Isaiah - Abigail Brand............... 5-15-1827
Hamilton, Arche - Hester Craft.............. 5-17-1832
Hamilton, William B. - Anselina D. Thompson.. 12-17-1826
Hammel, John - Helen Freneau................ 12-16-1816
Hammel, Laban - Sarah Brown................. 1-04-1838
Hammell, John - Amy Rogers.................. 7-18-1826
Hammell, John - Elizabeth Hults............. 12-03-1834
Hammell, Mahlon - Rebecca Dancer............. 2-01-1832
Hammilton, John - Sarah Reed................ 1-25-1800
Hammock, John - Elizabeth Hart.............. 9-30-1812
Hammond, John - Catherine Leming............ 2-05-1833
Hampton, Aaron - Mrs. Elizabeth Johnson...... 1-29-1811
Hampton, B. - Julia Morris.................. 7-05-1826
Hampton, James - Mary Patterson............. 3-04-1824
Hampton, James M. - Susan Hurley............ 4-23-1831
Hampton, John - Rachel Adenlem.............. 10-14-1815
Hampton, Kisis - Lydia Ann Riddle........... 9-12-1830
Hampton, Moses - Mrs. Margarete Lain........ 11-25-1820
Hampton, Timothy - Maria Mount.............. 2-21-1821
Hampton, William - Stacey Taylor............ 12-08-1832
Hamten, John - Hannah Pettet................ 11-01-1798
Hamton, John - Ann Cotteral................. 12-11-1799
Hanaway, Samuel - Suzannah Mount............ 2-07-1829
Hance, Asher - Ann Borden................... 2-01-1831
Hance, Borden - Rebeccah Woolley............ 1-17-1837
Hance, Cornelius - Catherine Clayland....... 2-20-1804
Hance, Cornelius - Deliverance Brown........ 6-22-1830
Hance, Edward - Sarah Conrow................ 12-23-1821
Hance, Isaac - Charlotte White.............. 5-19-1798
Hance, John - Elizabeth Auston.............. 11-29-1801
Hance, John - Nany Borden................... 12-15-1800
Hance, Joseph - Caroline Borden............. 9-12-1825
Hance, Robert of New York City, N. Y. -
    Elizabeth Hance......................... 2-01-1837
Hance, Timothy - Heather Hance.............. 3-01-1807
Handford, William H. - Elizabeth W. Borden... 2-03-1834
Handley, James - Ann Nugent................. 9-27-1807
Hankenson, Kenneth - Elizabeth Vanderveer.... 5-08-1803
Hankenson, William - Pheby Ker.............. 12-13-1807
Hankerson, Joseph - Ann Beers............... 5-07-1826
Hankins, Abraham - Catherine Burke.......... 5-09-1807
Hankins, Bemsun - Rejoice Chamberlain....... 11-08-1829
Hankins, Caleb - Ann Hopkins................ 12-24-1827
Hankins, Charles - Margaret Woodward........ 12-24-1831
Hankins, Charles - Sarah Hulshart........... 4-12-1834
Hankins, Cornelius - Nancy White............ 12-19-1840
Hankins, Daniel - Catherine Van Horn........ 8-14-1829
Hankins, Daniel - Hannah Clayton............ 10-23-1841
Hankins, Daniel - Matilda Clutch............ 9-27-1815

```
Hankins, Elias - Margaret Hendrickson........  2-10-1820
Hankins, Gilbert - Sarah Reynolds............  4-24-1817
Hankins, Isaac - Rachel Drew.................  6-05-1829
Hankins, James - Sarah Wainwright............  3-09-1821
Hankins, John - Frantynche Voorhees..........  8-02-1836
Hankins, John - Margaret Lawrence............ 10-01-1818
Hankins, Richard - Amey Soper................  2-18-1837
Hankins, Richard - Catherine Emens...........  3-26-1806
Hankins, Samuel - Elizabeth Hays............. 12-04-1810
Hankins, Thomas - Rebecca Chemard............ 12-08-1804
Hankins, William - Abigail Shin..............  9-20-1810
Hankins, William - Jane Buckelew.............  4-02-1829
Hankins, William - Mahala Hankins............ 12-02-1819
Hankinson, Kenneth - Catrine Bowne...........  1-12-1797
Hankinson, Lewis F. - Ann Stout..............  3-11-1833
Hankinson, Theodore - Charity Burk...........  2-02-1837
Hankinson, William - Mariah Matthews.........  3-10-1841
Hankinson, William W. - Mary Perrine......... 12-13-1814
Hanse, David - Phebe Vankerk................. 10-24-1798
Hansell, Joseph - Mrs. Juleyan Pharo.........  1-22-1815
Harber, Abner - Abegail Huntsinger...........  3-16-1831
Harbert, Henry - Mrs. Anny Stout.............      1807
Hargrove, Samuel - Lydia Covert.............. 10-28-1842
Harker, Daniel - Hannah Wallin...............  9-30-1809
Harker, John H. - Mary Sager................. 12-09-1830
Harker, William - Elizabeth Perrine.......... 12-26-1826
Harris, Abraham - Catherine Hopkins.......... 12-06-1838
Harris, Benjamin - Mary Ann Stout............  9-13-1835
Harris, George Sr. - Patty Stratton..........  5-06-1832
Harris, Henry - Hannah Hendrickson...........  1-09-1809
Harris, Isaias of Burlington Co., N. J.
    - Mary Sill.............................. 12-24-1827
Harris, John - Hannah Mount..................  6-29-1826
Harris, Robert - Leay Michael
    both of Burlington Co., N. J............. 11-17-1821
Harris, Starkey - Nancy Hendrickson..........  5-25-1812
Harrison, John - Charity Cowperwaite.........  7-31-1796
Harrison, Matthias of Philadelphia, Pa.
    - Rebecca Waln........................... 9-07-1795
Harrison, Thomas C. - Alithael Hawker........  5-11-1834
Harrison, Thomas Jr. - Margaret Homer........ 12-07-1809
Hart, Jacob - Anna Vanderveer................ 12-13-1805
Hart, Jacob - Uphemia Thorp..................  2-14-1805
Hart, James - Frances Lippincott.............  2-02-1798
Hart, John - Ann Traffor.................... 10-22-1809
Hart, Samuel - Mary Conrow...................  3-27-1834
Hartinhine, Ezekiel - Ellen Bowne
    dg. of James............................  6-07-1838
Hartman, Garret - Anne Stover................ 12-16-1841
Hartman, James - Deborah Wilkinson........... 12-25-1814
Hartman, Peter - Jane Shearman...............  1-09-1834
Hartman, Stephen - Elizabeth Jackson......... 11-22-1809
Hartsgrove, John - Mrs. Cathryne Clayton..... 12-22-1827
Hartshorn, James - Jane Ann Bowne............  5-01-1834
Hartshorne, Joseph - Achsah Rodgers..........  1-10-1810
```

Hartshorne, Richard S. - Ann Stevenson....... 8-03-1822
Harvey, Benjamin - Catherine Hyer............ 12-21-1795
Harvey, David - Abigail Riddle............... 12-24-1807
Harvey, Gavine - Sarah Jackson............... 2-11-1815
Harvey, Hawthorne - Ann Matthews............. 8-14-1836
Harvey, Jacob - Hannah Johnson............... 1-26-1822
Harvey, James M. - Abigail Street............ 8-05-1834
Harvey, Jesse - Lucy Lemming................. 7-27-1814
Harvey, John - Mary Van Note................. 4-21-1842
Harvey, Samuel - Anne Longstreet............. 8-30-1804
Harvey, Samuel - Maria Wooley................ 12-13-1837
Harvey, William - Catherine Miller........... 4-09-1839
Hathaway, Isaac - Margaret B. Woodward....... 12-24-1829
Hathaway, William - Jane Smith............... 7-31-1830
Haughman, William - Rebeckah Niverson........ 9-06-1818
Hausman, Christian - Elizabeth Standup....... 12-15-1836
Haven, Abraham - Mary Johnson................ 10-10-1810
Haven, Clark - Elizabeth Caxon............... 2-22-1838
Haven, Jacob - Edney Morton.................. 9-27-1834
Haven, Sylvester - Ann Brewer................ 4-27-1840
Havens, Aaron - Jemimah Newberry............. 8-25-1800
Havens, Abraham - Ann Davison................ 11-08-1826
Havens, Abraham - Elizabeth Herbert.......... 2-03-1841
Havens, Abraham - Sarah Osburn............... 2-08-1827
Havens, Charles - Elizabeth Sutphin.......... 3-09-1840
Havens, Charles - Rebecca Pierson............ 3-09-1837
Havens, Courtenias - Mary Curtis............. 2-13-1822
Havens, Curtis - Elizabeth Tilton............ 2-23-1826
Havens, Daniel - Margaret Ketcham............ 3-01-1827
Havens, Daniel - Nelly Wainwright............ 7-19-1801
Havens, David - Charity Johnston............. 4-30-1831
Havens, Ezra - Macey Brown................... 12-29-1832
Havens, Ezra - Mahala Hulse.................. 5-03-1814
Havens, George R. - Mary Hulse............... 4-18-1828
Havens, Jacob - Ann Chamberlain.............. 8-03-1807
Havens, Jacob - Edney Morton................. 9-27-1834
Havens, Jacob - Elizabeth Gifford............ 2-28-1839
Havens, Jesse - Mary Ann Morris.............. 8-29-1832
Havens, John son of Jacob - Amy Johnson...... 1-13-1801
Havens, John - Aner Osborn................... 5-30-1798
Havens, Joseph - Hannah Johnson.............. 1833-1834
Havens, Joseph - Jemima Worth................ 5-20-1837
Havens, John - Dinah Eslick.................. 6-04-1803
Havens, John - Mary Chamberlin............... 11-16-1802
Havens, John - Polly Pearce.................. 10-07-1833
Havens, John - Rachel Polhemus............... 1-24-1833
Havens, Richard - Catherine Ann Truax........ 10-24-1831
Havens, Robert - Margaret Barkalow........... 10-11-1828
Havens, Samuel - Amy Bennett................. 2-22-1822
Havens, Samuel C. - Rebeccah Fisher.......... 9-13-1827
Havens, Seeliah - Sarah Soper................ 10-08-1825
Haviland, John - Ann Kelly................... 7-14-1832
Haviland, John - Rebekah Emley............... 12-19-1807
Haviland, Joseph - Hanah White............... 2-21-1802
Haviland, Joseph - Sarah Ann King............ 12-08-1830

Haviland, Nicolas - Jane Lewis...............	7-11-1802
Hawthorne, Ezekiel - Eleanore Bowne..........	6-07-1838
Hayley, Aaron - Sarah Mesler.................	3-31-1805
Haymen, James - Elizabeth Phillips...........	10-08-1814
Hays, Horasha - Margaret Moore...............	1-22-1832
Hays, Samuel - Sarah Stricklin...............	12-18-1822
Hayward, James - Amy Warran..................	10-22-1809
Haywood, Davdi - Hope Oliphant...............	7-19-1827
Haywood, Joel - Lydia Pharo..................	3-22-1821
Haywood, Joel - Pernima Crane................	12-24-1805
Haywood, John - Ceany Headly.................	12-29-1808
Haywood, Nathan - Mrs. Sarah Crane...........	12-27-1818
Haywood, Thomson - Nancy Falkenburg..........	3-24-1817
Hazelhust, Abraham - Catherine B. Holmes.....	8-09-1830
Hazelton, Benjamin - Eliza Lippencott of	
Burlington, Co., N. J....................	1-13-1834
Hazelton, Jarves - Rachel Lets...............	8-11-1795
Headden, John - Hannah Cook..................	10-30-1810
Headley, James - Rachel Arnold...............	2-26-1820
Headley, Richard - Asseneth Conkley..........	9-17-1804
Heaviland, Amos - Phebe Craig................	4-26-1829
Heaviland, Thomas - Rebecca Applegate........	1-01-1815
Hedges, William W. (Dr.) - Jane English......	2-24-1814
Heeley, John - Eliza Ellison.................	5-28-1832
Helmore, Ames - Elizabeth Browne.............	12-27-1800
Hemphill, Lockwood - Margaret Stewart........	12-31-1840
Henderson, John - Alice Anderson.............	5-08-1824
Henderson, Joseph - Elizabeth Warding........	6-19-1819
Henderson, Samuel - Hannah Kniveson..........	4-06-1814
Henderson, Thomas - Matilda Ann Mitchell.....	5-04-1837
Henderson, William S. - Catherine Vincent....	12-03-1800
Hendrick, James E. - Hannah Morris...........	3-03-1813
Hendrick, James W. Harriet Anderson..........	4-28-1835
Hendricks, John - Christeanna Vanderventer...	8-15-1802
Hendricks, Peter of Philadelphia, Pa. -	
Phebe Thompson.........................	3-12-1818
Hendrickson, Amos - Eliza Middleton..........	2-25-1836
Hendrickson, Cornelius - Anne Smith (wid.)...	4-11-1802
Hendrickson, Cornelius - Catherine Reynolds..	8-25-1799
Hendrickson, Cornelius - Mary Taylor.........	3-17-1836
Hendrickson, Cornelius - Sarah Ann Strickland	9-07-1833
Hendrickson, Cyrenus - Ida Van Mater.........	9-18-1823
Hendrickson, Daniel - Deborah Tilton.........	1-12-1813
Hendrickson, Daniel - Mary Applegate.........	11-29-1836
Hendrickson, Daniel - Phebe Harmer...........	8-28-1841
Hendrickson, Daniel - Sarah Covenhoven.......	12-21-1797
Hendrickson, Denice - Susan Snyder...........	9-23-1830
Hendrickson, Enoch - Acha E. Parker..........	4-09-1834
Hendrickson, Forman - Theodosia Hendrickson..	3-06-1823
Hendrickson, Garret - Hannah Wikof...........	12-10-1829
Hendrickson, Garret - Jane Hendrickson.......	3-10-1808
Hendrickson, Gilbert - Alice Conover.........	12-13-1821
Hendrickson, Gilbert - Hannah Wilber.........	3-23-1837
Hendrickson, Hendrick (Esq.) -	
Helenah Longstreet.....................	10-18-1806

```
Hendrickson, Jacob - Mary Davis..............  8-11-1832
Hendrickson, Jacob - Sarah Vanderveer........  2-18-1811
Hendrickson, James - Hannah Matthews......... 11-14-1826
Hendrickson, James - Pollina Cotteral........  1-25-1821
Hendrickson, John - Catherine Fisher......... 10-16-1839
Hendrickson, John - Matildah West............ 11-22-1834
Hendrickson, John D. - Ellen Hyer............  3-01-1830
Hendrickson, John L. - Elizabeth Forman...... 10-04-1829
Hendrickson, Joseph - Catherine Anderson..... 11-20-1803
Hendrickson, Joseph - Elizabeth Hendrickson..  6-01-1816
Hendrickson, Lloyd - Adeline Crawford........ 12-16-1822
Hendrickson, Michael - Ann Eliza Wikoff......  1-27-1830
Hendrickson, Michael - Elizabeth Wikoff...... 12-25-1834
Hendrickson, Pearson - Sarah Van Dorn........  8-07-1823
Hendrickson, Peter - Catherine Cox........... 12-19-1807
Hendrickson, Richard - Mary Thomas...........  2-02-1828
Hendrickson, Samuel - Catherine Imlay........  1-29-1824
Hendrickson, Samuel - Deborah Combs.......... 12-06-1803
Hendrickson, Samuel - Ellen Layton...........  5-12-1832
Hendrickson, Samuel - Lydia Leeming..........  3-23-1840
Hendrickson, Tobias - Idah Conover...........  2-10-1813
Hendrickson, Tobias - Margaret Perrine.......  5-27-1824
Hendrickson, William - Alice Hendrickson..... 11-12-1828
Hendrickson, William - Eleanor Du Bois.......  1-21-1811
Hendrickson, William - Elenor Emmons.........  4-04-1800
Hendrickson, William - Elizabeth Van Der Rype 11-26-1797
Hendrickson, William - Hannah Middleton......  2-07-1796
Hendrickson, William - Ruth Horsefull........  6-03-1804
Hendrickson, William - Sarah Luyster.........  5-08-1816
Hendrickson, William H. - Hannah Van Mater...  4-02-1827
Hendrickson, William Henry -
    Elizabeth Woodward......................  2-28-1839
Hennisee, John - Elizabeth White............. 10-11-1840
Henry, Alexander - Elizabeth Williams........  3-13-1817
Henry, James - Susan Forman..................  6-   -1837
Henry, William - Charlotte Stillwell......... 11-05-1837
Herbert, Abram - Hannah Hampton.............. 12-11-1805
Herbert, Benjamin - Lydia Craddock...........  6-28-1795
Herbert, Charles - Sarah Warrick.............  8-31-1834
Herbert, Daniel - Catherine Hendrickson......  5-31-1809
Herbert, Davis - Mary Shepherd...............  6-29-1811
Herbert, Francis - Nancy Van Brunt...........  1-02-1817
Herbert, Hampton - Mrs. Mary Kernagtion......  1-01-1838
Herbert, Hance - Anne Havens.................  5-04-1806
Herbert, Hugh - Elizabeth Johnson............  8-23-1825
Herbert, Isaac - Mrs. Aletta Bancker......... 10-10-1819
Herbert, Isaac - Sarah Morris................  7-12-1806
Herbert, Jacob - Margaret Hall...............  3-28-1824
Herbert, Jacob - Mary Mount.................. 10-10-1804
Herbert, Jacob - Nelly Bailey................  8-26-1802
Herbert, James - Charlotte Laird............. 10-09-1810
Herbert, James - Ellen Davison of
    Middlesex Co., N. J.....................  2-28-1839
Herbert, James - Mary Johnson................  5-09-1833
Herbert, James - Mary Longstreet.............  2-06-1825
```

```
Herbert, James - Sarah Anderson..............   3-15-1832
Herbert, John - Ann Groom...................  10-11-1818
Herbert, John - Lucy Ann Penn...............   9-30-1832
Herbert, Joseph - Elizabeth Dayton..........   3-24-1827
Herbert, Joseph (Capt.) - Esther Woolf......  11-11-1809
Herbert, Joseph - Margaret Chambers.........  12-30-1832
Herbert, Littleton - Rachael Hopkins........  12-12-1796
Herbert, Robert - Elizabeth Sebrooks........   4-03-1821
Herbert, Thomas - Grace Lefetra.............   3-30-1809
Herbert, William - Ellener Covenhoven.......   1-31-1801
Herbert, William - Hannah Campbell..........  12-31-1841
Herbert, William - Hannah Hankinson.........   1-20-1802
Herbert, William D. - Margaret Denise.......   2-12-1828
Herley, Albert - Catherine West.............  12-23-1822
Herr, Samuel - Sarah Marls..................   1-13-1811
Herring, Jacob - Jane Butler................  12-03-1842
Heulitt, Samuel - Isediah Brower............   5-14-1808
Heveland, Joseph - Ledia Sutphin............  12-04-1805
Heverland, Joseph - Sarah Ann King..........  12-08-1830
Heviland, Myndert - Afia Claton.............   8-16-1795
Hewet, Jacob - Rachel Sprigg................   1-01-1821
Hewlitt, Samuel - Eliza Ann Osborn..........   3-30-1842
Heyers, Garret (Capt.) - Williampe Cook.....   5-15-1830
Heywood, Joell - Mary Ann Farrow............   6-27-1842
Hibbets, William - Betsey Smith.............   6-05-1797
Hicks, John - Ellette Ann Chumerille........   9-08-1831
Hickson, John - Abigail Browne..............   3-04-1815
Hier, Forman - Sarah M. Stillwell...........  10-06-1836
Hier, James L. - Eliza Herring..............   9-11-1841
Hiers, Joseph - Margaret Sutphin............  12-23-1835
Higgens, John - Annas Osborn................   4-25-1830
Hight, Daniel - Elizabeth Begle.............   2-15-1809
Hight, Robert - Mary Riddle.................   5-14-1809
Hill, Theadore of Burlington Co., N. J. -
    Elizabeth Hart of Hunterdon Co., N.J.....  11-07-1833
Hill, William B. of Philadelphia, Pa. -
    Deborah T. Lawrence.....................  10-25-1829
Hillard, Thomas C. - Eleanor Shearman.......  12-01-1832
Hillyer, Lawrence - Sarah Suydam............   7-17-1800
Hilyer, John - Sarah Ryder..................   3-10-1805
Hinis, William - Sarah Duchell..............   7-06-1811
Hire, John - Alice Maps.....................   8-21-1798
Hire, Peter - Mary Vannortwick..............   9-17-1795
Hires, Aaron - Gertrude Cottrell............   3-03-1816
Hires, Edward - Ann Barnes..................   5-03-1806
Hires, Garret - Harriet Conk................  12-29-1825
Hires, Gilbert - Mary Throgmorton...........   8-02-1801
Hires, John - Miss Mary Buck................   9-27-1813
Hires, Joseph - Rachel Estell...............   2-03-1827
Hisler, William - Emiline McChestney........  11-08-1834
Hithcart, Samuel - Lydia Rozel..............   1-31-1805
Hix, Oliver - Lucy Stout....................  11-14-1806
Hoagland, Peter T. - Mary Croxson...........  11-05-1834
Hobart, Thomas of New Brunswick, Middlesex
    Co., N. J. - Mary R. English............   1-04-1827
```

```
Hoddy, John - Phebe Lampson..................  7-12-1829
Hodge, Samuel - Clemence Horner..............  12-18-1804
Hoe, Zenas - Anna Walling....................  11-09-1808
Hoff, George - Zimnetta Bedle................  9-15-1830
Hoff, Isaiah - Mary Thorne...................  3-25-1840
Hoff, John - Sarah M. Down...................  11-21-1821
Hoff, Samuel - Elizabeth Aumack..............  7-05-1837
Hoff, Taylor - Eliza Dorset..................  2-05-1829
Hoff, Thomas - Joanna Truax..................  2-19-1828
Hoff, Thomas T. - Merran ----................  4-18-1827
Hoff, William - Ann Seabrook.................  11-15-1821
Hoffman, John - Eleanor Chambers.............  12-26-1829
Hoffman, William - Lydia Knott...............  6-14-1801
Hoffmier, Conrad - Sarah Ann Jackson.........  2-17-1842
Hoffmire, William - Patience Lippencott......  11-09-1824
Hogan, James - Catherine Williams............  2-05-1800
Hoglen, John - Ann Hankins...................  3-10-1835
Holdman, James - Ann Johnson.................  12-27-1828
Holeman, Robert - Elinor Johnson.............  5-29-1805
Holeman, William - Catherine Van Hise........  10-31-1832
Hollock, Shepherd Koziusko -
    Hannah Pinford Tilton....................  11-09-1833
Holloway, Aaron - Ann Arnold.................  11-09-1837
Holloway, John - Sarah Vanderveer............  1-28-1834
Holloway, Robert - Ann Kester................  9-09-1809
Holman, John - Ann Eliza Maccabee............  4-01-1837
Holman, Robert- Mary Skidmore................  1-18-1807
Holman, William - Mary Runnells..............  6-19-1812
Holmes, Abraham - Grace Wykoff...............  3-15-1838
Holmes, Adam - Julia Ann Johnson.............  10-29-1832
Holmes, Asher - Lydia Wallen.................  9-17-1808
Holmes, Benjamin - Sarah Malah...............  4-14-1823
Holmes, Charles - Hagar Job..................  9-22-1825
Holmes, DAniel - Rhoda Van Mater.............  11-15-1815
Holmes, Elijah - Anitha Conover
    (widow of William S. Conover)............  2-23-1839
Holmes, Elisah - Jane Van Dorn...............  2-17-1819
Holmes, Henry - Dinah Johnston...............  6-08-1826
Holmes, Jacob - Nelly Overfield..............  3-14-1803
Holmes, Jacob - Nelly Polhemus...............  11-27-1810
Holmes, Jacob - Sarah Worden.................  2-04-1829
Holmes, John - Deborah Holmes................  1-07-1821
Holmes, John - Rachel Bowles.................  8-01-1839
Holmes, John - Rachel Combs..................  2-22-1803
Holmes, John L. - Anne Golden................  12-28-1821
Holmes, Jonathan - Eleanor Schenck...........  12-07-1824
Holmes, Joseph - Ann Stout...................  2-14-1824
Holmes, Josiah - Deborah Bassett.............  12-31-1831
Holmes, Josaih - Hannah Martin...............  2-22-1812
Holmes, Josiah - Mary Ann Errickson..........  1-31-1814
Holmes, Lewis - Charlotte Anderson
    (both black).............................  6-18-1836
Holmes, Moses - Sarah Jefery.................  1-06-1816
Holmes, Stephen - Mary Worden................  5-16-1824
Holmes, Stout - Mary Bray....................  6-06-1799
```

```
Holmes, William - Catherine Edwards.........  1-23-1800
Holstan, Lemuel - Mary Van Note.............  10-21-1836
Homan, Benjamin - Hannah Andress............  12-12-1840
Homer, John - Eliza Chaffee.................  2-10-1830
Homer, Richard - Elizabeth Le Munyon........  9-13-1804
Homer, Silas - Jane Well....................  1-31-1805
Honce, David - Jane Ann Vancleef............  4-08-1831
Honse, Hendricks - Elizabeth Rogers.........  2-06-1813
Hoofmire, Michael - Deborah Tilton..........  6-29-1807
Hook, William - Martha Dye..................  10-22-1806
Hooper, Thomas - Alice Hendrickson..........  1832-1833
Hooper, Thomas of Burlington Co., N. J. -
     Ann Steward............................  2-15-1834
Hope, Cornelius - Euphemia Kerr.............  6-23-1830
Hopkins, Anthony - Sarah Horner.............  11-11-1819
Hopkins, Daniel - Agnes Hopkins.............  11-29-1838
Hopkins, Daniel - Mary Moore................  3-01-1827
Hopkins, Ezekiel - Lydia Gravatt............  9-11-1825
Hopkins, George - Elizabeth Grover..........  7-04-1830
Hopkins, George - Margaret Jones............  3-21-1818
Hopkins, John - Hannah Loveless.............  2-25-1817
Hopkins, John - Mary Tilton.................  5-08-1805
Hopkins, John - Sarah More..................  7-23-1821
Hopkins, Joseph - Agnes Lafettra............  1-17-1828
Hopkins, Joseph - Mary Johnson..............  9-01-1831
Hopkins, Levy - Lenzer Stackhouse...........  7-13-1796
Hopkins, Thomas - Massa Horner..............  7-27-1810
Hopkins, William - Elenor Crofford..........  10-11-1817
Hopkins, William Jr. - Margaret Hopkins.....  1-26-1823
Hopmire, Salter - Eliza Emmons..............  1-25-1827
Hopmire, William - Sarah Swort..............  4-27-1797
Hopper, Abraham - Deborah McGregor..........  2-08-1814
Hopper, James - Charlotte Rogers............  11-09-1837
Hoppin, James - Patience Tilton.............  4-02-1808
Hopping, James - Mary Eastmond..............  2-10-1836
Hopping, Primrose - Fanny Hankinson.........  9-27-1831
Hopping, Primrose - Nancy Chacy.............  1-06-1814
Horn, William - Nancy Watson................  2-06-1798
Hornbeek, Thomas - Sarah Barton.............  5-26-1802
Horner, Aaron - Anna Cooper.................  5-31-1841
Horner, Freedom - Mary Messler..............  8-08-1840
Horner, Fuller - Damarias Harker............  7-24-1808
Horner, Isaac - Ann West....................  2-15-1821
Horner, Isaiah - Eliza ----.................  6-05-1818
Horner, Jacob - Lyddia Hurley...............  11-07-1832
Horner, Jeremiah - Sary Gaskin..............  12-31-1819
Horner, John - Margaret Ann Smith...........  12-07-1822
Horner, John - Phebe Spragg.................  4-20-1823
Horner, John - Sarah Ridgeway...............  5-10-1828
Horner, Jonathan - Susan John...............  8-13-1834
Horner, Joseph - Elizabeth Conover..........  5-16-1841
Horner, Joseph - Margaret Jonson............  1-05-1820
Horner, Joseph - Mary Salter................  3-27-1837
Horner, Joshua - Rachel Parker..............  8-14-1842
Horner, Moses - Leonah Rogers...............  12-24-1810
```

Horner, Samuel - Mary Ann Dunfee............. 5-02-1839
Horner, Thomas - Sarah Ann Pullen............ 7-29-1840
Horner, Thomas - Sarah Worth................. 1-20-1797
Horner, Wesley - Allice John................. 8-07-1830
Horner, William - Hannah Hurley.............. 11-16-1829
Horner, William - Sarah Fowler............... 12-13-1841
Horsfield, Ezekiel - Margaret Hurr........... 11-05-1829
Horsfield, Jacob (Capt.) - Lucy Ann Blake.... 1-10-1833
Horsfield, Richard - Elizabeth Hnedrickson... 11-15-1826
Hough, Gesham - Mary Longstreet.............. 1-05-1825
Hough, Oliver - Elizabeth Megill............. 1-17-1836
Houghby, James - Hannah Parker............... 5-21-1809
Housler, Abraham - Catherine Sutten.......... 1-16-1809
Howard, Joseph - Ann Conover................. 12-31-1837
Howel, James M. - Hannah Youmans............. 2-03-1820
Howell, John - Catherine Estile.............. 9-09-1826
Howell, Samuel - Charity Hendrickson......... 8-09-1841
Howell, William - Rachel Thorp............... 3-31-1805
Howland, Asher - Caroline Wooley............. 5-09-1825
Howland, Asher - Zilphia Allgor.............. 10-18-1834
Howland, Cook - Anna Harvey.................. 9-29-1802
Howland, Gilbert - Mary Morrell.............. 12-20-1836
Howland, James - Mariah Brown................ 5-04-1836
Howland, James - Phaney Slocum............... 2-11-1808
Howland, Jesse - Meribah White............... 3-15-1821
Howland, Michael - Zemima Lane............... 1-03-1822
Howland, Thomas - Elizabeth Woolcott......... 12-22-1814
Howler, John - Elizabeth Woolley............. 1-06-1816
Howlett, Barney - Rachel Ridgway............. 4-22-1827
Hubbard, Abraham - Mary Morton............... 1-30-1824
Hubbard, James (Dr.) - Charlotte Corlies..... 11-04-1824
Hubbard, William H. - Ellen Cook............. 10-10-1836
Hubbert, Elias - Hulda Holmes................ 1-14-1801
Hubbert, Elisa - Nellie Hendrickson.......... 3-26-1811
Hubbert, Jacobus - Catherine Hendrickson..... 5-02-1798
Hubbert, John - Nelly Gusten (wid.).......... 2-05-1817
Hubbert, Samuel - Margaret Stoutonburrow..... 2-16-1818
Hubbert, Tunis - Margaret Covenhoven......... 1-05-1797
Hudson, Thomas - Caroline Conover............ 1-09-1840
Huff, David - Prisilla Buckalew.............. 1-01-1802
Huff, Thomas - Hannah Van Wyke............... 12-27-1797
Huff, Thomas - Tudea Wellet.................. 11-07-1835
Huff, William P. of New York -
    Elizabeth W. Edwards..................... 4-19-1834
Hughes, James - Lydia Bunting................ 3-12-1833
Hughes, John - Hariet Bordon................. 9-15-1821
Hughes, Lambert R. - Elizabeth G. Labow...... 4-04-1832
Hughes, Randall - Julia Ann Vannest.......... 1831-1832
Hughes, Richard - Acsah Cubberly............. 3-06-1830
Hughs, Elisha - Hannah Rouse................. 8-31-1810
Hughs, Joseph - Mariah Rybins................ 1-18-1816
Huggins, William - Emmeline Aker............. 2-25-1837
Hulce, Anthony - Hannah Ann Shepherd......... 11-12-1834
Hulce, Garret - Ann Johnson.................. 7-20-1822
Hulce, John - Elizabeth Harvey............... 6-15-1805

Hulek, James - Anne Dey..................... 9-07-1803
Hulet, William - Rebecah Burch.............. 1-22-1797
Hulick, Charles - Mary Hampton.............. 1-14-1841
Hulick, Cornelius T. - Elizabeth Combs....... 6-14-1807
Hulick, John - Edna Woolcote................ 1-25-1840
Hulings, Isaac of Burlingotn Co., N. J. -
    Achsa Woodward.......................... 12-20-1827
Hulit, James - Harriet Brown................ 4-11-1835
Hull, James - Ann Emmens.................... 10-25-1795
Hull, Thomas C. - Valaria Norris............ 12-14-1825
Hullick, Cornelius P. - Elizabeth Hampton.... 10-24-1813
Hulls, James - Linda Havens................. 4-04-1802
Hulsart, Sidney - Ann Bennett............... 2-24-1820
Hulse, Aaron - Grace Street................. 5-19-1836
Hulse, James - Mary Ely..................... 11-11-1835
Hulse, James - Sarah Adley.................. 11-03-1797
Hulse, John - Jane Mains.................... 11-24-1822
Hulse, John - Mary Mason.................... 11-24-1838
Hulse, Joseph D. - Margaret Voorhees........ 6-26-1819
Hulse, Ralph - Margaret Stillwell........... 11-20-1828
Hulse, William - Sarah Forman............... 1-13-1799
Hulshart, Cornelius - Rebecca Covert........ 12-30-1837
Hulshart, David - Lydia Jane Patterson...... 4-08-1839
Hulshart, Garret Sr. - Mrs. Alice Mackcabe... 11-04-1812
Hulshart, Gidian - Caty Thompson............ 12-29-1821
Hulshart, Hendrick - Esther Patterson....... 4-24-1841
Hulshart, James - Jane Voorhees............. 11-08-1827
Hulshart, John - Mary Chatman............... 2-06-1813
Hulshart, John - Mary Foster................ 7-12-1829
Hulshart, Samuel - Mary Emmons.............. 8-11-1796
Hulshart, Stephen - Sara Matthew............ 6-28-1829
Hulshart, Thomas - Annadolphe Hulshart...... 8-11-1828
Hulst, Hendrick (wid'r.) -
    Margaret Yetman (wid.).................. 12-30-1816
Hulstward, Joseph - Mayard Voorhees......... 2-22-1811
Hultry, John - Unice Emmons................. 6-14-1827
Hultz, William - Faithful Smith............. 3-09-1796
Huluck, Cornelius P. - Elizabeth Coombs..... 6-04-1807
Hunsinger, Peter - Martha Vanderipe......... 2-08-1797
Hunt, Abraham V. of New York -
    Margaret Nevius......................... 1-22-1818
Hunt, Asa - Susan Bruere.................... 6-15-1839
Hunt, John - Susan Pitman................... 9-11-1823
Hunt, Jospeh - Amy Tindal of Middlesex Co.,
    New Jersey.............................. 6-14-1832
Hunt, Thomas - Ann Mariah Newman............ 1-26-1830
Hunter, John - Ruth Jones................... 3-14-1813
Huntsinger, John - Katherine Erwin.......... 7-30-1809
Huntsinger, Matthias - Euphama Willson...... 10-27-1805
Hurley, Benjamin - Elizabeth Roman.......... 8-23-1842
Hurley, Cornelius - Hester Remine........... 11-01-1827
Hurley, David - Lidia Johnston.............. 4-29-1826
Hurley, Hudson - Eleanor Bennett
    dg. of William.......................... 2-14-1842
Hurley, Jacob - Catherine Van Note.......... 2-12-1833

Hurley, John - Alice Newbury................ 11-18-1820
Hurley, John - Elizabeth Banton............. 10-14-1843
Hurley, John - Elizabeth Bonbath............ 10-11-1833
Hurley, John D. - Sarah Ann White........... 1-13-1831
Hurley, Robert, Elizabeth Jones............. 4-17-1813
Hurley, Robert - Phebe Bennett.............. 6-01-1831
Hurley, Sylvester - Ann Marie Blake......... 11-20-1836
Hurley, Thomas - Mary Bennett............... 3-30-1811
Hurley, William - Rhoda Remine.............. 1-16-1826
Hurly, Henry - Eliza Ann Allger............. 11-23-1833
Huro, Hiram of New York City -
     Phebe Corlies Edwards.................. 6-20-1825
Huston, James - Ann Everingham.............. 4-13-1839
Hutchinson, Aaron - Elizabeth Davison....... 3-23-1837
Hutchinson, Abraham - Ann W. Robbins........ 1-24-1830
Hutchinson, Peerson - Ann Crickee........... 5-10-1831
Hutchinson, Sylvanus - Phebe Ann Thompson... 11-15-1837
Hutts, Enoch T. - Elizabeth Parmer.......... 12-13-1837
Huylemen, Andrew - Barbara R---............. 1841
Huylen, Aden - Elizabeth Robert............. 12-01-1842
Hyde, Zenas of New York City - Alice Wikoff.. 9-03-1825
Hyer, Gilbert - Perlina Miller.............. 1-07-1843
Hyer, Kortenus - Catherine Buck............. 5-21-1815
Hyer, William - Eleanor Waggoner............ 11-29-1828
Hyer, William - Margaret Hill............... 9-26-1799
Hyers, Daniel - Mrs. Margaret Pullen........ 10-02-1841
Hyers, Gilbert - Mary Jackson............... 11-19-1837
Hyers, Gisbert - Phebe Hankins.............. 4-13-1833
Hyers, Gorden - Elizabeth Allen............. 10-13-1838
Hyers, John - Amy Ann De Bow................ 1841-1842
Hyers, John - Sarah Connars................. 1-01-1814
Hyers, John Jr. - Jerimah Johnson........... 10-20-1832
Hyers, Joseph - Catherine Barnes............ 3-02-1801
Hyers, Joseph - Lavinia Wilbur.............. 3-23-1843
Hyers, Joseph - Margaret Johnson............ 7-28-1832
Hyers, Peter - Phoebe Pettit................ 3-29-1800
Hyland, Thomas - Ann Shreve................. 9-10-1836
Hyns, Joseph - Rachiel Estile............... 2-03-1827
Hyrley, James - Rebecah Newberry............ 3-14-1807
Idle, John - Ann Derby...................... 1-30-1809
Imlay, Elisha - Eleanor Taylor.............. 4-25-1802
Imlay, John - Mary Hanes.................... 10-20-1798
Imlay, Joseph - Elizabeth Stout............. 11-09-1836
Imlay, Peter - Catherine Hendrickson........ 2-03-1816
Imlay, William L. - Amey Anderson........... 3-17-1814
Ingersoll, Daniel - Sally Barry............. 10-28-1799
Inman, John - Elizabeth West................ 8-01-1818
Inman, John - Mary Headly................... 12-04-1813
Inman, John Stafford - Elizabeth Lippincott.. 10-23-1796
Inman, Michael - Hannah Inman............... 5-28-1824
Inman, Steven - Doryter Rutters............. 4-15-1819
Inman, William - Phebe Perrin............... 12-12-1840
Ireland, Robert - Margaret Vorhees.......... 12-31-1836
Ireland, William - Sarah Giberson........... 7-20-1820
Irons, Aaron R. - Elizabeth Ford............ 10-18-1829

```
Irons, Edward - Eliza Hyers.................. 12-24-1814
Irons, Francis - Elener Brewer............... 3-25-1814
Irons, Garret - Deborah Taylor............... 12-05-1841
Irons, Garret - Loas Brewer.................. 12-29-1821
Irons, Gilbert - Ledida Hyres................ 8-06-1825
Irons, James - Zilpha Clayton................ 12-02-1841
Irons, John - Abigail Applegate.............. 8-22-1840
Irons, John W. - Hester Applegate............ 12-15-1821
Irons, Joseph - Lydia Van Note............... 4-08-1837
Irons, William - Ann Crawford................ 8-01-1829
Ivins, David M. - Ann Lloyd.................. 12-08-1814
Ivins, Ezekiel - Charlotte Allen............. 12-04-1808
Ivins, George - Eliza Applebee both of
      Burlington Co., N. J.................... 1-29-1825
Ivins, George - Martha Burtis................ 10-08-1842
Ivins, Gilbert - Jacy Jackson................ 3-02-1809
Ivins, James - Mary Covenhoven............... 6-03-1818
Ivins, James - Sarah Rulong.................. 11-22-1829
Ivins, Joseph - Rachel Silvers............... 9-16-1835
Ivins, William - Mary Hazelton............... 11-22-1807
Jackson, Benjamin - Ann Lane................. 10-01-1836
Jackson, Benjamin B. - Hannah Longstreet..... 4-21-1814
Jackson, Benjamin Jr. - Catherine Longstreet. 3-06-1800
Jackson, Daniel - Mrs. Catherine Harvey...... 12-05-1812
Jackson, Edwin - Mary Wilbur................. 2-14-1826
Jackson, George - Emma Reed.................. 3-23-1832
Jackson, George - Mary Burden................ 11-15-1806
Jackson, Hartson - Elizabeth Osborn.......... 11-05-1818
Jackson, Henry - Mary Riddle................. 12-15-1825
Jackson, Hugh - Sarah Woolley................ 9-03-1799
Jackson, Hugh Jr. - Ann Forman............... 3-01-1815
Jackson, Isac - Phebe Cox.................... 8-29-1804
Jackson, James - Catherine Dangler........... 2-23-1842
Jackson, James - Sarah Wainwright............ 3-10-1836
Jackson, John - Ann Glen..................... 12-31-1837
Jackson, John - Hager Johnston (both black).. 4-12-1834
Jackson, Joseph - Deborah Elmer.............. 1-31-1821
Jackson, Joseph - Elizabeth Mitchell......... 12-27-1813
Jackson, Lambert - Sarah Dover............... 3-20-1819
Jackson, Lawrence - Deborah Brinley.......... 12-19-1806
Jackson, Samuel - Phebe Parker............... 4-25-1801
Jackson, William - Ann Conover............... 10-18-1819
Jackson, William - Rebecca Green............. 12-24-1797
Jackson, William A. - Mary Ann Clayton....... 8-08-1834
Jacobs, George - Clanah (negro).............. 12-20-1829
Jacobs, William - Barbary Dillon............. 9-01-1821
Jaggard, Walter - Catherine Eggleston........ 6-06-1837
James. Dunahay - Jane Heaveland.............. 6-06-1835
James, George of N. Y. - Mary Borden........ 7-29-1824
James, Henry - Catherine Craig (both black).. 8-13-1841
James, Imlay - Amanda Applegate.............. 3-16-1839
James, John - Rhoda Robbins.................. 1-17-1831
James, Lewis - Harriet Hammell............... 2-19-1824
James, Lewis - Lucy Niveson.................. 11-15-1823
James, Richard - Lidia Ford.................. 1-23-1819
```

James, Robert - Alice Longstreet............. 9-21-1831
Jane, Gilbert - Sarah Aumack................ 1-10-1796
Janes, William - Sarah Sexton............... 3-10-1814
Jaques, Samuel R. - Catherine Emmons........ 2-05-1829
Jaques, William A. - Elizabeth Allen........ 3-05-1829
Jefferson, Sexton - Rose Williams........... 3-15-1842
Jeffery, David - Elizabeth Rogers........... 1-10-1824
Jeffery, Francis - Elizabeth Martin......... 2-26-1801
Jeffery, Jesse - Alice Rogers............... 4-30-1800
Jeffery, Nathen - Lydia Rogers.............. 4-20-1830
Jeffery, William - Elizabeth Barklow
  (wid.) of Howell......................... 2-25-1830
Jeffery, William - Margaret Childs.......... 3-12-1801
Jeffery, William - Mrs. Sarah Luker......... 4-12-1817
Jeffree, James - G. Brand................... 11-29-1804
Jeffree, John - Mary Jeffree................ 7-20-1802
Jeffrey, Daniel - Anna Saltman.............. 12-03-1798
Jeffrey, Elihu - Catherine Lane............. 3-11-1820
Jeffrey, Elisha - Lydia Vunck............... 3-15-1816
Jeffrey, Francis - Eleanor Irons............ 9-29-1803
Jeffrey, Lewis - Mary Akins................. 6-17-1822
Jeffrey, Oliver - Elizabeth Lewis........... 5-07-1805
Jeffrey, Richard - Charlotte White.......... 12-07-1837
Jeffrey, William - Ruth Allen............... 1-10-1804
Jeffry, Lewis - Margaret White.............. 7-07-1825
Jemerson, Clayton - Harriet Girton.......... 8-14-1833
Jemson, Abraham B. - Rachel Debow........... 10-16-1827
Jemson, Jacob - Lydia Evernham.............. 10-27-1825
Jenson, Peter - Hannah Newman............... 11-16-1812
Jewel, John - Catherine Reed................ 4-19-1798
Jewel, Richard - Sarah Reid................. 2-15-1801
Jewell, Elisha - Mary Mount................. 4-05-1826
Jey, William - Hanah Vanderveer............. 7-13-1812
Job, Robert Jr. - Sarah Williams (both black) 4-01-1828
Jobs, Clayton - Charlotte Stedpole.......... 2-27-1815
John, E. Gordon - Lydia Hampton............. 2-24-1823
John, William - Jane Jonson................. 8-21-1796
Johne, Revoe - Mary Wells................... 7-31-1841
Johnson, Abraham - Mary Clayton............. 1-30-1811
Johnson, Adam - Elizabeth Leonard
  (both black)............................. 12-27-1834
Johnson, Amos - Charlot Kay................. 3-05-1806
Johnson, Andrew - Agibal Money.............. 12-08-1810
Johnson, Andrew - Margaretta Johnson........ 10-19-1839
Johnson, Benjamin - Anna Cooper............. 3-20-1800
Johnson, Benjamin - Temperance Soper........ 1-03-1839
Johnson, Charles - Margaret Simons.......... 7-22-1841
Johnson, Charles - Sarah Matthews........... 3-18-1837
Johnson, Daniel - Catherine Stutts.......... 5-24-1837
Johnson, Daniel - Sarah Green............... 12-24-1816
Johnson, David - Catherine Lloyd............ 1-04-1801
Johnson, David - Cornelia (black)........... 3-14-1839
Johnson, David - Mary Giberson.............. 12-09-1816
Johnson, David - Sarah Allen................ 11-13-1802
Johnson, Edmund - Sarah Estele.............. 8-30-1828

```
Johnson, Edward - Phebe (black).............. 10-06-1816
Johnson, Ephraim - Mary Cooke................ 12-27-1809
Johnson, Ezekiel - Hannah Riddle............. 1-26-1837
Johnson, Ezekiel E. - Elizabeth Skidmore..... 3-07-1818
Johnson, Francis - Charlotte Smires.......... 3-14-1821
Johnson, Francis - Margaret Saxon............ 2-10-1812
Johnson, George - Emma Granden............... 7-04-1840
Johnson, George - Mary McGill................ 8-20-1797
Johnson, Henry - Hannah Tilton............... 1-21-1818
Johnson, Henry - Mary Disborough............. 2-17-1811
Johnson, Henry - Rebecca Williams............ 10-28-1817
Johnson, Hugh - Ann Potter................... 1830-1835
Johnson, Isaac - Mary Ann Henderson
     (both black)........................... 5-23-1834
Johnson, Isaac - Sarah Preston............... 1-05-1830
Johnson, Jacob - Hannah Johnson.............. 5-17-1809
Johnson, Jacob - Mary Bray................... 9-18-1808
Johnson, James - Ann Arose................... 11-02-1833
Johnson, James - Elizabeth Rouse............. 2-25-1804
Johnson, James - Euphame Lucas............... 4-24-1813
Johnson, James - Louisa Nailer............... 12-02-1835
Johnson, James - Mary Bond................... 1-19-1798
Johnson, James - Mary Ann Irons.............. 5-30-1832
Johnson, James - Mary Mount.................. 12-12-1821
Johnson, James - Mary Pierce................. 6-16-1796
Johnson, James - Sarah Ely................... 9-07-1836
Johnson, James - Sarah Russell............... 4-23-1836
Johnson, Jobe - Phebe Mills.................. 9-05-1821
Johnson, John - Catherine Bird............... 3-07-1796
Johnson, John - Cloe Morroco (both black).... 12-05-1830
Johnson, John - Grace Likens................. 11-27-1810
Johnson, John - Hannah Reynolds.............. 3-25-1820
Johnson, John - Harriet Worth................ 7-22-1801
Johnson, John - Martha Stillwell............. 1830-1835
Johnson, John - Mary Gifford................. 12-18-1806
Johnson, John - Mary Holmes.................. 4-06-1796
Johnson, John - Mary Sutphin................. 7-04-1798
Johnson, John - Rachel Horner................ 7-28-1798
Johnson, John - Valeria Morris............... 3-25-1803
Johnson, Jonathan - Charity Phillips......... 1-24-1801
Johnson, Jonathan - Rachel Mitchell.......... 6-08-1799
Johnson, Jonathen - Rebecca Brewer........... 10-09-1836
Johnson, Jonathan - Sarah Tilton............. 12-07-1806
Johnson, Joseph - Elizabeth Wynant........... 6-22-1837
Johnson, Joseph - Hannah Philips............. 3-27-1803
Johnson, Joseph - Letta Algour............... 7-07-1831
Johnson, Joseph - Mariah Deouty.............. 2-06-1830
Johnson, Joseph - Mary Gifford............... 12-03-1809
Johnson, Joseph - Mary Shinn................. 2-23-1836
Johnson, Joseph - Silva Irons................ 3-07-1840
Johnson, Joseph - Susan Osborne.............. 1-16-1841
Johnson, Joseph Jr. - Zilpha Emmons.......... 3-21-1825
Johnson, Joseph T. - Elizabeth Curtis........ 10-27-1830
Johnson, Mathias - Judith Tice............... 4-27-1802
Johnson, Michael - Ann Chamberlin............ 8-30-1840
```

Johnson, Michael - Mary Phillips............. 2-09-1817
Johnson, Phineas - Charity Vaughn............ 3-15-1842
Johnson, Richard - Deborah Layton............ 1830-1835
Johnson, Robert - Mary Thompson dg. of John.. 6-04-1834
Johnson, Ruliff - Mary Shepherd.............. 5-20-1837
Johnson, Ruliff - Nancy Borden............... 7-27-1816
Johnson, Samuel - Elizabeth Coward........... 11-22-1802
Johnson, Samuel - Julia J. Grover............ 4-28-1839
Johnson, Simon - Harriet Little.............. 9-19-1835
Johnson, Taylor - Mary Applegate............. 9-08-1831
Johnson, Thomas - Abiga Rue.................. 7-28-1810
Johnson, Thomas - Amy Hendrickson............ 2-27-1840
Johnson, William - Deborah Allen............. 5-26-1839
Johnson, William - Hannah Giberson........... 9-29-1838
Johnson, William - Lois Giberson............. 4-27-1811
Johnson, William - Luezur Huggins............ 2-12-1836
Johnson, William - Lydia Baird............... 4-29-1806
Johnson, William - Margaret Perrine.......... 6-04-1818
Johnson, William - Nancy Throgmorton......... 2-11-1796
Johnson, William - Rebecca Tone.............. 11-26-1806
Johnson, William - Sarah Chamberlin.......... 1-11-1837
Johnson, William - Sarah Soper............... 1-11-1837
Johnson, William Jr. - Phebe Liming.......... 8-17-1806
Johnston, Aaron - Rachel Chambers............ 6-13-1822
Johnston, Abraham - Catherine Howard......... 4-22-1826
Johnston, Andrew - Leah Robbins.............. 1-09-1828
Johnston, Anthony - Rachel Coward............ 4-15-1828
Johnston, Benjamin - Catherine Harris........ 9-19-1812
Johnston, Daniel - Nancy Collins............. 9-05-1818
Johnston, Edwin - Mary Ann Schenck........... 10-07-1827
Johnston, Elisha - Catherine Cook............ 4-20-1833
Johnston, Elisha - Jane Hulse................ 12-15-1830
Johnston, Ezekiel - Deborah Morris........... 3-30-1816
Johnston, George - Catherine Huelitt......... 10-11-1809
Johnston, George Jr. - Nancy Vannote......... 6-01-1811
Johnston, Hance - Elizabeth Hulse............ 7-12-1832
Johnston, Henry - Rebecca Berry.............. 2-14-1841
Johnston, James - Jane Van Cleaf............. 12-13-1825
Johnston, James - Mary Wilbur................ 7-30-1831
Johnston, Job - Elizabeth Warwick............ 5-09-1841
Johnston, John - Ann Van Brockle............. 2-19-1831
Johnston, John - Anne Kirby of
    Burlington Co., N. J..................... 11-16-1826
Johnston, John - Mary Parker................. 10-09-1823
Johnston, John - Rachel Conover.............. 3-07-1799
Johnston, John - Mrs. Sarah Havens........... 5-07-1832
Johnston, Joseph - Lettee Brand.............. 4-30-1828
Johnston, Joseph - Mary Seabrook............. 1-04-1822
Johnston, Joseph son of Ruliff -
    Rachel Wilgus............................ 2-10-1799
Johnston, Joseph T. - Lidia Havens........... 8-16-1826
Johnston, Kenneth - Lydia Street............. 1-03-1828
Johnston. Lewis - Pauline Herbert............ 12-26-1829
Johnston, Lewis - Sarah Irons................ 12-12-1827
Johnston, Luke - Sarah Skidmore.............. 4-09-1825

```
Johnston, Ruben - Patience Woolley...........  9-02-1841
Johnston, Samuel - Ann Vanhise...............  6-09-1832
Johnston, Samuel - Mary Buckalew.............  8-27-1800
Johnston, Samuel - Sarah Jane Hays........... 11-27-1833
Johnston, Thomas - Martha Anderson...........  1-20-1816
Johnston, Thomas - Mary McAlvey..............  4-24-1802
Johnston, William - Lidde Bruer..............  1-25-1829
Johnston, William - Sarah Tilton.............  5-27-1810
Johnston, William G. - Elizabeth Estol....... 12-25-1824
Johnston, William T. - Mary A. Longstreet....  7-23-1829
Johntry, Abraham - Mary Maxzon...............  8-11-1835
Joline, George - Mrs. Hannah Howland.........  2-04-1828
Joline, Henry - Margaret Wardell............. 12-25-1823
Joline, James - Perselley White..............  9-09-1819
Joline, William H. - Margaret Wardell........ 12-25-1823
Jolly, John - Sarah Nesbit................... 10-31-1839
Jones, Adam - Ann Wordle..................... 11-14-1830
Jones, Benjamin - Eunice Emmons.............. 10-07-1810
Jones, David - Amelia Willis of
    Burlington Co., N. J....................  2-07-1819
Jones, David - Deliverance Leming............ 10-01-1836
Jones, David - Hannah Brown.................. 11-01-1800
Jones, David - Mary Ridgway..................  6-17-1823
Jones, David - Sarah Parker..................  3-18-1839
Jones, Ebenezer - Catherine Havens........... 10-15-1823
Jones, Elisha - Anna Harling.................  3-12-1818
Jones, Elisha - Charity Bennet...............  2-15-1823
Jones, Enoch - Elizabeth Stout...............  5-01-1830
Jones, Henry - Mary Cook.....................  7-12-1817
Jones, Jacob - Sarah Bonnet.................. 11-04-1810
Jones, Jervas - Elizabeth Crammer............ 12-01-1827
Jones, Jessie - Elizabeth Wooley.............  3-05-1807
Jones, John - Acsa Jones..................... 12-05-1820
Jones, John - Ann Hopkins....................  6-08-1823
Jones, John - Elizabeth Forgison.............  7-10-1803
Jones, John - Mary Stuart....................  6-26-1824
Jones, Phineus - Lydia Davis................. 10-21-1813
Jones, Richard - Mary B---...................  6-16-1821
Jones, Samuel of Burlington Co., N. J. -
    Alletta Smock...........................  9-17-1829
Jones, Samuel - Harriet Herbert..............  2-20-1837
Jones, Stacy - Bulah Crammer................. 11-22-1808
Jones, William - Bethur Gaskill..............  5-31-1800
Jones, William - Jane Havens.................  1-16-1828
Jones, William R. - Eliza R. Woodward........ 11-28-1833
Jonson, Joseph - Charity Adams...............  9-02-1797
Jonson, Robert - Sarah Jones.................  3-17-1810
Jonson, William - Mary Vernon................ 10-18-1817
Jonson, William - Sarah Barns................  1-21-1799
Joseph, John - Mrs. Mary Harris.............. 10-22-1826
Jurnis, Samuel of N. Y. - Lidia Thompson.....  4-18-1813
Karr, Abraham - Meriam Manes.................  3-02-1797
Karr, Andrew - Nancy Morris.................. 11-18-1820
Karr, Walter - Naomi Bennet.................. 10-04-1836
Keeler, James - Abigail McMichael............ 12-28-1831
```

Keeler, Jacob of Burlington Co., N. J. -
    Rachel Compton........................ 10-10-1818
Keepers, Joseph - Elizabeth Erixson.......... 2-17-1828
Keller, Jacob - Emmaline Rogers.............. 3-21-1837
Kelley, Alfred of Burlington Co., N.J. -
    May Jackson........................... 6-25-1842
Kelly, Cornelius - Mary Seamons.............. 10-21-1804
Kelly, Dennis - Phebe Simmons............... 4-04-1824
Kelly, Luke - Elizabeth Woolley............. 9-10-1802
Kelsey, James - Martha Herbert.............. 9-18-1796
Kembel, Henry - Sarah Ireland............... 3-22-1809
Kenvat, Robert - Mary Wilgust............... 5-24-1801
Kenworthy, John - Mrs. Jemima Rogers........ 10-16-1834
Ker, Joseph - Margaret Herbert.............. 2-06-1800
Kerby, William - Elizabeth Skidmore......... 9-01-1835
Kern, Aaron - Rachel Davison................ 11-17-1821
Kernaghan, William - Margaret Snider........ 2-10-1803
Kerr, David - Achsah Bennett................ 3-04-1809
Kerr, Job - Ann Hutts....................... 11-14-1839
Kerr, John - Susannah Coward................ 10-03-1822
Kerr, Walter Jr. (Capt.) - Sarah Thomas..... 1-10-1833
Kerry, Edward - Abigal Reoy................. 3-10-1810
Ketcham, John - Margaret Truex.............. 3-01-1810
Ketcham, Thomas - Elizabeth Longstreet...... 1-06-1817
Ketchem, Daniel B. - Mary A. Stillwell...... 3-03-1828
Ketchum, Benjamin - Harriet Taylor.......... 9-20-1823
Ketchum, John - Caroline Bowne.............. 4-18-1830
Ketchum, William - Margaret Havens.......... 12-30-1830
Kiddel, John - Rebarah Layton............... 10-10-1799
Kilts, Forman - Sarah Clevenger............. 10-11-1827
Kimble, Abraham - Elizabeth Haymen.......... 7-08-1816
King, Charles - Mary Ann Kittle............. 4-03-1827
King, John - Margaret Borden................ 11-10-1836
King, Joseph - Ann Worthley................. 12-03-1840
King, Joseph - Betsey Ridgway............... 3-01-1812
King, Joseph - Catherine Lippincott......... 9-18-1816
King, Mahlon - Sarah Stanton................ 6-11-1836
King, Rememberance - Letisha Kirley......... 2-04-1829
King, Samuel - Lucy Vanhise................. 7-22-1831
Kirby, Edmund B. - Margaret Antrim.......... 5-13-1830
Kirby, Job - Elizabeth Arney................ 11-25-1799
Kirby, Richard - Sarah Hurley............... 9-13-1827
Kirby, Peter - Alche Martin................. 6-09-1824
Kirby, Samuel - Clarica Kenada.............. 2-23-1822
Kirby, Thomas B. - Margaret Herbert......... 10-21-1833
Kirkpatrick, Jacob (Rev.) -
    Mary K. H. B. Sutfin.................. 9-23-1809
Kisner, Jacob - Lydia Cool.................. 4-17-1828
Kittle, Elijah - Adeline Woolley............ 8-29-1839
Kline, John - Rebecca Little................ 11-12-1838
Knott, Jacob - Sarah Pitcher................ 2-21-1822
Knott, Jeremiah - Isabella Perrine.......... 2-25-1826
Knott, Joseph - Elizabeth Wilson............ 3-27-1831
Kozciuski, Kollack - ---- Pintard........... 1833-1834

```
Labough, David - Sarah Barcalow..............  10-20-1799
Lacount, John - Elenor Mathews...............  12-25-1834
Lacount, Joseph - Sarah Ann Brown...........   7-12-1838
Lafetra, Benjamin - Rebecca A. Wainwright....  1-20-1825
Lafetra, George W. -
   Elizabeth S. Throckmorton.................  11-19-1814
Lafetra, Moses of N. Y. - Ann Eldridge.......  6-23-1811
Lafetra, Rylee T. - Marobah S. Woolcott......  8-01-1824
Lafetrer, Tyla W. - Catherine Haring.........  1-23-1817
Lafusge, Abraham of N. Y. - Catherine Bills..  12-05-1835
Lain, Abraham - Ann Brinley..................  2-22-1819
Lain, Cornelius Jr. - Mariah Chamberlain.....  1-06-1821
Lain, Jacob - Jane Hulshart..................  8-01-1813
Lain, Jacob - Lydia White....................  10-09-1813
Lain, Joseph - Ann Cook......................  10-01-1823
Lain, Samuel - Kathryn King..................  2-18-1799
Laine, John - Charity Martin.................  12-06-1815
Laine, Manning - Eleanor Lee.................  11-21-1840
Laird, Benjamin - Hannah Mount...............  1-17-1809
Laird, David - Elizabeth Herbert.............  2-23-1823
Laird, John - Alice Williams.................  6-28-1803
Laird, Samuel - Helena Tilton................  1-11-1815
Laird, William - Sarah Aux Newell............  11-29-1804
Lake, Joseph - Sarah Van Mater...............  7-07-1807
Lake, Samuel - Catherine Harvey..............  6-15-1816
Lake, Samuel - Mrs. Frances Mount of N. Y....  8-21-1842
Lake, William - Elizabeth Van Mater..........  1-11-1816
Lamberson, John - Mary Vorhees...............  4-19-1810
Lambert, Thomas - Mary Reed..................  3-19-1826
Lambertson, Joshua - Mary Britan.............  10-22-1799
Lampson, Edward - Catherine Bennett..........  2-10-1811
Lampson, William - Agnes Simmons.............  4-10-1825
Lane, Aaron - Jane Schenck...................  5-15-1816
Lane, Abraham - Mary Wooley..................  2-12-1806
Lane, Abraham - Sarah Thompson...............  8-21-1834
Lane, Cornelius - Catherine Davison..........  1-04-1829
Lane, Garret - Catherine Hendrickson.........  5-23-1803
Lane, George - Fetry Havens..................  9-18-1836
Lane, Gilbert - Deborah Morris...............  9-25-1824
Lane, Gilbert - Sarah Aumack.................  11-10-1796
Lane, Isaac - Sarah Mathews..................  5-11-1814
Lane, Isaiah S. - Mary Ann Lane..............  1-11-1834
Lane, John - Elizabeth Haven dg. of Howell...  7-07-1804
Lane, John - Jane Breece.....................  8-03-1806
Lane, John - Lydia Vancleef..................  11-15-1809
Lane, Joseph - Lettia Kerr...................  8-24-1824
Lane, Peter - Elmira Thompson................  7-12-1834
Lane, Peter - Mary Roberson..................  9-07-1816
Lane, Samuel - Mary Wilkeson.................  12-23-1799
Lane, William - Amela Irons..................  7-24-1803
Lane, William - Mary Nivison.................  9-28-1806
Langans, John - Catherine Cambern............  3-22-1832
Laquiar, John - Lucinder Belis...............  12-19-1839
La Roid, James - Mary Ann Perrine............  2-27-1837
Laroza, Zebulon - Mary Snyder................  9-13-1801
```

Latham, Calvin of N. Y. - Elizabeth Brown.... 10-15-1836
Lathrop, Randolph - Elizabeth Bowker......... 10-20-1838
Laton, Thomas - Mary Emons.................. 3-29-1803
Laurence, James S. - Mary S. Conover........ 2-10-1825
Lawrence, Alphred - Elizabeth Lyons of
    Burlington Co., N. J.................... 1-18-1832
Lawrence, Daniel - Althe Williamson......... 12-15-1814
Lawrence, Gilbert B. - Anna Newell.......... 5-27-1803
Lawrence, Jacob - Margaret Vancleve......... 11-18-1820
Lawrence, James - Ann Potts................. 9-01-1833
Lawrence, John - Hannah Vancleve............ 11-22-1822
Lawrence, John Jr. of Woodbury, Gloucester
    Co., N. J. - Mary Ann Waddell........... 1-24-1796
Lawrence, Joseph - Mary Newell.............. 11-28-1802
Lawrence, Joseph - Rachel Borden............ 10-20-1833
Lawrence, Samuel - Ann Ayers................ 8-15-1822
Lawrence, Samuel - Lizabeth Reynolds........ 9-05-1818
Lawrence, Samuel - N. Hankins............... 9-09-1832
Lawrence, William - Elizabeth Gifford....... 10-14-1837
Lawrence, William - Margaret Hanes.......... 5-08-1825
Lawrence, William - Permelia Everingham..... 9-17-1810
Laws, David - Mrs. Eliza Ann Holland........ 1-06-1838
Lawyer, George - Mary Pullen................ 11-02-1829
Lawyer, Thomas - Catherine Herbert.......... 9-05-1839
Layton, Aaron - Catherine Williams.......... 11-10-1821
Layton, Aaron - Sarah Barber................ 6-24-1814
Layton, Albert - Catherine Wagoner.......... 9-06-1828
Layton, Andrew - Mary Ann Southerd of
    Burlington Co., N. J.................... 3-15-1834
Layton, Anthony - Sarah Perrine............. 11-24-1832
Layton, Charles - Hannah Johnson
    (both black)............................ 12-28-1836
Layton, David - Phebe Reynolds.............. 12-22-1827
Layton, Edward - Barbara Marks.............. 3-17-1832
Layton, Francis - Margaret Ann Waggoner..... 11-24-1832
Layton, Hendrick - Sarah Woolley............ 11-21-1841
Layton, James - Elizabeth Murray............ 2-23-1818
Layton, James T. - Sarah Magill............. 3-18-1826
Layton, James W. - Charlotte Ayres.......... 12-24-1833
Layton, John - Esther Truex................. 3-28-1818
Layton, John - Lydia Jones.................. 10-12-1836
Layton, John of N. Y. - Martha M. Burdge.... 10-31-1827
Layton, John - Mary Sickels................. 1-01-1822
Layton, Lewis - Deborah Allger.............. 2-22-1826
Layton, Michael - Sarah Patterson........... 9-21-1836
Layton, Nathaniel - Ann Layton.............. 1-17-1838
Layton, Peter - Mary Reynolds............... 3-18-1833
Layton, Peter - Mary Wardell................ 5-25-1821
Layton, Safety - Abigail Alegor............. 4-02-1829
Layton, Safty - Mary Alger.................. 4-13-1820
Layton, Thomas - Anna Newberry.............. 2-09-1800
Layton, Thomas - Catherine Ellis............ 6-24-1804
Layton, Thomas - Deborah Burdge............. 9-07-1799
Layton, Thomas - Ellen Runyon............... 1-08-1827
Layton, Thomas - Rebecka Matthews........... 10-02-1803

```
Layton, Tunis - Mrs. Lydia Hulsart...........  12-12-1809
Layton, Walton - Elizabeth Price.............   8-19-1798
Layton, William - Anna McCormick.............   2-22-1837
Layton, William - Mrs. Catherine Voorther....  12-15-1821
Layton, William - Jane Vorhees...............  12-29-1802
Layton, William - Phebe Brewer...............   3-07-1818
Layton, William N. - Rebecca Reed............   1-18-1827
Lazarlee, Pennington - Sarah R. Blake of
     Middlesex Co., N. J.....................  12-21-1836
Lead, William - Sylvia Bennett...............   3-08-1808
Leadbeater, Edward - Agnes Freneau...........   5-25-1816
Leaman, Thomas - Catherine Johnson...........   5-20-1816
Leamon, Ezekiel - Rebecca Cole...............   6-02-1813
Leamon, Hazelton - Sarah Pharo...............   3-08-1834
Leander, John - Hannah Lucas.................   2-11-1827
Leavenworth, William - Mary Debow............   8-11-1830
Le Compte, William - Elizabeth Applegate.....   5-06-1804
Lecow, Francis - Mary Ann Conover............  12-24-1831
Lee, Aaron - Eliza Hutchinson................   9-25-1826
Lee, Aaron - Mary Brevy......................   1-06-1827
Lee, Andrew - Elizabeth Combs................   4-11-1835
Lee, Cabel - Mary Parker (both black)........   6-16-1799
Lee, David of Trenton, N. J. -
     Mary Ann Lane...........................   2-16-1822
Lee, James - Lydia W. Imlay..................  11-08-1821
Lee, Stacy - Rebecca Cowperthwaite...........   3-15-1828
Lee, Talbout - Mary Walling..................  11-18-1835
Lee, William - Mary Morris...................   4-20-1825
Leetts, John Jr. - Elizabeth Bennett.........   7-29-1830
Lefetra, James - Elizabeth Tabor.............   8-09-1821
Lefetra, James - Sarah Wolcott...............   5-29-1831
Lefetra, William T. - Elizabeth Woolley......  11-10-1827
Lefferson, William - Elenor Robinson.........  12-18-1832
Lefferts, H. (Dr.) - Ellen Conover...........   6-19-1831
Leffertson, Leffert - Jane Wikoff............   9-26-1803
Legar, John - Eleanor Lewis..................   3-20-1825
Leigh, Stout - Anny Lanning..................   3-15-1815
Leister, Cornelius - Catherine Poland........  10-28-1833
Lemen, Garet - Huldah Maines.................   3-09-1832
Leming, Epherem - Hannah Robbins.............   1-20-1817
Leming, Job - Elizabeth Cornelius............  11-14-1837
Leming, Job - Mary Gifford...................   8-09-1825
Leming, Job - Rebecca Posure.................  10-12-1833
Leming, John - Elizabeth Bird................  11-27-1796
Leming, Joseph - Ruth Van Horn...............  11-26-1817
Leming, Lewis - Mrs. Martha Johnson..........   5-06-1834
Leming, Thomas - Sarah Giberson..............   3-05-1814
Lemmin, William - Hannah Street..............   9-15-1827
Lemming, Isaiah - Alles Wells................  12-16-1822
Lemming, William - Mary Newman...............  11-23-1808
Lemmon, Charles - Phebe Wilgus...............       1816
Lemmon, Ephraim - Catherine Hiers............   2-13-1838
Lemmon, John - Charlotte Snieves.............   8-30-1837
Lemmon, John - Phebe Applegate...............   9-03-1803
Lemmon, Thomas - Anna Banks..................   1-26-1841
```

```
Lemon, Job - Elizabeth Philips...............  8-18-1801
Lemon, Thomas - Perthene Cox................  1-04-1801
Le Monyon, David - Dejiah Cranmer...........  4-11-1837
Lenard, John S. - Trissa Lane...............  6-24-1841
Leonard, John - Mary Brown..................  1-06-1836
Leonard, Joseph - Sarah Matthews............  1-14-1809
Leonard, Nathaniel - Diadame Hendrickson.....  8-30-1807
Leonard, Richard - Elizabeth Roberts........  3-14-1833
Leonard, Samuel - Lydia Madden..............  3-19-1804
Leonard, Thomas - Mary Hopping..............  2-05-1840
Leonard, Thomas - Phebe Davis...............  9-18-1825
Leonard, William - Elizabeth Applegate.......  12-31-1810
Leonard, William - Elizabeth Conover.........  11-29-1838
Lester, Ezekiel - Mary Crane................  4-17-1806
Letson, Joseph - Hannah Towers..............  9-28-1837
Letson, Thomas - Rachel McCain..............  8-01-1841
Letts, Charles - Elizabeth Stout............  10-20-1832
Letts, Francis - Rebecca Stout..............  2-17-1827
Letts, Isaac - Anna Hoffman.................  10-19-1800
Letts, James - Mary Silbers.................  6-24-1837
Letts, James - Mary Soper...................  12-29-1821
Letts, Job - Neomy Garrison.................  3-16-1826
Letts, John - Mary Benett...................  2-02-1815
Letts, John - Mary Clevenger both of
    Burlington Co., N. J....................  2-10-1827
Letts, John - Mary Platt....................  6-08-1800
Letts, Joshua - Melleney Warn...............  11-30-1805
Letts, Moses - Rachel Spragg................  2-01-1807
Letts, Tobias - Content Allen...............  3-17-1802
Letts, William - Mary Fortenbury............  5-20-1810
Lettson, William - Catherine Van Bruntt......  11-21-1802
Levison, Benjamin - Hannah Conover..........  11-10-1836
Lewis, ---- - Mary Ammerman.................  8-06-1820
Lewis, Aaron - Elenor Vorhees...............  10-03-1835
Lewis, Benjamin - Elizabeth Mount...........  3-03-1827
Lewis, Benjamin - Hannah De Hart............  12-18-1802
Lewis, Benjamin - Jane Johnson..............  6-15-1839
Lewis, Benjamin S. - Rachell Allen..........  11-21-1835
Lewis, Elias - Julia Simpson................  3-03-1832
Lewis, Elias - Phebe Lewis..................  8-08-1809
Lewis, Jacob - Mary Brown...................  3-25-1800
Lewis, James - Deborah Stough...............  12-21-1796
Lewis, James - Effa Bennett.................  6-19-1816
Lewis, Joel - Ann Laton.....................  12-17-1806
Lewis, John - Catherine Conk................  3-26-1803
Lewis, John - Margaret Garrett..............  1-04-1842
Lewis, John M. - Fanney Thomas..............  5-04-1833
Lewis, John P. - Catherine Wooley...........  12-29-1811
Lewis, Jonathan - Mary Johnston.............  1841-1842
Lewis, Joseph - Caroline Robbins............  1-24-1829
Lewis, Joseph - Edith Well..................  2-23-1828
Lewis, Joseph - Elizabeth Wilkins...........  12-22-1840
Lewis, Joseph - Liza Ann Berlin.............  1-02-1833
Lewis, Joseph - Mary Allen..................  3-19-1834
Lewis, Joseph W. - Mary Ann Mc Elvey........  11-08-1834
```

```
Lewis, Michiel - Elizabeth Ekbulk............  11-03-1823
Lewis, Robert - Elizabeth Morris.............   4-10-1802
Lewis, Robert Patterson -
    Frances Ann Atkinson Cochron.............   1-02-1831
Lewis, Samuel - Mrs. Catherine Lake.........    9-29-1831
Lewis, Samuel S. (Rev.) - Lydia G. White.....   3-16-1814
Lewis, Thomas - Sarah Smith..................   3-04-1838
Lewis, Uriah - Elizabeth Gifford.............   7-10-1821
Lewis, Uriah - Lidia Haviland................   8-09-1801
Lewis, William - Elizabeth Patterson.........  11-27-1819
Lewis, William - Mary Barber.................  10-02-1825
Lewis, William - Mary Britton................  12-02-1802
Lewis, William - Sarah W. Applegate..........   1-08-1821
Lewker, Barzillai - Harriet Burk.............  10-26-1822
Lewker, Keneth - Elssey Hulse................  12-28-1816
Lifison, Jack(free negro) - Lidia Reap
    (free negro).............................   4-09-1797
Liker, George - Mary Meslar..................   3-25-1823
Lilly, James - Elizabeth Primmer.............   9-06-1797
Limmery, Enoch - Jemima Groom................   2-24-1805
Lines, Abraham of N. Y. -
    Amelia Lippincott........................   1-26-1804
Lippencoat, Joseph - Nancy Fox...............  12-12-1808
Lippencott, Henry - Abigail Hulit............   3-01-1832
Lippencott, Remembrance - Ann White..........   1-23-1797
Lippencott, Sylvester - Mary Brown...........   2-05-1816
Lippencott, William - Emeline West...........  11-  -1833
Lippincott, Benjamin — Lydia Williams........   2-15-1821
Lippincott, Charles - Sarah Worthley.........   5-25-1822
Lippincott, Curtis - Elsie Van Brunt.........   4-16-1826
Lippincott, Elisha - Ann Wardell.............  12-09-1814
Lippincott, Ezra of Burlington Co., -
    Eliza Crammer............................  12-23-1827
Lippincott, Henry - Mary West................   9-13-1827
Lippincott, James - Deborah Morris...........   5-08-1806
Lippincott, John - Elizabeth M Cain..........   8-31-1820
Lippincott, John W. - Ann Morris.............   9-09-1814
Lippincott, Joseph - Mary Taylor.............   4-30-1832
Lippincott, Manly - Mary Crammer.............   8-08-1832
Lippincott, Robert - Lydia Johnson...........   3-29-1798
Lippincott, Robert - Mary Tilton.............   6-24-1836
Lippincott, Samuel - Rachel Brewer...........   2-21-1827
Lippincott, Samuel - Rebecca Steward.........   5-30-1835
Lippincott, Sulvester - Catherine Jackson....   4-02-1804
Lippincott, Sylvester - Hannah Allen.........   2-26-1797
Lippincott, William - Nancy Bell.............  12-12-1810
Little, Charles - Margaret Ann Crawford......  11-07-1831
Little, Danile - Nellie Covenhoven...........   3-22-1797
Little, John - Eleanor Williamson............  11-24-1814
Little, John - Mary Thompson.................   2-16-1842
Little, John - Masey Harbart.................   1-02-1800
Little, Olis - Susannah Borden...............  11-12-1812
Little, Samuel A. - Elizabeth Hough..........   1-07-1836
Little, Wade - Molly Allen...................   3-10-1811
Little, William - Ann Knott..................   4-30-1814
```

```
Little, William - Deborah Scott..............  1-09-1814
Little, William - Harriet Ann Mulat..........  6-24-1832
Little, William - Nancy Jeffrey.............. 11-15-1807
Livingston, John - Elizabeth Ryle............  2-02-1829
Lloyd, Charles - Sarah Emmons................ 10-18-1828
Lloyd, Corlis - Anne Forman.................. 12-06-1797
Lloyd, Corlis - Mrs. Sara Clayton............  3-27-1826
Lloyd, David - Ann Carson both of
    Burlington Co., N. J.....................  9-01-1833
Lloyd, Elisha - Mary Morris..................  4-10-1814
Lloyd, Peter - Sarah Errickson............... 12-04-1806
Lloyd, Robert - Lydia Corlies dg. of
    Timothy..................................  2-18-1804
Lloyd, William - Hannah Throckmorton.........  2-06-1830
Lloyd, William L. - Mary Van Mater........... 11-18-1812
Lobb, Isaac of New York City -
    Catherine Hamilton of Hunterdon Co. N.J..  6-17-1829
Locason, Barzilla - Rebecca Chaffey.......... 10-01-1842
Locason, Samuel - Mrs. Maria Wilson.......... 10-27-1842
Locerson, Daniel - Rachel Chappy.............  2-22-1817
Lofins, Francis - Philis Van Maiter.......... 10-18-1827
Logan, Peter - Eleanor Layton................  1-17-1827
Logan, Robert - Lydia Brinley................  9-17-1804
Lokason, John - Mrs. Catherine Buckelew...... 12-29-1821
Lokerson, Cabel - Nelly Ann Stricklin........ 12-30-1826
Lokerson, John - Mrs. Alice Clayton..........  7-30-1838
Lokeson, John - Catherine Schenk.............  2-12-1797
Lokinson, David - Sarah Stillwell............  6-27-1824
Lonam, Edward - Phebe Premore................  8-25-1838
Longstreet, Aaron - Deborah Hulse............  5-16-1813
Longstreet, Aron - Mary Morton...............  6-24-1826
Longstreet, Benjamin - Mary Brinley..........  5-15-1837
Longstreet, Cornelius - Isabella W. Clayton..  3-07-1831
Longstreet, David - Mary McChesney...........  6-13-1798
Longstreet, Garret - Elizabeth Rogers........  1-24-1820
Longstreet, Garret (Esq.) - Lydia Baraclow... 12-16-1802
Longstreet, Gilbert - Margarate Keels........  5-31-1804
Longstreet, Gilbert - Rebecca Mors...........  1-06-1825
Longstreet, Hendrick - Catherine Haviland....  8-06-1807
Longstreet, Hendrick - Mary Holmes........... 10-18-1804
Longstreet, Jacob - Catherine Longstreet.....  2-06-1840
Longstreet, Jacob - Mary Hewlett.............  3-11-1842
Longstreet, James M. - Elizabeth Huff........  1-08-1834
Longstreet, John - Elizabeth Emmons..........  1-04-1838
Longstreet, John - Elizabeth Stoutenborrow...  5-26-1812
Longstreet, Joseph B. - Rebecca Coombs.......  1-05-1835
Longstreet, Lloyd - Amanda Vanmater..........  9-23-1829
Longstreet, Richard - Zilpha White........... 11-12-1812
Longstreet, Samuel - Anner Allen.............  6-11-1799
Longstreet, Samuel A. - Ann Sutphin.......... 11-12-1826
Longstreet, Sylvanus - Ida Leming............  5-04-1842
Longstreet, Thomas - Ann Huff................  3-22-1837
Longstreet, Timothy - Hannah Longstreet...... 11-29-1826
Longstreet, William - Christian Little.......  3-09-1809
Longstreet, William - Deborah Kinney.........  7-04-1804
```

```
Longstreet, William - Lydia Hampton.........   1-06-1817
Longstreet, William P. - Catherine Smith.....   5-10-1823
Looken, William - Sarah Brown...............   8-27-1803
Loper, Anthony - Ellen Camburn..............   1-25-1817
Loreman, Charles of Burlington Co., N. J. -
  Catherine Pearce........................   7-31-1818
Loreman, James - Elizabeth Grover...........   7-01-1804
Lounsberry, Jeremiah - Hannah Parker.........  11-14-1804
Loveborough, Richard - Ann Taylor...........   3-21-1830
Lovelace, Joseph - Ann Bishop...............   1-23-1836
Lovelace, Thomas - Sarah Ann Sprowlis........  12-31-1811
Loveland, Robert - Caty Cross...............   3-04-1798
Low, Andrew - Eliza Helsey..................  12-26-1826
Low, William - Isabella Emons...............   3-18-1800
Lucas, Archiblad of N. Y. -
  Catherine Morris........................   5-22-1837
Lucas, John - Catherine Clinton.............  12-31-1799
Lucas, William - Ann M. Given...............   3-02-1817
Lucer, James - Elizabeth Chambers...........   1-22-1842
Luffborough, Charles - Deborah Burge........   5-06-1828
Lukas, James - Sarah Jones..................   6-24-1810
Luker, Charles - Alice Karr.................  10-22-1832
Luker, Edmund - Mary Stackey................  11-01-1835
Luker, Enock - Amy Burke....................   9-15-1821
Luker, Jacob - Mary Seper...................  12-04-1800
Luker, Ralph - Martha Patten................  10-21-1815
Lukor, John - Abigail Matthews..............   5-12-1838
Luts, Henry - Sarah Johnston................   1-19-1842
Luyster, David - Amelia Hank................  10-07-1840
Luyster, Hendrick - Margaret Conover........   3-02-1841
Luyster, Peter - Emeranda Suydam............  12-20-1829
Lydia, Matthew - Elizabeth Lewis............   7-10-1802
Lyons, Joseph - Hannah White................   3-01-1826
Lyster, John C. - Catherine Vanderveer......  12-12-1812
M'Gee, Jonathan - Ann Barclay...............  11-27-1824
Mac Clain, John - Mrs. Lydia Covert.........  12-22-1822
Mace, Abraham - Eliza Chambers..............  10-19-1812
Machning, Joseph - Mary Hays................   2-14-1827
Mack, Elijah S. - Abigail Voorhees..........   6-04-1834
Mackey, Alexander - Caty Roberts............   2-03-1797
Mackqueen, Charles - Sarah Lefetra..........   4-16-1802
Maclain, Moses - Elizabeth Cooper...........   9-18-1796
Macleass, Cors - Ann Matthews...............   9-17-1795
Macnab, Thomas - Ezebellar Robinson.........   2-18-1828
Madden, Daniel - Elizabeth Ross.............   2-24-1812
Madden, James - Mary Ayers..................  10-21-1815
Madden, William - Rachel De Bouse...........   4-01-1804
Magee, James - Catherine Muckelvane.........   1-21-1808
Magee, James - Lucritia Nailor..............   2-17-1033
Magee, John - Mary Mucklewane...............   7-26-1812
Magee, Jonathan - Elizabeth Hulse...........   1-25-1810
Magee, Robert - Anne Emmons.................   4-08-1804
Ma Gill, Brittian - Louisa Brinley..........   7-15-1841
Magill, David - Anna Patterson..............   1-04-1837
Magill, Joseph - Catherine Longstreet.......   1-12-1822
```

Magill, William - Deborah Emmons............. 7-22-1841
Maguire, Lewis - Margaret Miller............. 11-13-1838
Mahan, Joshua of Pa. - Clarissa Mattison of
    Trenton, N. J........................... 10-02-1820
Maidanial, William - Catherine Anderson...... 10-16-1801
Malard, Fayette of Vermont - Marion Herbert.. 11-10-1831
Malat, James - Helener Cooper................ 10-03-1802
Malbough, Asa - Anne Simmons................. 2-03-1799
Malcome, John - Margaret Grant............... 4-03-1822
Mallard, Lyman - Phebe Matthews.............. 5-21-1842
Mallard, Simon - Lydia Matthews.............. 7-10-1832
Mallard, Stacy - Mary Fisher................. 10-10-1840
Malsberry, Thomas - Mercy Chamberlin......... 1-10-1829
Malsbury, Caleb - Lutisha Leming............. 11-21-1833
Malsbury, Caleb - Margaret Dennis............ 5-20-1821
Malsbury, Jacob - Rebecca Leaming............ 4-28-1838
Malsbury, James - Mary Gullie................ 2-28-1827
Malsbury, John - Catherine Pullen............ 1-22-1835
Malsbury, John M. - Elizabeth Perine......... 3-21-1822
Malsbury, William - Mary Elison.............. 7-03-1824
Malsby, Gilbert - Sarah Burgess.............. 1-09-1798
Malsby, Samuel - Nancy Brown................. 1-22-1804
Mames, Frederick - Sarah Ann Cooper.......... 7-22-1838
Manning, Daniel - Anna Stillwell............. 11-18-1802
Manning, John - Mary Ann Thomas.............. 9-24-1838
Manning, Stephen - Sarah Taylor.............. 2-22-1813
Maoer, Richard - Hannah Brewer............... 4-25-1827
Map, Solomon - Hannah Woolley................ 6-19-1823
Maple, Hezekiah - Margaret Atchley........... 9-27-1799
Maps, Lewis (Rev.) - Eunice Ferguson......... 7-08-1840
Maps, Michael son of Frederick -
    Hannah Throgmorton dg. of John........... 2-11-1806
Maps, Zenas - Nancy Howland.................. 2-04-1809
Margening, Edwin G. - Rebecca Rosewell....... 3-10-1842
Marinor, John - Abigail White................ 1-01-1834
Mark, William - Nancy Morris................. 12-20-1830
Markes, Benjamin - Lydia Brown............... 6-22-1833
Marks, Abial of New York City -
    Jane Thomas.............................. 8-06-1838
Marks, Andrew - Lydia Gaunt.................. 4-24-1815
Marks, Gideon - Maria Mount.................. 11-12-1842
Marks, Richard - Christian Riddle............ 12-06-1823
Marlatt, John - Willimpy Marlatt............. 8-05-1813
Marles, William - Nancy Shinn................ 1-17-1830
Marlin, Nathaniel - Sarah Garrison........... 5-05-1812
Marshall, Frederick of Philadelphia, Pa. -
    Sarah Willets of Burlington Co., N. J.... 3-04-1813
Marshall, Isaac - Edith Brown................ 2-07-1838
Marshall, John of Philadelphia, Pa. -
    Phebe Steepy............................. 11-15-1810
Marshall, William H. - Abagail Lepincott..... 2-17-1831
Martin, Dennis - Gertrude A. White........... 10-28-1829
Martin, James - Lydia Parker................. 4-07-1816
Martin, Jeptha - Eleanor Mann................ 2-14-1814
Martin, Jesse - Maria Harvey................. 1-22-1842

```
Martin, John - Jerusha Wainright.............  2-03-1841
Martin, John - Mariah Callehan..............  8-13-1833
Martin, Joseph F. - Sarah Remson............ 11-25-1832
Martin, William - Hester Grevat (wid.).......  9-21-1815
Martin, William - Lydia Curtis..............  4-20-1833
Martin, William - Mary Throckmorton.........  3-05-1796
Marton, Jesse - Hannah Tucker...............  1-06-1827
Mascion, John - Sally Fielder...............  1-27-1814
Mash, Elias - Catherine Pryor............... 10-09-1802
Mason, James - Ann Shepherd................. 1836-1837
Mason, John - Leana Williamson.............. 12-22-1805
Mason, John - Lucy Combs.................... 11-28-1802
Mason, Samuel - Eliza Welch.................  8-28-1825
Mason, Thomas Letson - Deborah Craddik......  3-23-1807
Matchet, Richard - Rachel Vandusen..........  3-04-1810
Mater, Garret - Elizabeth Lake..............  7-07-1807
Mather, Gilbert - Catherine Emmons.......... 12-07-1816
Mathew, Charles - Nancy Hevalin.............  1-26-1817
Mathews, Benjamin - Rhoda Ann Lewis.........  8-23-1832
Mathews, Charles T. - Catherine Clayton......  8-30-1831
Mathews, David - Mary Emmons................ 10-30-1831
Mathews, David D. - Catherine Johnson........ 10-13-1835
Mathews, Hubbard - Lydia Morris.............  1-30-1834
Mathews, Joseph - Eliza A. Herbert.......... 12-10-1823
Mathis, Charles - Thankful Dunham...........  4-02-1797
Mathis, Job - Cathrin White.................  4-21-1817
Mathis, Thomas - Mary Van Pelt..............  4-09-1839
Matilyn, William - Ann Eliza Gaskil......... 12-05-1829
Matson, Aaron - Mary Bennett................  8-14-1800
Matthew, David - Sarah Estell...............  5-07-1809
Matthew, Garret - Lydia Emmons.............. 12-14-1808
Matthew, James - Sarah Britton..............  1-22-1825
Matthew, John - Mary Carter.................  3-10-1799
Matthew, John - Sarah Hulse.................  1-20-1821
Matthew, William - Elizabeth Matthews........  6-13-1809
Matthews, Charles - Anadotia Hultshart.......  9-02-1837
Matthews, Charles - Sarah Ann Robins........  1-23-1833
Matthews, Cornelius - Ann Anderson..........  5-31-1816
Matthews, Cornelius, Jane Barkalow..........  1-06-1822
Matthews, David Sr. - Mrs. Ann Preston....... 11-20-1825
Matthews, David Sr. - Mischa Preston......... 11-20-1825
Matthews, Edward - Catherine Miller.......... 10-01-1836
Matthews, James - Deborah Howland...........  2-07-1807
Matthews, John - Rachel Ford................  9-17-1819
Matthews, John - Sarah Giberson.............  6-18-1808
Matthews, Joseph - Gitty Truax..............  2-22-1821
Matthews, Joseph Jr. - Mary Thompson.........  3-23-1822
Matthews, Samuel - Catherine Emmons..........  4-05-1828
Matthews, Samuel - Jerucy Lawrence.......... 10-07-1840
Matthews, Samuel F. - Jane Boud.............  5-25-1833
Matthews, Thomas - Eliza Haveland........... 11-08-1815
Matthews, William - Ann Scott...............  2-01-1829
Matthews, William - Elizabeth Chasey........  5-25-1836
Matthews, William - Elizabeth Matthews.......  6-13-1809
Matthews, William - Phebe Ann Burge.........  2-04-1840
```

```
Matthews, William - Polliver Johnston........   2-08-1830
Mattock, Aaron - Elizabeth Grante............   7-11-1835
Maulott, William - Mary Tilton...............   9-28-1841
Maxeon, Joseph - Mary Quirburg...............   3-15-1813
Maxson, Charles - Cornelia Cook..............   1-09-1816
Maxson, George - Mrs. Esther Fish............   6-13-1825
Maxson, Jonathan - Elizabeth ----............  12-28-1830
Maxson, Robert - Elinor Applegate............  10-04-1806
Maxson, William - Margaret Mount.............  12-31-1836
Maxwell, John W. - Mary Laird................  11-22-1815
Mc ----, John - Phebe Rue....................   6-06-1811
Mc Alvey, Richard - Rebuiah Tilton...........   2-21-1802
Mc Bride, John Jr. - Margaret Homer..........  12-25-1809
Mc Cabe, Elisha - Julian Heveland............  12-30-1821
Mc Cabe, George - Sarah Bennett..............   9-25-1828
Mc Cape, John - Hanner West..................   5-07-1823
Mc Carthy, James of Philadelphia, Pa. -
    Nancy Page...............................   8-17-1820
Mc Chesney, John - Catherine Egbert..........   7-29-1798
Mc Chesney, John - Mary Shepherd.............  12-03-1835
Mc Cintire, John - Lydia Dennis..............   9-09-1841
Mc Clain, Douglas - Deborah Morris...........  12-03-1829
Mc Clain, Jesse - Mary Walling...............   1-23-1834
Mc Clain, John - Elizabeth Everngam..........   6-10-1809
Mc Clane, Moses - Margaret Coil..............  12-30-1818
Mc Clane, William - Mary Leonard.............  12-20-1838
Mc Clay, Andrew - Rachel Van Note............   3-20-1834
Mc Clean, Jacob - Mary Burrowes..............   5-19-1836
Mc Clees, Aaron - Jane Low...................  10-05-1815
Mc Clees, James - Rebecca Lewis..............  10-20-1829
Mc Clees, John - Nancy Mc Cless (wid. of
    Peter Mc Cless)..........................  11-15-1796
Mc Clow, Joseph - Lecritia Wooly (both black)  1-23-1840
Mc Coy, Ezekiel - Hannah Applegate...........  10-10-1814
Mc Coy, James - Deborah Ann Rulong...........   5-24-1834
Mc Coy, William - Eliza Burch................   6-09-1807
Mc Coy, William - Martha Hadley..............  10-12-1815
Mc Culley, George - Nancy Williams...........   9-30-1807
Mc Culley, George - Sarah Janeway............   6-17-1813
Mc Daniel, George - Matilda Walton...........  11-07-1841
Mc Daniel, George - Rachel Challender........   6-04-1826
Mc Daniel, Thomas - Mary Covert..............   2-27-1830
Mc Daniel, William - Sarah Nutt..............  10-24-1829
Mc Dannel, Robert - Elizabeth Thorp..........  12-13-1806
Mc Dannel, William - Abigail Hulse...........   6-24-1798
Mc Dermott, Mathis - Mary Cooper.............   4-12-1800
Mc Duffe, Robert - Aultye Emmons.............  10-13-1795
Mc Elvy, William - Mahala Smith..............   4-02-1836
Mc Fargner, Alexander - Hannah Cotteral......   9-26-1807
Mc Gaskins, Michael - Tinty Stillwell........   5-02-1835
Mc Gattan, Michael - Margaret Yetman.........   1-01-1809
Mc Gill, Charles - Rebecca Bennett...........   1-20-1805
Mc Gill, William - Sarah Patterson...........   5-02-1833
Mc Henry, Archibald - Lydia Grimes...........   1-18-1810
Mc Kean, David - Mariah W. Steward...........   1-24-1830
```

```
Mc Kean, Washington - Margaret Ivins......... 11-11-1828
Mc Kelvey, Gemit - Getty Ann Halsey.......... 12-14-1840
Mc Kelvey, Jonathan - Hester Ann Irons....... 3-19-1842
Mc Kelvey, Robert - Mary Johnson............ 11-28-1836
Mc Kinney, William - Abigail French both of
    Burlington Co., N.J..................... 3-21-1840
Mc Kinty, Charles - Mary Smith.............. 4-10-1835
Mc Knight, Joseph - Anner James............. 3-27-1803
Mc Knight, Joseph - Mary Green.............. 10-09-1816
Mc Knight, Joseph - Mary Johnson............ 1-01-1823
Mc Knight, William - Amey Zenas............. 2-10-1808
Mc Lane, Moses - Christiana Paxson........... 3-02-1813
Mc Lean, Jonathan - Eleanor Burdge........... 1-21-1810
Mc Ninny, Joseph - Mary Hays................ 2-14-1827
Mc Quig, Thomas - Nancy Grover.............. 12-26-1809
Meal, Jacob - Jane Shumard.................. 5-05-1811
Measure, Felix - Alice Fowler............... 2-28-1822
Meeny, Abijah - Deborah Dillon (both black).. 1-24-1835
Megahon, John - Catherine Jones............. 1-19-1806
Megill, Christopher - Margaret Brisinghan.... 12-27-1838
Megill, David - Ackey Benet................. 11-30-1811
Megill, Joseph - Sarah Ayres................ 10-20-1810
Megill, Tyler - Jane Emmons................. 6-14-1827
Megill, William - Mary Genner............... 9-25-1814
Meires, Apollo - Anne Burtis................ 3-02-1805
Meirs, Charles - Sarah Ann Cox.............. 12-05-1833
Meirs, John - Lucretia Gaskill of
    Burlington Co., N. J.................... 1-17-1828
Meirs, Thomas - Rebecca H. Conover.......... 12-17-1823
Meirs, William - Catherine G. Conover....... 12-20-1827
Mendile, Job - Ann Cook..................... 12-13-1825
Menee, Tilus - Margaret Jefferey............ 8-28-1817
Meny, Humphrey - Hannah ----................ 1-11-1800
Merlott, Garret - Mary Smith................ 10-28-1840
Merrill, Cornelius - Joanna Mason........... 5-13-1828
Meslar, Garret - Pheobe Webb................ 3-25-1819
Messler, Ocke - Mary Lippincott............. 10-18-1833
Messler, William - Christiana Rogers........ 10-17-1840
Micham, John - Elizabeth Layton............. 12-18-1834
Michel, Jonathan - Catherine Burl........... 9-06-1804
Middleton, Anthony - Miriam Middleton....... 9-26-1837
Middleton, Edward - Eliza Ann Burtis both of
    Burlington Co., N. J.................... 11-04-1824
Middleton, Gideon - Abigail Tilton.......... 8-05-1814
Middleton, Hudson - Hannah Middleton of
    Burlington Co., N. J.................... 5-27-1822
Middleton, Joel - Idah Ann Molatt of
    Burlington Co., N. J.................... 5-19-1832
Middleton, John - Sarah Shinn............... 11-21-1795
Middleton, Montgomery - Sarah Bennet........ 7-12-1823
Middleton, Nathan - Hannah Reid............. 10-09-1809
Miers, George C. - Lucy Parent.............. 12-31-1828
Miers, Nickolus - Mary Fisher............... 9-25-1819
Miers, Nicolus - Hester Maxan............... 12-20-1831
Miers, Robert - Rachel Worth................ 9-09-1801
```

```
Miller, Amos - Lydia Carr...................  12-21-1801
Miller, Brittian - Mary Ann Worthington......   3-28-1842
Miller, Caleb - Ann Hulse....................  12-16-1824
Miller, David - Deborah Brand................   2-27-1803
Miller, David - Elizabeth Woolley............  11-05-1842
Miller, George W. - Mary Hulet...............   9-22-1834
Miller, Gilbert - Kitturah Morris............   8-16-1821
Miller, Gilbert of Burlington Co., N.J. -
   Mrs. Rebeckah Lokason.....................   4-04-1822
Miller, Jacob - Ann Matthews.................  10-12-1832
Miller, Jacob - Susanna Wainright............   3-30-1797
Miller, James - Abigail Robins...............  10-29-1834
Miller, James H. - Sarah Jane Finison........   2-07-1838
Miller, John - Ann Eliza Davison.............   2-22-1837
Miller, John - Anner Parker..................   1-16-1812
Miller, John - Elizabeth Applegate...........  11-13-1839
Miller, John - Sarah Allen...................   5-31-1834
Miller, John - Sarah Mac Anine...............   4-27-1828
Miller, Joseph - Hannah Scidmore.............  12-25-1805
Miller, Josiah - Rachel Van Mater
   (both black)..............................   5-03-1830
Miller, Nimrod - Hannah Clark................  10-19-1823
Miller, Redding - Margaret Carver............   2-06-1842
Miller, Robert - Catherine Conover...........   4-03-1833
Miller, Robert - Lucy Clayton................  11-21-1835
Miller, Robert E. - Eliza Ann Potts..........  12-07-1831
Miller, Thomas - Tabitha Britton.............   2-11-1823
Miller, Westley - Catherine Newman...........   9-21-1836
Miller, William - Charity Johnson............   4-23-1836
Miller, Wilson - Mary Norton.................   2-20-1828
Milley, James - Mary Caye....................   3-21-1829
Mills, Thomas - Nancy Inman..................   9-05-1821
Mils, Joshua - Luce Corlis...................   1-15-1798
Milton, Joel - Mary Hulse....................   9-17-1804
Minna, Henry - Fanny Schanck.................   7-23-1840
Minor, Orsen - Esther Applegate..............   6-12-1842
Mintard, Andrew - Mary Pew...................   2-14-1825
Mitchell, Edward - Sarah Hulse...............   1-10-1839
Mitchell, Jacob - Lucy Rulon.................   2-26-1808
Mitchell, Joseph - Ann Murphee...............   8-30-1795
Mitchell, Samuel - Amanda Wainwright.........  11-26-1836
Mitchell, William - Margaret McKinney........  10-27-1836
Mitten, William - Ann Smith..................  12-23-1820
Mittors, Joel - Cate Emmons..................   3-31-1796
Moffitt, Henry - Cathrin Lisk................   3-09-1802
Molatt, Joseph - Agnes Heyer.................   9-20-1828
Molden, Cato - Luticia Jones.................   3-12-1830
Monson, Jacob - Lydia Cook...................   5-13-1807
Moonday, Michael - Hannah Cottrell...........   9-04-1798
Mooney, Joseph - Rebecca Clinton.............   1-27-1830
Moor, John B. - Meriba Meguere...............   5-04-1818
Moor, Nickolas - Catherine Mitchell..........   5-15-1820
Moore, Garret - Phebe Pharo..................   2-21-1841
Moore, Henry - Ann Horner....................  11-28-1814
Moore, James - Elizabeth Horner..............   3-29-1827
```

Moore, John - Jemima Horner both of
   Burlington Co., N. J..................... 8-29-1839
Moore, John - Lucy Lawrence................. 10-25-1804
Moore, Jonathan - Sarah Van Note............. 4-29-1840
Moore, Thomas - Frances Blake................ 8-14-1814
More, Hugh - Rachel Horner................... 6-01-1822
More, Peter - Hannah Chambers................ 12-22-1825
Morehouse, David - Leiha Stout............... 12-13-1795
Morelat, John - Ducretia Hartman............. 1-21-1826
Morford, Austin W. - Mary Osborn............. 11-28-1833
Morford, Charles - Susan Herbert............. 10-05-1832
Morford, Elias - Fanny Taylor................ 11-22-1831
Morford, Garret - Catherine White............ 4-02-1818
Morford, Jesse - Eliza Herbert............... 11-01-1840
Morford, John - Ann Hulsehart................ 4-30-1816
Morford, John - Eliza Osborn................. 3-24-1831
Morford, Thomas - Lydia Tilton............... 1-27-1829
Morford, Thomas - Rebecca West............... 12-30-1801
Morford, William - Elizabeth Willet.......... 12-30-1818
Morford, William - Joanna Johnson............ 10-09-1836
Morgan, Adam - Rebecca Tomlinson............. 8-24-1817
Morgan, James - Martha Ellison............... 10-03-1798
Morgan, William - Anna Clark................. 11-06-1802
Morlat, John - Alice Boice................... 9-15-1828
Morrell, Eliezer - Elizabeth Pauling......... 2-18-1827
Morrell, Jacobus - Mary Hyer................. 1-08-1797
Morrill, John - Nancy Cotrell................ 6-11-1797
Morris, Abraham - Hannah Dohn................ 11-10-1821
Morris, Adam - Lydia Matthews................ 3-09-1811
Morris, Asher - Elizabeth Herbert............ 2-26-1799
Morris, Benjamin - Margaret Chadwick......... 8-26-1829
Morris, Charles - Ann Elisa Holmes........... 6-08-1829
Morris, Charles - Ellen Van Kirk............. 4-14-1816
Morris, David - Susannah Lanery.............. 1-16-1806
Morris, Elisha - Elizabeth Smith............. 2-13-1798
Morris, Ezekiel - Mary Kirby................. 2-06-1817
Morris, Ezekiel - Mary Wilson................ 3-22-1813
Morris, Garret - Polly Sydam................. 4-27-1797
Morris, George - Amy Woolley (both black).... 1-15-1837
Morris, George - Jedidah Newman.............. 2-22-1817
Morris, George - Nelly Covenhoven............ 12-07-1796
Morris, Henry - Esther Wilson................ 3-05-1833
Morris, Hugh - Catherine Emmens.............. 12-02-1816
Morris, Hulbank - Eliza Tanner............... 1-01-1835
Morris, Jacob - Amelia Tracy................. 10-02-1837
Morris, Jacob - Hannah Wolcott............... 11-21-1799
Morris, Jacob W. - Marie M. Wardell.......... 11-06-1830
Morris, James - Ann D. Little................ 11-16-1829
Morris, James - Eliza Fleming dg. of James... 6-04-1829
Morris, James - Eliza Randolph............... 11-29-1817
Morris, James - Ezebella Clayton............. 3-14-1803
Morris, James - Susanna Lippencott........... 12-07-1805
Morris, John - Alice Chamberlain............. 4-04-1827
Morris, John - Catherine Lane................ 10-22-1803
Morris, John - Eliza Reed.................... 3-02-1819

```
Morris, Jonathan - Sarah Conck...............  6-23-1836
Morris, Jopphia - Lydia Morris...............  10-29-1811
Morris, Joseph - Deborah Bennett.............  2-18-1821
Morris, Joseph - Mary Brewer.................  6-16-1805
Morris, Joseph - Mary Hendrickson............  1-14-1834
Morris, Joseph - Mary Patterson..............  12-31-1838
Morris, Joseph - Sarah Hiliard...............  3-09-1828
Morris, Josiah - Ann Elmer...................  6-22-1825
Morris, Lewis - Catherine Wooley.............  12-30-1800
Morris, Lewis - Lydia Johnston...............  1-10-1828
Morris, Peter - Mary Van Cleve...............  1-22-1814
Morris, Richard B. - Alice Snowden...........  11-30-1839
Morris, Robert - Catherine Conover...........  2-01-1827
Morris, Robert - Lydia Cooper................  4-05-1830
Morris, Robert - Rebecca Jackson.............  4-10-1804
Morris, Robert - Rebecca Youmans.............  8-16-1821
Morris, Robert L. - Elizabeth Allen..........  7-27-1834
Morris, Robert P. - Mary Johnson.............  2-08-1830
Morris, Rubin - Ann Wyckoff..................  9-08-1841
Morris, Samuel - Rebeckah Smith..............  1-20-1796
Morris, Samuel - Rhoda Ann Van Mater.........  3-04-1830
Morris, Samuel S. - Sarah W. Sutphin.........  6-01-1820
Morris, Stephen - Elizabeth Cole both of
    Burlington Co., N. J.....................  8-15-1812
Morris, Stephen - Mary Compton...............  11-09-1815
Morris, William - Hannah Gardener............  7-03-1806
Morris, William - Hannah Lafetra.............  10-22-1840
Morris, William - Mariah Wright..............  9-15-1817
Morris, William - Sarah Smith................  7-12-1833
Morris, William Henry - Lydia Smith..........  1-24-1841
Morrocco, George - Rebecca Harris
    (both black).............................  11-04-1830
Morse, Joseph - Rebeckah Soper...............  7-23-1819
Morton, David - Hester Hagerman..............  3-17-1830
Morton, Herbert - Elizabeth Johnson..........  4-18-1799
Morton, Joseph - Hannah Longstreet...........  8-29-1833
Morton, Joseph - Phebe Barber................  1-05-1795
Morton, Theofilas - Deborah Shibla...........  10-02-1828
Morton, Thomas - Edne Avey...................  9-05-1813
Morton, Thomas - Mary Curtis dg. of
    Captain Garret...........................  8-11-1841
Morton, Timothy - Jane Journee...............  3-02-1820
Morton, William - Hannah Howland.............  12-31-1822
Morton, William - Sarah Milne................  9-02-1841
Morton, William D. - Elizabeth Allen.........  1-29-1824
Mossbrook, Jonathan - Charity Miskelly.......  9-03-1836
Mott, John - Anne West.......................  7-01-1797
Mount, Aaron - Lydia Stillwell...............  4-02-1814
Mount, Abijah - Mary Chamberlin..............  2-06-1817
Mount, Button - Ann Curtice..................  1-29-1818
Mount, Cornelius - Elenor Hankenson..........  1-26-1809
Mount, Cornelius - Mary Casner...............  9-29-1829
Mount, David - Ann Hutchinson................  2-10-1830
Mount, Ely - Frances Reade...................  10-22-1837
Mount, Ezekiel - Margaret Denise.............  2-24-1814
```

Mount, Ezekiel - Margaret Gaston............. 3-12-1814
Mount, Hezikiah - Catherine Taylor Mount..... 4-21-1840
Mount, James - Deborah Swart................. 11-06-1814
Mount, Jesse - Phebe Phillips................ 8-23-1837
Mount, Jesse - Sarah Parker.................. 8-14-1824
Mount, John - Lydia Chamberlain.............. 10-31-1804
Mount, John - Mary Swan...................... 12-25-1842
Mount, John - Matilda Perine................. 3-21-1838
Mount, John H. - Nancy Boude................. 12-24-1829
Mount, Joseph - Catherine Clayton............ 7-21-1821
Mount, Joseph - Elizabeth Allen both of
   Middlesex Co., N. J....................... 9-13-1828
Mount, Joseph - Elizabeth O Donald........... 4-25-1829
Mount, Joseph - Rebecca Roberts.............. 4-23-1826
Mount, Mathias - Matilda Bell................ 3-01-1801
Mount, Michael - Abigail Cooper.............. 5-10-1809
Mount, Michael - Hannah Clayton.............. 4-02-1827
Mount, Michael - Louiza Wyckoff.............. 12-21-1822
Mount, Peter - Margaret Rue.................. 12-29-1803
Mount, Richard - Deborah Perine.............. 3-11-1840
Mount, Richard - Susan Wilson................ 2-13-1821
Mount, Thomas - Margaret Cook................ 1-21-1802
Mount, Thomas - Phebe Harley................. 7-15-1798
Mount, Timothy B. - Mary T. Walling.......... 1-18-1835
Mount, William - Belinda Ely................. 1-31-1839
Mount, William - Elizer Lewis................ 1-10-1821
Mount, William of Middlesex Co., N. J. -
   Lydia Pearce.............................. 11-16-1827
Mount, William - Mary Hankins................ 2-21-1835
Mount, Zachariah - Ann Mount Bouth........... 8-03-1833
Muckelvane, John - Esther Bowman............. 9-24-1815
Muler, John - Sarah Allen.................... 5-31-1834
Mulford, William - Lydia Tilton.............. 10-02-1834
Munyon, John - Alice Parker.................. 8-20-1795
Murdoch, Joseph - Buley ----................. 3-26-1837
Murdock, Abraham - Lydia Boker............... 5-04-1828
Murdock, Ephram - Rachel Price of
   Burlington Co., N. J...................... 10-13-1831
Murphy, Francis - Ann Bray................... 4-18-1812
Murphy, John - Elizabeth Chandler............ 6-30-1840
Murphy, John - Elizabeth Smith............... 2-11-1841
Murphy, Joseph - Alice Holmes................ 1-01-1820
Murry, John - Meriah Gardner................. 7-21-1817
Murry, William Jr. - Mary Crawford........... 11-20-1817
Myers, Isaac - Lydia Compton................. 1-10-1818
Myers, James - Margaret Benett............... 12-23-1833
Nafie, Abraham G. - Sarah Ann Smith.......... 12-29-1825
Nailor, Jacob - Mary Ann Anderson............ 11-08-1821
Neal, John - Elizabeth Logan................. 3-17-1829
Negro, George - Negro Lettiss (both black)... 6-08-1798
Neilson, Alexander - Charlotte Mushelee...... 7-23-1832
Neilson, William - Mellicent Reed............ 7-26-1827
Nelson, Andrew - Phebe Vanhise............... 8-08-1829
Nelson, Elisha - Jane Errickson.............. 2-12-1810
Nevison, John - Charlotte Freeman............ 9-21-1842

MARRIAGES OF MONMOUTH COUNTY, NEW JERSEY

Nevius, James - Hannah Bowne................	5-31-1837
Newberry, David - Prudence Crown............	3-09-1809
Newberry, Jacob - Elizabeth Harvey..........	5-19-1816
Newberry, Lawrence - Lydia Brannen..........	1-07-1826
Newberry, Stephen - Zupha Curtis............	5-25-1800
Newberry, Walter C. - Lydia Lawrence........	4-12-1828
Newbold, Alexander - Harriet Allen..........	12-18-1834
Newbury, Stephen - Mary Harvey..............	4-18-1829
Newbury, Taylor - Martha Birdsall...........	4-05-1837
Newel, William - Mary Chamberlain...........	5-06-1802
Newell, James - Alice Page..................	10-20-1810
Newell, Thomas - Rebeckah Treuax............	1-18-1798
Newil, Samuel - Martha Haviland.............	8-09-1801
Newland, John - Elenor Aumack...............	6-23-1835
Newman, Aaron - Elizabeth Layton............	4-12-1810
Newman, Abit - Abigail Layton...............	5-30-1842
Newman, Abbitt - Cornelia Devoe.............	9-25-1841
Newman, Abolt - Deborah Martain.............	1-03-1820
Newman, Benjamin - Ann Thorne...............	7-19-1834
Newman, Bloomfield - Mary Woolley...........	2-19-1834
Newman, Charles - Elizabeth Aumack..........	2-29-1832
Newman, Correll - Mary Devose...............	6-21-1837
Newman, David - Ann Harris..................	1-11-1821
Newman, Dennis - Rebeckah Tice.............	12-11-1827
Newman, Edon - Elizabeth Shearman...........	12-24-1842
Newman, Elijah - Jane Latony................	4-15-1816
Newman, Elijah - Sarah Rogers...............	5-05-1830
Newman, Ferdinand - Mary Dunwell............	4-18-1835
Newman, Francis - Mary Ann Barener..........	11-09-1831
Newman, Garret - Hannah Smith...............	9-21-1824
Newman, Jeremiah III - Rebecah Halloway......	6-08-1816
Newman, Jesse - Aecdery Baily...............	11-10-1808
Newman, John - Catherine Mc Guyrs...........	6-18-1809
Newman, John - Catrine Shearman.............	10-20-1811
Newman, Joseph - Ann Remind.................	11-02-1815
Newman, Joseph - Faith Herbert..............	9-19-1822
Newman, Morris - Ann Gray...................	9-27-1822
Newman, Morris - Mary Gray..................	3-16-1836
Newman, Nelson - Jane Holloway..............	11-14-1836
Newman, Robert - Ann Clark..................	3-27-1795
Newman, Samuel - Blainy Berry...............	5-01-1840
Newman, Samuel - Hester Thorn...............	2-06-1836
Newman, Silas - Elizabeth Cooper............	11-27-1831
Newman, Stephen - Elizabeth Smith...........	8-16-1841
Newman, Washington - Sarah Taylor...........	2-08-1834
Newman, William - Ellen Mathews.............	9-26-1835
Newmon, Ezekiel - Christian Dilby...........	1-27-1831
Newmon, John - Sarah Halaway................	9-05-1812
Newson, William - Hope More.................	11-18-1806
Neynolch, Henry - Hannah White..............	1-01-1834
Nickells, Peter G. - Elizabeth Bennett.......	4-03-1824
Nickson, James - Harriet Truax..............	1-02-1836
Nicolas, William - Francyntie Schenck........	2-05-1803
Niel, Benjamin - Elizabeth Bennett..........	4-08-1800
Nisbet, James - Lydia Vancleaf..............	10-30-1832

```
Nively, Allen - Deborah Hurley...............    3-26-1831
Nivison, Aarone - Jane Posty.................    2-25-1805
Nivison, William O. - Sarah F. Throckmorton..    1-11-1831
Nixon, Levy - Rachel Dove....................   11-25-1831
Nixon, Samuel Jr. - Susan Case of Trenton,
    N. J. (both black)......................    9-28-1833
Noble, Andrew of Phildelphia, Pa. -
    Alice Conover...........................   12-29-1836
Norcross, John A. - Harriet Kerby............   11-26-1835
Norcross, Joshua - Theodocia Gaskill.........    2-02-1839
Norris, Joseph - Rosetta Craft...............   10-21-1804
Norris, Richard - Altie Hendrickson..........   12-12-1797
Norris, William - Mariah Price...............   10-21-1813
Norstrand, Isaac - Patience Hendrickson......   12-23-1841
Norton, Daniel D. - Almira Thompson..........    3-20-1833
Norton, John - Mrs. Ann Van ----.............    1-11-1826
Norton, Joshua - Sarah Cox...................   12-08-1825
Nortret, Dennis - Anna Wooley................    6-18-1805
Nowlan, Henry - Mary Morris..................    3-17-1829
Nowlan, William - Annie Kite.................   10-22-1803
Nowland, Austin - Nancy Tyson................   10-19-1818
Nowman, John (Minister) - Ann M. Guger.......    6-04-1807
Nulet, Daniel - Catrin Scott.................   12-03-1816
O'Neal, Henry - Deborah Newman...............    8-10-1804
Oakerson, James - Mrs. Rhoda Attison.........    9-20-1827
Oakerson, John - Catherine Luguiere..........   12-20-1832
Oaks, John Walter - Deliah Eayres............    8-04-1813
Ockerman, Charles - Elizabeth Edwards........    5-19-1816
Odill, Nathaniel L. - Lydia Mc Michael.......    1-01-1825
Ogburn, William - Susan Parent...............    7-08-1825
Okerson, David - Nancy Schenck...............    1-25-1800
Oliphant, William - Eleanor Pharo............   12-19-1828
Ormsby, Leonard - Gertrude Roberts...........    7-09-1830
Osberne, Allen - Sarah Allen.................   10-24-1839
Osborn, Abraham - Christian Johnston.........   12-29-1821
Osborn, Isaac - Lydia Clayton................    8-04-1830
Osborn, Jacob - Phebe Johnson................    5-08-1834
Osborn, James - Elizabeth Johnston...........    3-15-1818
Osborn, James son of William -
    Elizabeth Longstreet....................    1-22-1823
Osborn, John - Martha Allin..................   11-12-1817
Osborn, Samuel H. - Hannah Falkenburgh.......    3-26-1826
Osborne, Abraham - Deborah Havens............    2-27-1842
Osborne, Abraham - Mary Rankins..............    3-21-1839
Osborne, Benager - Caroline Allen............   11-30-1842
Osborne, Forman - Elizabeth Baley............    2-04-1836
Osborne, Henry of New York City, N. Y. -
    Clementine Dennis.......................   11-13-1839
Osborne, John - Ida Newman...................   10-23-1817
Osburn, William - Catherine Fish.............    5-20-1802
Ostley, Michael - Aecha Phillips.............   11-11-1823
Outgelt, John - Hannah Voutyn................    9-13-1795
Page, Edward - Susan A. Vaughn...............   11-13-1834
Page, Elijah - Eleanor Warner................    3-26-1837
Page, Elijah - Mary Tantum...................    2-21-1822
```

Page, James - Amelia Yearling................ 1-01-1827
Page, John - Susanna John.................... 2-11-1796
Painter, Isaac - Ann Borden.................. 11-13-1804
Painton, Tobious - Cornelisann Hall.......... 9-14-1820
Paintor, Samuel - Mary Snyder................ 11-08-1829
Pakeson, John D. - Elissa Voorhees........... 1-01-1816
Palmer, Gilbert - Hannah Forman.............. 10-30-1836
Palmer, John - Hannah Taylor................. 1-21-1836
Palmer, Stern - Mary Palmer.................. 4-15-1827
Palmmer, Forman - Phebe Cottrell............. 1-05-1828
Panling, Elisha - Catherine A. Scott......... 10-28-1834
Parent, James - Theodocia Coward............. 1-13-1830
Parent, William Jr. - Mary Smith............. 9-09-1819
Parham, William - Julia Busbee............... 2-28-1833
Parker, Anthony - Pheby Hough................ 3-01-1798
Parker, Benjamin - Hannah Lippincott......... 5-22-1827
Parker, Benjamin - Martha Chapman............ 10-13-1821
Parker, Benjamin - Mary Stillwell............ 4-23-1832
Parker, Caleb - Isabelle Lawrence............ 7-24-1825
Parker, Charles - Alice Lawyer............... 9-15-1842
Parker, Charles - Mary M. White.............. 6-21-1829
Parker, Charles - Sarah Coward............... 8-17-1808
Parker, Daniel - Mary Springsteen............ 11-14-1838
Parker, Edmund - Sarah G. Smith.............. 12-11-1832
Parker, Elijah - Anna Schenck................ 6-13-1836
Parker, Ephraim - Johannah Ayres............. 11-15-1800
Parker, Eric - Mary Lacompt.................. 1-19-1826
Parker, George - Ann Hendrickson............. 12-31-1835
Parker, Jesse - Martha Foreman............... 1-05-1825
Parker, John - Anna Button................... 10-04-1826
Parker, John - Elizabeth Swanbeth............ 3-15-1836
Parker, John - Jane Van Pelt................. 5-13-1820
Parker, John - Joanny Demmott................ 5-11-1831
Parker, Jonah - Susanna Lloyd................ 8-12-1805
Parker, Jonathan - Phoebe Stratten........... 12-20-1810
Parker, Joseph - Hannah Castler.............. 2-28-1811
Parker, Joseph - Mary Matthews............... 3-30-1816
Parker, Joseph C. - Mariah Craven............ 3-30-1824
Parker, Josiah - Elisabeth Burden............ 2-05-1797
Parker, Lewis - Mary Smith................... 11-07-1827
Parker, Marcus Jr. - Mahala Applegate........ 1-05-1811
Parker, Michael son of William -
    Ann Wooley............................... 9-29-1803
Parker, Nathaniel - Sarah Hatfield........... 11-08-1803
Parker, Richard - Mary Steepy................ 12-15-1813
Parker, Riley - Margaret Leming.............. 1-07-1838
Parker, Samuel of Cape May Co., N. J. -
    Caroline Cranmer......................... 10-04-1842
Parker, Samuel - Elizabeth Craddock.......... 1-16-1806
Parker, Samuel - Mary Bird................... 12-25-1815
Parker, Samuel - Mary Ann Throckmorton....... 2-12-1831
Parker, Samuel - Rebecca Garavatt............ 12-25-1834
Parker, Thomas - Sarah Patten................ 12-10-1825
Parker, William - Margaret Anderson.......... 12-03-1811
Parker, William - Mary Wooley................ 5-06-1805

```
Parker, William - Sarah Shepherd............  9-08-1799
Parkus, John - Jemica Brewer................ 12-09-1810
Parmer, William - Emiline Burdge............  9-14-1842
Parrent, Edward - Rachel Applegate..........  3-03-1815
Parseoue, John - Mary Chamberlin............  3-27-1805
Parsons, Walter - Mary Morford..............  3-28-1829
Paterson, Dennis - Sarah Webb............... 11-20-1831
Paterson, Thomas - Catherine Kerney.........  4-08-1822
Patrick, George - Alizabeth Garent..........  9-02-1820
Patten, John (wid'r.) - Catherine Wilson
  (widow)...................................  3-18-1815
Patten, John - Sarah Platt..................  3-17-1811
Patten, Lewis - Jane Mannahan...............  6-19-1800
Patten, Samuel - Mary Rue................... 11-08-1798
Patterson, Aaron - Catherine Clayton........  2-25-1808
Patterson, Charles - Sarah Brown............  5-02-1840
Patterson, Charles G. - Cathrin Wainwright...  9-21-1816
Patterson, Cornelius -
  Catherine Ann Paterson.................... 12-22-1836
Patterson, Cornelius - Jaein Covenhoven......  2-07-1812
Patterson, Courtenius - Pheby Hers..........  5-29-1814
Patterson, David - Zilpha Riddle............ 10-  -1838
Patterson, Enock - Mary Brewer..............  3-29-1819
Patterson, Francis - Elizabeth Cottrell......  4-27-1840
Patterson, George - Phebe Archer............  8-15-1842
Patterson, Hiram - Abigail Brewer...........  3-31-1841
Patterson, Isaac - J. Layton................  3-15-1828
Patterson, Isaac - Luhana Hall..............  2-24-1842
Patterson, Jacob - Carolyn Loukerson........  5-12-1838
Patterson, James - Deborah Conover..........  1-22-1840
Patterson, James - Debrah Trafford.......... 10-12-1817
Patterson, James - Leah Patterson........... 12-17-1796
Patterson, James - Lydia Walling............  1-22-1831
Patterson, James - Mary Covenhoven.......... 12-31-1806
Patterson, James B. - Sarah Smith........... 10-11-1842
Patterson, Job - Sarah Snyder...............  5-30-1839
Patterson, John - Hannah Emmans.............  2-12-1835
Patterson, John - Mary Robinson.............  8-04-1832
Patterson, John - Mary A. Patterson.........  8-13-1835
Patterson, John - Nancy Potter..............  7-26-1806
Patterson, John - Sarah Stout...............  2-23-1834
Patterson, John L. - Mary H. Clayton........  8-12-1835
Patterson, Joseph - Eliza Smith.............  7-27-1829
Patterson, Joseph C. - Sarah Ann Connet...... 11-20-1828
Patterson, Moses - Mrs. Eliza White.........  2-07-1839
Patterson, Robert - Eleanore Burdge......... 12-17-1835
Patterson, Robert - Olivia Ann Morris
  both of New York..........................  1-15-1840
Patterson, Safety - Phebe Davis.............  8-26-1798
Patterson, Stillwell - Jannet Vanschoeck..... 12-29-1836
Patterson, Sylvester - Sarah Thompson........  1-09-1841
Patterson, William - Caroline Ketchem........  3-07-1839
Patterson, William - Hetty Lippincott........  1-14-1804
Pattison, John C. - Sarah Riddle............ 11-14-1813
Patton, Joseph - Mary Horner................  2-11-1808
```

MARRIAGES OF MONMOUTH COUNTY, NEW JERSEY

Patton, William - Ann Blake................. 12-26-1824
Paul, Benjamin Jr. - Betsy Crane............. 8-02-1808
Paul, William - Lea Lippincott............... 11-08-1795
Pauling, Elisha - Catherine Scott............ 10-28-1834
Peacock, John - Sarah Conover................ 12-23-1819
Pearce, Adam - Catherine Helmore............. 10-29-1796
Pearce, Amon - Mary Cross.................... 1-11-1839
Pearce, Barzilla - Sarah Parker.............. 2-20-1819
Pearce, Benjamin - Caroline More............. 7-20-1833
Pearce, Benjamin - Catherine White........... 8-13-1817
Pearce, Benjamin - Elizabeth Newberry........ 3-31-1799
Pearce, Danice - Jane Estie.................. 6-14-1812
Pearce, Elisha - Sarah Clayton............... 4-23-1827
Pearce, Herbert C. - Margaret Wooley......... 11-25-1824
Pearce, James - Ann Shinn.................... 9-03-1820
Pearce, James - Caroline Newman.............. 11-01-1834
Pearce, James - Hannah Morris................ 12-20-1821
Pearce, James - Rachel Stout................. 1-27-1827
Pearce, James - E. Prudence Longstreet....... 6-05-1817
Pearce, John - Claricy Gant.................. 8-28-1828
Pearce, John - Grace Simson.................. 6-22-1824
Pearce, Jonathan - Rintha Conover............ 12-17-1821
Pearce, Joseph T. - Rebecca Clayton.......... 4-10-1820
Pearce, Joshua - Elizabeth Lawrence.......... 2-10-1831
Pearce, Leonard - Ida Bennett................ 2-06-1842
Pearce, Richard - Elizabeth Jane Riley....... 1-31-1839
Pearce, Richard - Sarah Rively............... 10-02-1802
Pearce, Robert - Deborah Peace............... 1-08-1827
Pearce, Thomas Charclay - Lenah Helmore...... 1-26-1801
Pearce, Thomas C. - Sally Harvey............. 10-06-1833
Pearce, William - Meraber Chadwick........... 3-22-1815
Pearce, William - Meribah Cossel............. 1-02-1823
Pearce, William - Sarah Parker............... 2-27-1798
Pearce, William W. - Deborah Ann Hankinson... 5-15-1827
Pearce, Zephaniah - Elizabeth Hulse.......... 4-15-1840
Pease, Josiah - Elizabeth Nailor............. 7-14-1821
Peckworth, Isaac of Philadelphia Pa. -
    Hannah Gray.............................. 4-07-1822
Peer, Jose - Easther ----................... 7-03-1808
Pees, Jossa - Elizabeth Anderson............. 4-25-1801
Peirson, Thomas - Lorance Slack.............. 6-03-1795
Pelhemus, Daniel - Ledia Covenhoven.......... 1-22-1807
Penn, Jesse - Rebeckah Headley............... 3-09-1830
Penter, William - Mary Clayton............... 11-10-1803
Peppinger, Baines - Pheby Heveland........... 1819
Perce, Richard - Elizabeth Gordon............ 12-16-1802
Perine, Daniel - Susannah Garrison........... 5-21-1806
Perine, Enock - Ann Holeman.................. 1-04-1798
Perine, Henry - Margaret Herbert............. 6-02-1799
Perine, Joseph - Amy Thompson................ 10-02-1828
Perine, Joseph - Anne Vanhise................ 5-15-1804
Perine, Joseph - Mary Erricson............... 10-21-1815
Perine, Matthew - Hannah Morford............. 2-03-1798
Perine, Samuel - Nancy Slown................. 9-05-1821
Perrin, Barzilla - Sarah Ann Heyers.......... 2-13-1841

80

MARRIAGES OF MONMOUTH COUNTY, NEW JERSEY

```
Perrin, Enoch - Caroline Ford................  2-27-1841
Perrin, Ezekiel - Theodosia Hebberson........ 10-16-1842
Perrine, Henry of Middlesex County, N. J. -
    Ann Mercerole...........................  3-11-1835
Perrin, James - Deborah Dey..................  3-08-1838
Perrin, James - Sarah Hutchinson.............  1-03-1838
Perrin, John - Mary Ann Drummond.............  1-16-1840
Perrin, John - Matilda Mount.................  9-05-1833
Perrin, Joseph - ---- Rue....................  9-21-1836
Perrin, William of Middlesex Co., N. J. -
    Harriet Baker...........................  1-04-1838
Perrin, William - Mary Conover...............  3-10-1840
Perrine, David - Elizabeth Tilton............  1-05-1831
Perrine, David - Mary Conover................  1-09-1811
Perrine, Henry - Phebe Nielson............... 11-28-1831
Perrine, Joseph - Hannah B. Anderson........ 10-07-1819
Perrine, Peter son of Daniel -
    Anne Garrison...........................  2-12-1809
Perrine, Peter - Elizabeth Johnson........... 12-19-1818
Perrine, Solon - Jane Thompson...............  7-07-1839
Perrine, Thomas W. - Mrs. Ellen Woodward.....  5-03-1829
Perrine, William - Ann Roberts...............  3-19-1836
Perrine, William - Catherine Davis........... 12-20-1810
Peterson, Benjamin - Hattie Dunfee...........  3-08-1798
Petit, Jacob - Nancy Ware....................  1-26-1842
Petit, John - Ann Chamberlin.................  7-03-1822
Petitt, Thomas - Hannah Sutten............... 12-23-1812
Pette, William - Elizabeth Applegate.........  5-24-1812
Pettet, John - Catherine Hays................ 10-13-1799
Pettet, William - Rebecca Clayton............  1-06-1799
Pettit, James - Hannah Havens................ 12-25-1820
Pettit, John - Catherine Johnston............  1-30-1823
Pettit, Joseph - Mary Ann Bird............... 10-21-1826
Pettit, William of New York City -
    Hannah Strickland.......................  1-11-1834
Phar, William - Mary Ann Hazelton............ 11-20-1814
Phares, Robert - Mary Clevenger..............  6-28-1795
Pharo, Amos Jr. - Desiah Burdsall............  2-06-1830
Pharo, Benjamin - Sarah Kelley...............  5-19-1822
Pharo, Borden - Susanne Larigaux.............  2-24-1842
Pharo, Charles - Elizabeth Haywood...........  8-16-1820
Pharo, James - Elizabeth Hall................  2-23-1843
Pharo, James - Mary Elsworth................. 12-01-1826
Pharo, John - Zilphay Ivins..................  3-22-1821
Pharo, John Jr. - Edith Crammer..............  2-09-1828
Pharo, Samuel - Annaliza Mires...............  3-01-1834
Pharo, Samuel - Huldah Lewis.................  1-18-1843
Pharo, Samuel - Sarah Caping ................  6-28-1838
Pharo, Servis - Elizabeth Crainer............  8-18-1803
Pharo, Stephen - Mary Jones..................  1-01-1826
Philips, Jacob - Rachel Forgason.............  7-17-1803
Phillips, Garret - Hilda Russel..............  3-26-1807
Phillips, Jacob - Emeline Luker..............  9-19-1835
Phillips, John - Lydia Kinne.................  3-08-1802
Phillips, John - Sarah Midleton..............  5-05-1804
```

```
Phillips, Joseph - Ursula Throckmorton......    3-10-1810
Phillips, Richard - Margaret Luker..........   10-31-1835
Phillips, Richard Jr. - Mary Tilton.........   10-29-1815
Phillips, Thomas - Abigail Mc Kelvey........    5-02-1811
Phillips, Thomas - Catherine Morris.........    9-09-1815
Phillips, Thomas - Mariah Cornelius.........    6-11-1831
Phillips, William - Lydia Phillips..........         1815
Phillips, William G. - Elizabeth Crawford...    2-05-1825
Pier, Jacob - Jane Clark....................    9-13-1838
Pierce, John - Josephine Morgan.............   12-30-1842
Pierson, Aaron - Anna Hulfish...............    4-21-1822
Pierson, Thomas - Rebecca Hughs.............   10-18-1836
Pigot, William of New York Cuty -
    Mariah Schanck..........................   12-06-1838
Pile, Simon - Abegal Sharp..................    4-27-1817
Pilyou, James - Jane Lewis..................   12-21-1807
Pinnington, Edward of Philadelphia, Pa. -
    Helena Lawrence Holmes..................    9-27-1798
Pintard, John - Hannah Parker...............    1-26-1843
Pitcher, Edwood - Mrs. Jane Pool............    6-30-1822
Pitcher, Elias - Mary Hurley................    1-01-1828
Pitcher, Stacey - Jane Anderson.............    2-02-1824
Pitenger, John - Mary Cheesman..............    3-04-1812
Pitman, Barzilla of Burlington Co., N. J. -
    Deborah Philips.........................    4-21-1832
Pitney, Aaron - Willampie Longstreet........    4-02-1804
Pitney, Samuel - Hannah Barkalow............    6-30-1800
Pittenger, David - Hannah Clayton...........    8-22-1816
Pittenger, Jacob - Helena Conover...........    5-28-1835
Pittenger, Jacob - Jane Sayers..............    3-12-1833
Pittenger, Joseph - Jerusha Erickson........    2-14-1828
Plaine, Charles of Boston, Mass. -
    Ann Eliza Thorpe of N. Y................    1-22-1831
Platt, Abel - Melah Letts...................    3-20-1796
Platt, Job - Eliza Ann Allen................    2-19-1831
Platt, Joel - Ruth Anderson.................    3-05-1815
Platt, Levi - Margaret Voorhees.............    5-09-1802
Platt, William - Deby Potter................    2-16-1812
Plumb, Joseph - Hannah Lippincott both of
    Burlington Co., N. J....................    9-26-1818
Plumer, Daniel - Martha Hains (both black)...   9-13-1829
Poast, Elias - Elnar Southard...............    1-01-1795
Poinset, Joseph - Sarah Mount both of
    Burlington Co., N. J....................    4-02-1825
Poinsett, Irick of Burlington Co., N.J. -
    Ann Nutt................................   12-08-1824
Poinsett, Joseph - Rhoda Chafee both of
    Burlington Co., N. J....................    4-26-1832
Poland, Peter - Mary Layton.................    1-01-1817
Poland, Richard - Leah Lamberson............    3-17-1834
Poland, Zephaniah - Eliza Lamberson.........   10-30-1833
Polemus, William - Mary Chadwick............    7-19-1797
Polhemus, Anthony - Catherine Riley.........    4-23-1841
Polhemus, Daniel D. - Elizabeth Bennet
    dg. of John W. Bennet...................    4-15-1828
```

```
Polhemus, Jacob - Ann Bennett...............    2-24-1819
Polhemus, James - Abigail Patterson
   (both black)...........................    7-25-1822
Polhemus, John - Mary Bennett...............   11-23-1831
Polhemus, Joseph - Diadema Irons............   10-21-1840
Polhemus, Laurence - Eleanor Mc Clain.......    3-26-1808
Polhemus, Levi W. - Maria Havens............    1-25-1832
Polhemus, Tobias - Sarah Meers..............    3-17-1821
Polhemus, William - Ann Hayden..............   10-31-1832
Polin, John - Mary Herbert..................    4-02-1812
Poling, Charles - Ann Kelsey................   12-31-1837
Pool, Cornelius - Abigail White.............    7-05-1818
Pool, George - Margaret Graham..............    1-27-1825
Pool, Joseph - Hannah C. Sear...............   11-10-1829
Post, George - Ann Taylor...................    1-15-1835
Post, John of N. Y. C. - Agnes Forman
   dg. of Ezekiel..........................   10-10-1796
Pots, John - Mary Vorhees...................    2-06-1800
Potter, Enoch - Hannah Borden...............    4-06-1826
Potter, Ephraim - Frances Garrett...........    8-26-1813
Potter, Ephraim - Hannah Woodmancy..........    1-25-1806
Potter, James - Mary Pease..................    9-14-1803
Potter, Jesse - Catherine Morris............    3-20-1828
Potter, Joel - Sarah Smith..................    9-14-1812
Potter, John - Mary Martin..................    9-14-1834
Potter, Joseph - Leadia Pette...............    4-29-1802
Potter, Reubin - Euphemia Lawrence..........    7-31-1841
Potter, Ruben - Ann B. Applegate............    1-06-1836
Potter, Samuel - Rebecca Hendrickson........    5-20-1830
Potter, Samuel - Ulsey Leuker...............   10-06-1827
Potter, Thomas - Rebeckah Platt.............    1-31-1813
Potter, William - Margaret Newman...........   10-12-1830
Potter, William - Rachel Wells..............    2-28-1818
Potter, William - Rebecca Arrants...........   11-05-1822
Pottor, Nathaniel - Mary Fieldor............   12-25-1796
Potts, Charles - Mary Potts dg. of William...   7-01-1823
Potts, Samuel - Mary Riggs..................    7-18-1815
Potts, Thomas - Priscilla Hooper............    2-10-1825
Potts, William W. - Mary Vann...............    3-23-1833
Poynton, William - Ann Barker...............   11-17-1822
Predmore, Job - Elizabeth Soper.............   12-29-1838
Predmore, John - Asenah Chamberlin..........    1-12-1833
Predmore, William - Fanny Camburn...........    1-24-1819
Predmore, William - Mary King...............    8-25-1838
Preston, Jacob - Rachel Preston.............    2-21-1807
Preston, Joseph - Elizabeth Conover.........    9-23-1834
Preston, Robert - Elizabeth Flemmon.........    8-22-1830
Preston, Samuel - Anna Clayton..............    6-19-1803
Preston, Samuel - Lucy Ann Dey..............    2-27-1834
Preston, Samuel - Mariah Hankins............   11-20-1824
Preston, William - Elizabeth John...........    7-24-1815
Preston, William - Sarah Hutchinson.........    6-28-1801
Price, ---- - Anna Little...................   10-29-1818
Price, James Jr. - Sarah Crammer............    6-01-1806
Price, Jeremiah - Huldah Salter.............    5-06-1834
```

```
Price, John - Mary Lain....................  1-27-1827
Price, Joseph - Jemima Smock................  2-22-1795
Price, Lawrence - Catherine Taylor.......... 11-08-1798
Pricket, Stacy - Jane Covenhoven............  6-15-1809
Prickett, Levi - Sally Ann Smith............  1-01-1827
Pridmore, Benjamin - Phebe Brown............  1-31-1814
Pridmore, Ephraim - Mary Brown..............  2-15-1810
Prine, Daniel - Zilfe Holman................ 11-04-1795
Probasco, Abram - Jane Baraclow.............  2-17-1799
Proctor, John - Amy Woodmanse...............  7-18-1808
Provost, David - Elizabeth Norris........... 11-05-1800
Pru, Zephemah - Hopy Headley................  9-03-1827
Pulen, George - Rachel Stevens..............  1-24-1815
Pullen, Charles - Catherine Young...........  7-24-1828
Pullen, Clark - Mary Applegate..............  6-21-1837
Pullen, Davison - Elizabeth Lane............ 11-02-1816
Pullen, Ellison - Leah Bearmore............. 11-14-1842
Pullen, George S. W. of Middlesex Co., N. J.
  - Lydia A. Reid...........................  4-11-1835
Pullen, William - Elizabeth ----
  both of Burlington Co., N. J.............  8-04-1832
Pullien, Elijah - Phoebe Atchley............  3-03-1798
Pulling, Stogdon - Margaret Horsefield......  6-03-1830
Purdy, Harper - Sarah Chamberlin............  8-25-1822
Purdy, John - Rebecca Van Note.............. 12-18-1819
Purnal, Williams - Mary Johnson............. 10-01-1800
Purpel, Edward - Alice Shumard..............  8-26-1813
Pyle, Samuel - Emmeline Morford............. 11-19-1823
Quackenbush, William - Gette Vorhees........ 10-09-1814
Quail, James (Rev.) - Susan Lippincott......  4-14-1813
Quay, John - Agnes Remson...................  6-06-1799
Queen, Asher - Hannah Brinley............... 10-25-1830
Queen, Miles - Margaret Hays................  4-16-1814
Quero, Anthony - Catherine Still
  (both black)............................. 12-05-1836
Quick, Henry of Somerset Co., N. J. -
  Jane Smock...............................  3-22-1812
Quicksel, John - Sarah Hopkins both of
  Burlington Co., N.J...................... 10-06-1832
Quig, William - Ann Tetman..................  6-08-1837
Quigley, Azariah - Sarah James..............  3-24-1825
Quin, Roger - Deborah Griskey...............  2-18-1807
Quizley, John - Ann Van Horn................  1-03-1816
Radford, Aaron - Altie Vanderbylt........... 12-31-1814
Rainer, Jonathan - Caroline Jones
  (both black).............................  3-01-1838
Ralph - Francis - Mrs.Elizabeth Kenada...... 11-29-1834
Ralph, Francis - Rachel Smith............... 12-06-1806
Ralph, Jacob - Merible Warrick..............  5-23-1832
Ralph, Joseph - Jannetta Thomas............. 10-30-1842
Ramsay, Alexander - Ann Millne..............  1-26-1841
Ramsey, John - Edith Brown..................  6-11-1797
Randolph, Bennington - Eliza Forman......... 11-25-1840
Randolph, Joseph - Ann Forman............... 11-19-1828
Randolph, Phineas - Sarah Davidson.......... 11-17-1837
```

```
Randolph, William - Rachel Inman............   8-12-1801
Rankin, James - Rebecca Ann Longstreet.......   3-06-1834
Rapalje, George - Elizabeth Smock............  11-21-1821
Raynols, Samuel - Betsey Brewer..............   5-11-1825
Reader, Amos - Mariah Stillwell..............   4-30-1795
Real, Robert - Rebecca Richardson
   (both black)..............................   3-23-1822
Reckhow, David (Rev.) - Isabel Morris........  12-23-1802
Redman, William - Fanny White................  10-14-1840
Reed, Aaron - Elizabeth Combs................  12-07-1797
Reed, Benjamin - Lydia Mount.................   7-05-1835
Reed, Charles - Ann Sutphen..................   2-06-1830
Reed, Charles (Elder) - Martha Claypole......   2-07-1830
Reed, Doughty - Phebe Spragg.................   3-05-1804
Reed, Eliphalet (Rev.) - Mary Throckmorton...   4-03-1823
Reed, George - Catherine Joely...............   6-30-1798
Reed, George - Lucy Cheeseman................   3-11-1809
Reed, George - Sarah Wright..................  11-30-1816
Reed, George W. - Mary Nesbit................  12-  -1823
Reed, Hugh of New York City -
   Mrs. Catherine Tapscott...................   8-10-1818
Reed, Jacob - Hannah Johnson.................   9-23-1802
Reed, James - Sarah Davison..................   3-06-1805
Reed, James M. - Maria Birdsall..............   3-25-1835
Reed, John - Ann Marks.......................   1-18-1827
Reed, John - Catherine Dillintach............   3-21-1840
Reed, John - Eliza Hankinson.................   3-11-1835
Reed, John - Elizabeth Fisher................   6-13-1838
Reed, John A. - Hannah Johnston..............  11-18-1798
Reed, Noble - Adaline Logan..................   8-30-1834
Reed, Robert - Mary Tilton...................   9-27-1832
Reed, William - Elizabeth Perrine............  12-03-1834
Reed, William C. of Burlington Co., N. J. -
   Hester Brown of Middlesex Co., N.J.......   4-19-1834
Reeder, David - Amy James....................   2-20-1839
Reeve, John - Margaret Blackwell.............   1-01-1829
Reeves, Samuel - Hannah Chambers.............   1-24-1823
Reeves, Thomas - Ann Steward of
   Burlington Co., N. J......................   2-15-1834
Refine, George - Lucy Cawood (both black)....   4-23-1833
Reid, James - Cornelia Ann Bower.............   6-02-1822
Reid, John - Ann Hulshart....................   1-19-1833
Reid, John - Hannah Miller...................   1-30-1812
Reid, Peter - Eleanor Matthews...............   1-08-1834
Reid, Simon A. - Mary Walton.................   2-05-1818
Relyea, Peter - Rachel Brown both of N.Y.....   4-28-1833
Remine, Theophilus - Phebe Newman............   6-19-1821
Renny, Abraham - Catherine Preston...........   7-09-1803
Reulon, James - Mary Ann Furgeson both of
   Burlington Co., N. J......................   6-14-1828
Reulong, Joseph - Silence Preston............   8-20-1828
Reulong, Stephen - Ann Soper dg. of Ezekiel..   1-20-1827
Revey, Benjamin - Mary Ann Revey
   (both black)..............................   4-27-1830
Revey, Robert - Sarah Richardson.............   7-09-1836
```

```
Revy, Thomas - Margaret Revy................ 11-16-1800
Reyhuve, Francis - Matilda Dillen
   (both black)............................ 1-08-1829
Reynolch, Henry - Hannah White.............. 1-01-1834
Reynolds, Barzilla - Lydia Layton........... 9-15-1832
Reynolds, Corlies - Jane Morris............. 3-06-1828
Reynolds, James - Allice Milsbury........... 11-20-1816
Reynolds, James - Peggy Miller.............. 3-19-1797
Reynolds, James - Phebe Dangler............. 1-06-1836
Reynolds, John - Eliza Luker................ 1-14-1837
Reynolds, John - Rebecca Cook............... 9-20-1827
Reynolds, John - Mrs. Susan Cottrell........ 2-09-1839
Reynolds, John - Trenty Anderson............ 1-18-1823
Reynolds, John - Zilpha Webb................ 3-30-1815
Reynolds, Matthew - Mary Woodward........... 12-08-1803
Reynolds, Miles - Lydia Cottrell............ 9-17-1829
Reynolds, Peter - Mary James................ 3-18-1839
Reynolds, Robert M. - Mercy Pettit.......... 1-22-1825
Reynolds, Samuel - Deborah Jeffery.......... 11-14-1799
Reynolds, Samuel - Hannah Ashton............ 1-24-1802
Reynolds, Samuel - Lydia Applegate.......... 9-18-1837
Reynolds, Samuel - Nancy Grooms............. 12-31-1804
Reynolds, Samuel W. - Elizabeth Anderson.... 1-09-1819
Reynolds, William - Phebe Patterson......... 5-10-1801
Reynor, John - Alice Holmes................. 12-02-1826
Rice, John - Margaret Davison............... 5-30-1837
Richard, John - Elizabeth Parker............ 6-09-1813
Richards, Andrew - Anna Reve................ 12-25-1802
Richards, Joseph - Jemimy Manuel
   (both black)............................ 11-27-1824
Richardson, David - Mary Rile............... 8-31-1839
Richardson, Samuel - Jemthy Revey........... 9-05-1829
Richardson, William - Mary Holmes........... 9-16-1837
Richardson, William A. - Emeline Rivey
   (both black)............................ 1-24-1829
Richmond, Anthony - Mrs. Caty Holmes........ 10-26-1821
Richmond, David - Trisalah Patterson........ 2-24-1798
Richmond, Joseph - Esther Vancleaf.......... 10-30-1832
Riddle, David - Catherine Brannen........... 1-01-1829
Riddle, David - Hannah Burge................ 11-06-1802
Riddle, Hendrick - Charity Ayres............ 6-08-1822
Riddle, Thomas - Ellen Rulong............... 9-04-1819
Ridgeway, Clayton L. - Sarah Cornwall....... 11-06-1832
Ridgeway, Joseph - Phebe Pharo.............. 4-07-1827
Ridgeway, Lawrence - Charlotte Warner....... 11-16-1826
Ridgeway, Richard - Mary Ann Conover........ 6-15-1833
Ridgway, Asa - Elizabeth Newell............. 2-09-1835
Ridgway, Daniel - Lucy Burtis............... 4-17-1839
Ridgway, Joseph - Lydia Mc Cabe............. 2-19-1831
Ridgway, Joseph - Phebe Carr................ 10-25-1810
Rigaway, Lawrence - Mary Collins............ 11-01-1820
Riggs, Samuel - Elizabeth Atchley........... 5-11-1799
Right, Samuel - Hannah Horner............... 9-16-1838
Right, Thomas - Ethalind Herbert............ 3-04-1841
Right, Thomas - Mary Butterfield............ 5-01-1839
```

Riley, Johnathan - Martha Boyls
   (both black)........................... 12-31-1836
Riley, William - Hester Leonard.............. 1-10-1828
Rind, George - Sarah Mick.................... 6-25-1832
Rive, John - Nancy Buckalew................. 11-16-1795
Rively, Allen - Deborah Hurley.............. 3-26-1831
Riverley, James - Elizabeth Tilton........... 4-29-1841
Rivit, William - Emma Seely................. 9-10-1834
Roads, David - Patty Allen.................. 5-31-1797
Robberts, William - Lean Van Derbeck......... 11-04-1805
Robbins, Aaron - Eliza Robbins.............. 1-02-1822
Robbins, Aaron - Hannah Hepburn both of
   Middlesex Co., N. J...................... 8-19-1829
Robbins, Asher - Hannah ----................ 1835-1836
Robbins, Benajmin - Lydia Carr.............. 2-28-1839
Robbins, Charles - Sarah Laird.............. 3-06-1823
Robbins, Clayton - Angeline Applegate....... 1-16-1823
Robbins, Elisha - Ann Stoddard.............. 2-08-1841
Robbins, Enoch - Ann Willits both of
   Philadelphia, Pa........................ 5-15-1818
Robbins, Ephraim - Carolyn Stillwell........ 10-30-1840
Robbins, Garret - Prudence Lewis............ 11-01-1836
Robbins, George - Christiana Beatty......... 3-31-1840
Robbins, Jacob - Sarah Ann Warren........... 3-21-1829
Robbins, James D. - Angelina Hutchinson...... 2-23-1831
Robbins, John - Edneyetta Hutchinson of
   Burlington Co., N.J..................... 1-09-1834
Robbins, John - Margaret Van Derbeek........ 9-30-1830
Robbins, John B. - Jane Gravatt............. 12-12-1834
Robbins, Jonathan - Elizabeth Swart......... 1-27-1811
Robbins, Joseph - Cornelia Andrews.......... 6-30-1824
Robbins, Joseph - Mary Firman............... 11-24-1829
Robbins, Lewis - Mary Snowden............... 3-09-1825
Robbins, Lloyd - Maria Hall................. 12-18-1841
Robbins, Ravall - Jerusha Hutchinson........ 9-04-1834
Robbins, Vanroom - Margaret Blackwell....... 6-09-1828
Robbins, William Jr. - Susan Sinclair....... 3-17-1841
Robert, James - Susan Summerhays............ 3-22-1823
Roberts, Ezekell - Ellener Crawford......... 7-08-1795
Roberts, Henry - Elizabeth Scott
   dg. of Benjamin......................... 1-30-1842
Roberts, Joel - Barbary Elizabeth Morrison... 10-18-1802
Roberts, John - Ann Chambers............... 12-20-1824
Roberts, John - Hannah Scott................ 3-04-1811
Roberts, John - Jane Laqueer................ 2-09-1807
Roberts, Joseph - Betse Crawford dg.
   of David................................ 4-01-1804
Roberts, Matthias - Elizabeth Smith......... 9-21-1801
Roberts, Thomas - Mary Mott................. 7-16-1800
Roberts, Thomas Jr. - Mary Griggs........... 3-07-1833
Roberts, William - Eliza Voorhees........... 7-23-1831
Roberts, William - Leanor Johnson........... 6-13-1806
Robertson, Andrew - Elizabeth Fowler........ 1-29-1827
Robertson, Samuel - Lydia Shoby............. 2-09-1812
Robins, Augustus - Lucy Savage.............. 1-23-1840

Robins, Ephraim - Jane Wright............... 1-22-1815
Robins, James - Sarah Ann Potts.............. 12-02-1827
Robins, Joel - Ann Gravatt................... 8-28-1817
Robins, John - Charlotte Bowman.............. 1-10-1804
Robins, William - Abiah Wear................. 6-18-1809
Robins, William - Jane Robins................ 1-17-1816
Robinson, Edmond - Nancy Throckmorton........ 9-14-1816
Robinson, James - Sarah Applegate............ 10-06-1832
Robinson, John - Mariah Vanderbelt........... 3-11-1831
Robinson, John - Matilda Mount............... 12-04-1826
Robinson, Joseph - Ann Conover............... 1-12-1813
Robinson, Richard - Lidia Brinley............ 11-17-1798
Robinson, Thomas of Long Island, N. Y. -
  Margaret Burling........................... 8-23-1841
Robinson, William - Jolly Schenck............ 2-22-1819
Robinson, William H. - Sarah Lefferson....... 1-21-1829
Rockafellor, David - Elizabeth A. Haughawout. 7-20-1812
Rockerfeller, Hiram - Susan Little........... 9-19-1840
Rockhill, Joel - Euphame Lawrence............ 10-02-1833
Rodger, Britton - Sarah Newman............... 3-16-1825
Rodgers, Daniel - Phebe Preston.............. 9-19-1802
Rodgers, John - Eliza R. Walker.............. 6-25-1801
Rodgers, John - Elizabeth Wardell............ 4-10-1828
Rodgers, John - Sarah Flin................... 7-09-1801
Rodgers, William - Lucretia Horner........... 3-07-1807
Rodgers, William - Lucy Walton............... 1-13-1803
Roeyner, Jonathan - Anna Crammers............ 11-29-1829
Rogers, Abner - Lydia Ann Jeffery............ 2-04-1824
Rogers, Amos - Parmelia Tunis................ 9-26-1833
Rogers, Anthony - Elizabeth Hartshorne
  both of Burlington Co., N. J............... 12-13-1831
Rogers, Benjamin - Margit Ermine............. 12-19-1799
Rogers, Benjamin - Sarah Patterson
  both of Burlington Co., N. J............... 2-03-1828
Rogers, Britton - Eliza Howland.............. 1834-1835
Rogers, Charles - Harriet Ford............... 2-26-1840
Rogers, David - Susannah Chadwick............ 5-01-1796
Rogers, George - Rebecka Jeffrey............. 11-22-1820
Rogers, James D. - Rebecca Forman............ 12-16-1827
Rogers, Reuben - Deborah Jeffery............. 1-16-1823
Rogers, Samuel - Helena Hendrickson.......... 12-14-1797
Rogers, Samuel - Mary Howell Freeman......... 2-03-1802
Rogers, Samuel - Mary Potter................. 11-05-1831
Rogers, William - Cornelia Van Huys.......... 11-01-1837
Rogers, William - Deborah Hulsart............ 8-11-1796
Rogers, William - Deliverance Newman......... 10-20-1825
Rogers, William - Hannah Stout............... 2-28-1818
Rolf, Jacob - Meribe Warrick................. 5-09-1832
Rolfe, Jonathan - Susanah Elison............. 5-30-1799
Rolfe, Samuel - Hannah Elison................ 7-14-1799
Romain, James - Leah Headdon................. 5-19-1835
Roman, Jacob - Esther White.................. 2-26-1839
Ronnolds, John M. - Sarah Curtis............. 10-19-1820
Roop, Joseph - Elizabeth Stephens............ 3-02-1816
Rose, Ebenezier P. - Catherine C. Forman..... 12-03-1811

MARRIAGES OF MONMOUTH COUNTY, NEW JERSEY

Rose, Elijah - Margaret Arose............... 10-04-1837
Rose, Israel - Ann Rue both of
  Burlington Co., N.J...................... 8-22-1823
Rose, James - Elizabeth Handlin.............. 9-28-1836
Rose, Job - Mary Shoards.................... 9-30-1804
Rose, Nathan - Eliza Inger both of
  Burlington Co., N.J...................... 3-12-1828
Rose, Stephen - Sarah Wikoff................ 2-21-1837
Rosell, John - Mary Fitsimonds.............. 2-17-1811
Ross, John - Levinia Cheeseman.............. 12-15-1829
Roszel, Nathaniel - Ann Ford................ 1-05-1826
Roszell, Isaac - Lydia White................ 2-22-1832
Rote, David - Maria Boice................... 6-05-1827
Rouse, William - Elizabeth Fowler........... 3-22-1836
Rouze, Daniel - Alice Coward................ 5-16-1822
Rouze, Theodore - Mary Ashton............... 5-05-1803
Rowe, George of Long Island, N. Y. -
  Caroline Burling........................ 8-31-1840
Rowland, James - Hester Taylor.............. 2-09-1813
Rowland, Morris C. - Sarah A Vansciver....... 9-30-1830
Rubard, Samuel - Sarah Curtis............... 2-21-1835
Rue, Austin - Lydia Johnson................. 12-13-1837
Rue, Cornelius - Gertrude Leaming........... 12-15-1840
Rue, Edmond - Matilda Clayton............... 3-27-1833
Rue, George S. - Ellen Lucas................ 3-06-1834
Rue, Jacob - Alice Bowne.................... 2-28-1833
Rue, James - Luisa Hadden................... 4-19-1836
Rue, James - Margaret Sutphen...............   1835
Rue, James - Maria Abraham.................. 12-31-1805
Rue, James - Rebeckah Hooper................ 10-01-1813
Rue, John - Mary H. Sutphin................. 12-17-1806
Rue, John M. - Fransinkey Van Schoick....... 2-20-1833
Rue, Joseph of Middlesex Co., N. J. -
  Cornelia Mount.......................... 12-07-1836
Rue, Joseph - Eleanor Perrine............... 2-20-1822
Rue, Joseph - Hannah Covenhoven............. 12-12-1805
Rue, Joseph - Phebe Tone.................... 1-22-1799
Rue, Lewis - Mary Baker..................... 3-11-1835
Rue, Nathaniel - Elizabeth Tone............. 11-26-1806
Rue, Nathaniel Jr. - Ann Cox................ 5-30-1837
Rue, Samuel - Mary Potts.................... 2-21-1828
Rue, Samuel M. - Harriet Dey................ 7-29-1812
Rue, William - Ann Street................... 7-17-1816
Rue, William - Rebecca Holeman.............. 12-08-1796
Rue, William T. - Margaret Rue.............. 10-14-1823
Rulon, Joel - Cinthea Rose both of N. Y...... 7-26-1837
Rulon, Joseph - Manhaleth Chamberlin........ 2-18-1830
Rulon, Samuel - Rhoda Spragg................ 1838-1839
Rumson, Samuel - Lucretia Miller............ 2-03-1834
Rune, Zur - Rosanne Beal (both black)....... 11-23-1830
Runnels, John Jr. - Catherine Hart.......... 10-01-1813
Runnels, Joseph - Mary West................. 4-13-1817
Runnels, William - Hannah Hudson............ 3-16-1797
Runnels, William - Leanah Fransis........... 8-10-1795
Runyon, Henry - Lucrettia Grant............. 10-19-1820

```
Runyon, John - Dorothy Gant..................  8-06-1829
Runyon, Richard - Deborah Curtis.............  4-12-1820
Rupel, Abraham - Avis Stout.................. 12-20-1817
Rury, William - Dinah Booth (both black).....  11-15-1812
Rutters, Philip - Ruth Lines of
   Cold Springs, N. Y......................  3-14-1831
Ruttex, Philip - Abigail Haywood............. 10-10-1841
Ruttus, Robert - Pheabe Cranmer............. 10-18-1826
Ryall, Daniel B. - Juliet P. Scudder........  1-02-1828
Ryall, Daniel B. - Rachel B. Lloyd...........  9-18-1822
Ryark, Daniel - Elizabeth Mathis.............  2-29-1840
Ryder, Hendrick of Long Island N. Y. -
   Hannah Walling.........................  7-25-1838
Rynear, John - Elizabeth Tell of
   Philadelphia, Pa.......................  3-09-1835
Sadler, Henry - Margaret Cord...............  1-15-1825
Sagers, George - Hannah Barkalow............  6-10-1797
Said, William of N. Y. -
   Elizabeth Patterson.....................  3-22-1827
Salem, Barnt D. - Pateans Tilton both of      .
   Burlington Co., N. J...................  4-12-1820
Salmons, Barzilla - Rebecca Jones...........  8-16-1835
Salter, Richard - Elizabeth Jackson.......... 11-18-1815
Samford, David - Jane Woolcott..............  1-29-1823
Sammis, Ebenezer R. - Jane Vandevere........  3-04-1810
Sammons, Job - Sary Jones...................  6-17-1823
Samons, Nehemiah - Ruth Wiley...............  8-30-1795
Samons, William - Anne Reme.................  7-24-1803
Samson, Thomas - Mary Simmons...............  7-06-1823
Sanforce, Enoch - Jane Mount................  3-13-1839
Sanford, James - Elizabeth Ware.............  3-25-1830
Sanford, John - Eliza Ann Fielder...........  8-30-1829
Sanford, John - Sarah Roberts...............  1-13-1839
Sanford, William - Sally Shreve.............  1-28-1798
Sansbury, Wayne - Nancy Lawry...............  4-25-1832
Santfort, Joseph - Lucy Shreves.............  3-11-1802
Sareton, John - Margaret Fisher.............  7-04-1815
Savidge, William of Burlington Co., N. J. -
   Theodocia Hutchinson of Middlesex Co.
   New Jersey............................. 12-11-1833
Sawyer, John - Rachel Howell................  8-19-1813
Scaram, John - Hannah Morris................  9-11-1830
Schanck, Crynyonce - Maria Schanck..........  1-31-1811
Schanck, David - Ann Applegate..............  1-20-1814
Schanck, De Lafayette - Nelly Covenhoven..... 12-17-1805
Schanck, Elias - Harriet Newman.............  9-05-1835
Schanck, Jacob - Mary Ann Hall..............  1-10-1828
Schanck, James - Gertrude Jane Hampton.......  3-14-1839
Schanck, John C. - Margaret Polhemus........  2-14-1828
Schanck, Peter - Nellie Covenhoven..........  4-03-1811
Schanck, Peter - Sarah Ann Beers............ 10-29-1817
Schanck, William - Anne Covenhoven..........  3-11-1812
Schanck, William (Rev.) - Eliza Ann Scudder..  5-01-1811
Schenck, Daniel - Ellener Schenck...........  2-10-1801
Schenck, Daniel - Lydia Longstreet.......... 11-30-1831
```

Schenck, David - Lilly Smock................. 11-12-1818
Schenck, Denise - Margaret Polhemus.......... 10-31-1798
Schenck, Elisha - Catherine Craig............ 1-16-1829
Schenck, Elisha - Ida Schenck................ 12-16-1818
Schenck, Ephriam Lory - Nelly Covenhoven..... 9-15-1812
Schenck, Garret - Lydia Schenck.............. 4-04-1815
Schenck, Garret - Nelly Covenhoven........... 11-24-1797
Schenck, Garret - Sarah Ann Schenck.......... 12-22-1820
Schenck, Garret - Sarah Hendrickson.......... 1834-1835
Schenck, Hendrick - Sarah Schenck............ 12-09-1812
Schenck, James - Ann Covenhoven.............. 12-21-1809
Schenck, James - Har Tucker (both black)..... 5-12-1827
Schenck, John - Anne Vancleaf................ 12-14-1808
Schenck, John - Mrs. Margaret Schenck........ 10-17-1814
Schenck, John - Sarah Lane................... 12-20-1802
Schenck, John of Burlington Co., N. J. -
   Sarah Leach.............................. 4-17-1827
Schenck, John H.- Jane Covenhoven (wid.)..... 8-02-1812
Schenck, Jonathan - Ellener Schenck.......... 2-09-1815
Schenck, Jonathan - Sarah Pecock............. 3-03-1819
Schenck, Michael - Betsey S. Baldwin......... 10-05-1820
Schenck, Nathaniel - Rachel Dillon........... 1-31-1835
Schenck, Obadiah - Eleanor Longstreet........ 9-12-1802
Schenck, Peter V. - Elizabeth Smock.......... 12-05-1808
Schenck, Roelef - Sarah Bennett.............. 1-28-1798
Schenck, Ruler - Mary Stilwell............... 9-15-1814
Schenck, Ruliff - Ester Combs................ 9-09-1821
Schenck, Schyler - Margaret Covenhoven....... 2-18-1798
Schenck, William - Abby Polhemus............. 2-28-1821
Schenck, William - Ann Hankerson............. 2-10-1836
Schenck, William - Hager Schenck............. 1-30-1830
Schereman, James - Susan Wall................ 9-09-1817
Scholthorpe, James - Mary Brewer............. 9-07-1834
Schureman, John (Rev.) - Juliana Conover..... 5-12-1802
Schuyler, Aaron - Grace Norton............... 4-27-1839
Scidmore, John - Elizabeth Runyan............ 8-26-1815
Scoby, Samuel - Elizabeth Fisher............. 10-06-1800
Scofield, Jacob - Pelina Ann Maxen........... 12-31-1829
Scot, Charles W. - Martha L. Biles
   (both black)............................. 10-19-1837
Scott, Benjamin - Mariah Sanford............. 8-18-1824
Scott, Ebenezer - Anne Little................ 9-18-1836
Scott, Ebenezer - Eliza Thompson............. 8-05-1824
Scott, James - Anna Van Brunt................ 3- -1813
Scott, James - Mary Dowdy.................... 3-06-1842
Scott, James - Sarah Hoppey.................. 7-06-1827
Scott, William - Nancy Allen................. 1-31-1798
Scudder, Joseph - Hannah Applegate........... 9-06-1828
Scudder, Kenneth A. - Elizabeth C. Neely..... 1-28-1801
Scudder, William - Elinor Craig.............. 5-19-1816
Scull, James - Mary Harker both of
   Burlington Co., N. J..................... 3-21-1836
Sculthorp, Thomas - Elizabeth Rogers......... 1-18-1835
Scutcliffe, Robert - Ann Irons............... 3-01-1841
Seabrook, Andrew - Johannah Hulit............ 6-16-1799

```
Seabrook, Elias - Sarah Walley..............    6-25-1842
Seabrook, John - Catherine Hoffmire.........    9-15-1810
Seabrook, Stephen - Sarah Hankinson (wid.)...   2-26-1812
Seaman, Benjamin - Ann Pharo................   11-21-1838
Seaman, Benjamin - Hannah Commons...........    1-07-1826
Seaman, Hezilton - Sarah Pharo..............    3-08-1834
Seaman, Morris - Elizabeth Cramer...........   11-12-1801
Seamon, Isaac - Anney Sammons...............    3-10-1811
Sears, Obediah - Deborah Cook...............    4-01-1809
Sears, Zephaniah - Nancy Ireland............   10-06-1811
Seavers, Abraham - Ann Lemon................    9-18-1837
Sedam, Cornelius - Abigail Polhemus.........    3-08-1808
Sedam, Jacob - Mary Polhemus................    3-08-1808
Seeley, Robert - Swan Wilson................    2-06-1828
Seeley, Samuel - Mary Morris................    9-21-1828
Seely, Hyram - Deborah Compton..............    3-27-1827
Segers, Jobe - Sarah Friend.................    6-16-1802
Segoine, John - Lucy Smith..................    3-18-1835
Seigill, Thomas - Allice Hopkins both of
    Burlington Co., N. J....................    1-16-1828
Seily, Leonard - Levina Morris..............    4-14-1842
Seleck, Hawford - Catolina Cunningham.......   10-27-1842
Sexton, Ezekiel - Mareal Crane..............    1-29-1835
Sexton, Isaac - Catherine Allen.............    8-13-1826
Sexton, Thomas - Mary Wikoff................    1-05-1797
Shadwick, Taber - Catherine Chamberlin......    5-06-1797
Shafto, Anthony - Ann Harbor................    3-22-1829
Shafto, Anthony - Jane Brinley..............    2-14-1811
Shafto, John - Mary Eley....................    1-31-1827
Shafto, Robert - Isabel Carr................   12-14-1802
Shamard, Joseph - Mary Brewer...............   12-28-1820
Sharman, Abraham - Rebecca L. Reed..........    2-09-1832
Sharp, Henry - Sarah Murdock................    1-19-1800
Sharp, Philip - Susannah Gordon.............    1-28-1802
Shavor, Joseph L. (Rev.) - Diana Forman.....    4-07-1812
Shearman, Benjamin - Marthy Bennett.........    6-28-1824
Shearman, David - Frances Ann Smith.........    1-01-1822
Shearman, David H. - Sarah Gifford..........    8-28-1828
Shearman, Edward - Margaret Newman..........   10-28-1837
Shearman, Forman - Phebe Longstreet.........    2-06-1840
Shearman, H. - Ann Mex......................    1834-1835
Shearman, James - Mary Newberry.............    3-11-1809
Shearman, James G. - Hannah Mathews.........    7-01-1830
Shearman, John - Permellia Tice.............   12-06-1839
Shearman, Joseph - Harriet Worthly..........   10-13-1836
Shearman, Samuel - Catherine Hyland.........    1837-1838
Shearman, Talis C. - Ann Borden.............    9-25-1826
Shearman, Thomas - Cathern Bennett..........   11-19-1827
Shearman, Thomas - Else Smith...............    1-09-1823
Shearman, Thomas - Lucretia Gant............    1-15-1842
Shearman, Thomas - Margaret Curtis..........    4-04-1837
Shearman, Thomas - Mary Lane................    3-03-1810
Shearman, Thomas - Sarah Book...............    1-07-1808
Shebly, Ferdinan - Deborah Aumack...........    3-03-1796
Sheed, William - Elizabeth Roger............    3-15-1843
```

Shemard, Nathan - Anne Shreve............... 2-04-1796
Shepard, James - Annie Mathews............... 4-13-1816
Shepard, John - Sarah Thompson............... 9-19-1812
Shepard, Samuel - Anne Clayton............... 7-01-1809
Sheperd, Thomas - Helen Stout................ 4-11-1802
Shephard, William - Amey Matthews............ 12-02-1804
Shepherd, Elisha - Neely Van Kirk............ 12-24-1796
Shepherd, Joseph - Elizabeth Dorne........... 10-01-1834
Shepherd, Thomas - Lucy Fields dg. of Robert. 5-28-1839
Sheppard, David - Elizabeth Ely.............. 4-23-1836
Sheppard, Joseph - Sarah Pearse.............. 9-09-1815
Sheppard, Joseph M. - Lydia B. Craig......... 9-27-1823
Shereman, Theophilus - Ann North............. 1-01-1808
Sherman, William - Elizabeth Butler.......... 12-16-1835
Shermer, John - Ann Gifford.................. 4-10-1800
Shibla, Jacob - Deborah Bennett.............. 3-25-1835
Shibley, John - Phebe Brown.................. 3-29-1817
Shiblo, Ferdinand - Ackey Varemore........... 3-11-1840
Shilby, Theophilus - Mary Newman............. 3-10-1831
Shin, James - Elizabeth Allen................ 3-25-1809
Shin, Samuel - Rachel Clayton................ 10-23-1816
Shinn, Benjamin - Mary Loveman............... 1-19-1831
Shinn, Benjamin - Mary Singleton............. 2-18-1841
Shinn, Daniel - Ann Bongart.................. 1-07-1812
Shinn, Esick - Caroline Paterson............. 2-06-1840
Shinn, Job - Alice Chambers.................. 8-13-1815
Shinn, John of Burlington Co., N. J. -
    Lydia Burtis............................. 9-09-1818
Shinn, Joseph B. - Rebecca Stratton Cline.... 3-10-1831
Shinn, Noah - Nancy Burmell.................. 2-03-1831
Shinn, Samuel - Elizabeth Wagner............. 11-15-1815
Shinn, Viracom - Sarah Middleton............. 12-01-1810
Shinn, William - Elizabeth Brown............. 4-11-1818
Shire, Andrew of Western New York -
    Maria Russell............................ 9-05-1840
Shiunamonte, Samuel - Sallie Van Cleaf....... 1-19-1801
Shoney, William - Margaret Warrick........... 11-12-1814
Shomma, William - Catherine Mason............ 8-20-1818
Shotwell, John - Beulah Gaskill.............. 11-10-1836
Shreave, David - Charlotte West.............. 10-10-1803
Shreeves, Thomas - Lydia Anderson............ 9-12-1818
Shrevy, Thomas - Sarah West.................. 10-21-1816
Shults, David A. - Lydia Holeman............. 12-17-1834
Shumarr, Joseph - Lydia Johnson.............. 12-19-1810
Shumway, Nehemiah - Sarah Tyse............... 12-10-1795
Shuter, John - Rebecca Anderson.............. 2-01-1806
Shutts, John Jr. - Sarah Ann Cottrell........ 8-29-1840
Sickels, Elisha - Hannah Hulshart............ 8-10-1815
Sickels, George - Catherine White............ 6-27-1841
Sickels, John - Amanda Johnson............... 9-12-1840
Sickels, Joseph - Margaret Hyer.............. 5-29-1816
Sickels, Spafford - Deborah Pattern.......... 3-17-1842
Sickels, William - Sarah Ann Carson.......... 10-05-1821
Sickles, Hendrick son of Ann & James -
    Polly Tilton dg. of Alice & John......... 2-28-1820

```
Sickles, James - Ann Posty..................  4-16-1811
Sickles, John - Zilpha Drum.................. 12-10-1808
Sickles, William - Abigail Wood.............  9-18-1800
Sickles, William - Nelle Ketchum............ 10-29-1827
Silk, Thomas - Abigail Ponset of
    Burlington Co., N. J....................  5-31-1824
Sill, John - Edith Woodmanse................  5-17-1806
Sill, John - Elizabeth Bilyew...............  1-06-1825
Sill, Wesley - Susanna Rodgers.............. 10-13-1830
Sillcocks, John - Sarah Brown...............  9-29-1821
Silver, Elias - Lydia Ann Wall..............  1-05-1837
Silver, Garret - Sarah Applegate............  6-11-1825
Silvers, David - Nancy Robbins..............  4-05-1827
Silvey, Robert - Pamelia Anderson...........  9-02-1817
Simison, Christopher - Mercy Leigh
    (both black)............................  2-10-1799
Simmons, Charles of Hunterdon Co., N. J. -
    Edith Lee of Burlington Co., N. J....... 11-21-1833
Simmons, Isaac - Mary Buckalew.............. 10-20-1800
Simpson, Aaron - Hannah Smith...............  5-16-1812
Simson, Robert - Bethena Mc Clarkin......... 11-02-1797
Sinclair, John of Burlington Co., N. J. -
    Theodisia Rouze......................... 10-30-1819
Sinclair, Josiah - Lidea Fowler.............  1-31-1822
Singleton, Richard - Ann Moore both of
    Burlington Co., N. J....................  1-10-1818
Sinnickson, Seneca - Ruth Brewer............  3-11-1819
Skidmore, Benjamin - Valaria Eldridge....... 12-20-1812
Skidmore, James - Elizabeth Ware............  8-28-1817
Skidmore, Reuben - Elizabeth Johnston.......  4-09-1825
Skidmore, Robert - Hannah Hulman............ 10-30-1824
Skidmore, Robert - Mary Williams............  3-03-1822
Skidmore, Samuel of New York City -
    Mercy Edwards........................... 10-14-1814
Slack, Daniel - Meribah Mount...............  2-09-1829
Slatch, Barnet of Staten Island, N, Y, -
    Nancy Cramer............................ 12-06-1812
Slocum, Daniel - Mrs. Rebecca Wood.......... 12-26-1818
Slocum, Elijah - Anna Fleming dg. of James...  6-04-1829
Slocum, Elisha - Sarah Bennett..............  5-22-1824
Slocum, Ezekiel - Mary Wardell..............  3-07-1822
Slocum, James - Elizabeth Newman............  5-09-1812
Slocum, Joseph - Lydia Smith................ 11-11-1815
Slocum, Peter - Abigail Newman..............  2-22-1810
Slocum, Peter - Maria Maps..................  4-07-1830
Slocum, Thomas - Ruth West..................  6-09-1810
Slocum, William - Sarah Logan............... 10-08-1815
Slover, Daniel - Elizabeth Vanderhoff.......  3-17-1801
Slowim, John - Elizabeth Brand.............. 11-16-1799
Smally, Isaac - Helena Applegate............  8-28-1841
Smally, James - Ester Emmons................ 12-18-1813
Smires, John - Rebecca Richardson...........  1-19-1828
Smires, Joseph - Nancy Thomas...............  3-20-1796
Smith, Aaron - Alchey Gould.................  2-18-1830
Smith, Abraham - Lydia Layton............... 10-13-1799
```

Smith, Anthony - Elenor Morris............... 10-09-1819
Smith, Anthony - Elizabeth Crane............. 5-10-1815
Smith, Asher - Ann Pearson................... 3-14-1805
Smith, Baxter - Emily Chambers............... 5-22-1836
Smith, Baxter - Sarah Anderson............... 12-02-1841
Smith, Benjamin - Elizabeth Eddy............. 12-10-1804
Smith, Charles - Elinor Storey............... 4-09-1820
Smith, Cornelius - Eliza Van Derripe......... 10-10-1821
Smith, Cornelius V. - Louisa Tucker.......... 11-26-1840
Smith, Daniel - Elizabeth Bouice............. 11-08-1824
Smith, David - Mary Hurley................... 1-08-1823
Smith, Edward - Harriet Morris............... 6-21-1821
Smith, Ezekial - Mary Randolph............... 11-24-1822
Smith, Henry - Catherine Martin.............. 12-27-1837
Smith, Hezekiah - Ezilpha Lemman............. 3-13-1819
Smith, Hugh - Catherine Matchett............. 12-04-1803
Smith, Jacob - Melinda Pierce (Peese)........ 9-16-1840
Smith, Jacob - Rachel Newberry............... 2-20-1812
Smith, James - Idah Van Mater................ 2-25-1798
Smith, James - Rebecca Woolley............... 6-17-1827
Smith, James - Sarah White................... 6-16-1839
Smith, Job - ---- ----....................... 6-08-1828
Smith, Job - Rachel Rogers................... 1-02-1808
Smith, John - Ann Davy....................... 11-12-1816
Smith, John - Ann Gray....................... 6-24-1815
Smith, John of Gloucester Co., N. J. -
    Catherine Lallande of Germany............ 8-13-1842
Smith, John - Elizabeth Conover.............. 6-03-1841
Smith, John - Hannah Taylor.................. 12-09-1811
Smith, John - Lydia Polon.................... 12-24-1822
Smith, John - Magdalen Van Brunt............. 3-28-1815
Smith, John - Mary Anderson.................. 11-16-1835
Smith, John - Nancy Magee.................... 1-27-1803
Smith, John - Nancy Reed..................... 12-11-1805
Smith, John - Phebe Mertilda Wikoff.......... 12-16-1812
Smith, John - Phebe Pees..................... 1-31-1804
Smith, John - Sarah Archey................... 4-15-1828
Smith, John - Sarah Mathews.................. 4-27-1834
Smith, John G. - Sarah Isabela Decon........ 5-13-1811
Smith, John H. of Manchester, England -
    Catherine Nickey of Cornwall, England.... 10-16-1832
Smith, John P. - Rachel Walling.............. 11-25-1840
Smith, Jonathan - Elizabeth Riddle........... 11-10-1840
Smith, Joseph - Deborah Stillwell............ 11-26-1822
Smith, Joseph - De Bras Stillwell............ 8-08-1824
Smith, Joseph - Eliza Cord................... 8-19-1830
Smith, Joseph - Nancy Lafetra................ 10-27-1816
Smith, Joseph - Sarah Curtis................. 7-21-1831
Smith, Joseph D. - Hannah V. Horsfield....... 12-09-1827
Smith, Lewis - Hannah King................... 9-14-1805
Smith, Lewis - Mariah Hendrickson............ 12-23-1820
Smith, Mark - Ruby Walling................... 3-30-1836
Smith, Merriet - Sarah Horner................ 6-23-1833
Smith, Peter - Elizabeth Diskel.............. 6-04-1808
Smith, Peter - Mary Stillwell................ 4-15-1827

```
Smith, Richard - Ann Wardell................. 11-19-1795
Smith, Richard - Hannah Curtis............... 11-09-1823
Smith, Richard - Hannah Simmons.............. 7-29-1841
Smith, Richard C. of N. Y. -
    Henrietta Cranmer....................... 10-16-1826
Smith, Ruliff - Mrs. Catherine Hendrickson... 3-30-1826
Smith, Samuel - Mary Cottrell................ 1-06-1799
Smith, Sidney - Sarah Jane Armstrong......... 3-22-1837
Smith, Solomon I. - Hannah Smith............. 8-15-1798
Smith, Thomas - Betsey Randolph.............. 2-13-1812
Smith, Thomas - Rebecca Wilson............... 9-14-1797
Smith, Thomas - Eleanor Haley................ 12-24-1829
Smith, William - Ann Walling................. 4-23-1831
Smith, William - Catherine Wilson............ 7-27-1808
Smith, William - Margaret Bennett............ 10-31-1814
Smith, William - Mary Fowler................. 10-09-1829
Smith, William - Sarah Havens................ 1-30-1826
Smith, William - Susan Quail................. 11-05-1830
Smith, William P. - Eliza Cole............... 10-08-1828
Smock, Aaron - Sarah Schenck................. 11-28-1804
Smock, Archibald - Margaret Denise........... 2-24-1814
Smock, Barnes - Ledia Longstreet............. 1-30-1798
Smock, Daniel - Ann Schenck.................. 12-06-1838
Smock, Garrett - Rebecca Wallin.............. 11-20-1810
Smock, George - Sarah Smock.................. 12-19-1811
Smock, Harry - Margaret Johnston
    (both black)............................ 4-20-1841
Smock, Hendrick - Ann Vanderveer............. 12-22-1816
Smock, Jacob - Jane Schanck.................. 1-22-1818
Smock, John - Elizabeth Dubois............... 11-27-1804
Smock, John - Ellen Schenck.................. 1-10-1822
Smock, John - Hannah Shepherd................ 3-19-1795
Smock, John - Margaret Williamson............ 6-04-1824
Smock, John G. - Sarah Laird (wid.).......... 12-22-1814
Smock, Keneth - Mary Pees.................... 1-04-1808
Smock, Peter - Catherine Hendrickson......... 12-24-1821
Smock, Peter - Catherine Schenck............. 9-26-1816
Smock, William - Cornelia Stillwell
    dg. of Joseph........................... 11-20-1832
Smythe, Ickabud - Elizabeth Pearce........... 11-03-1803
Smythe, Matthew - Rachel Tallman............. 3-17-1801
Snedicer, Samuel - Susanne Davidson.......... 1-21-1836
Snediker, Jacob J. - Amy Lippincott.......... 7-25-1841
Snediker, Joshua - Mary Ann Hartman.......... 7-19-1838
Snider, Peter - Jane Walling................. 1-01-1822
Snowhill, Andrew - Hannah Solomon............ 12-22-1813
Snyder, Alexander - Eleanor Vanderhoff....... 11-13-1841
Snyder, Hendrick - Ann Smith................. 10-30-1826
Snyder, Peter - Amanda Cottrell.............. 5-16-1840
Snyder, Peter - Susanna Debore............... 2-20-1803
Snyder, William - Eleanor Lain............... 1-17-1818
Soden, George - Alice Hire................... 12-20-1815
Soden, John - Harriet Pittenger.............. 11-10-1840
Soden, William - Martha Van Deripe........... 1-26-1842
Solomon, Charles A. - Jane Burr.............. 12-31-1833
```

```
Solomon, Levi - Elizah Cook.................  8-  -1810
Soper, Biddel - Eliza Wells.................  8-13-1818
Soper, Charles - Amy Winner................. 10-27-1821
Soper, Howard - Phebe Spragg................ 12-29-1838
Soper, James - Hannah Bowker................  7-10-1823
Soper, Joseph - Phebe Bennet................  1-13-1824
Soper, Joseph - Rachel Conklin..............  2-03-1838
Soper, Solomon - Sally Camborn..............  7-02-1809
Soper, William - Mary Southard..............  5-02-1822
Sopher, Timothy - Deliverence Price......... 10-22-1831
South, Andrew F. - Acsah Hammell............  3-07-1826
South, Benjamin Jr. - Mary Gordon...........  1-10-1796
Southard, Abner - Ann Baily................. 12-25-1831
Southard, Amos Jr. - Mary Cranmer...........  3-20-1814
Southard, Caleb - Emley Stephens............  8-24-1834
Southard, Caleb - Mary Ginnings.............  9-22-1808
Southard, David - Rhoda Emmans.............. 11-03-1838
Southard, Job - Ann F. Randolph.............  2-01-1824
Southard, Job - Nance Johnson............... 11-24-1801
Southard, John - Unity John................. 10-10-1829
Southard, Joseph - Lydia Ann Hays........... 12-31-1826
Southard, Joseph - Mary Ann Dough...........  1-29-1826
Southard, Solomon - Paty Brown..............  2-24-1795
Southard, Wesley - Lidia Stout of
    Burlington Co., N. J....................  8-10-1823
Southwick, James - Sarah Errickson of
    Philadelphia, Pa........................  3-23-1824
Spencer, John of England - Nancy Jones......  7-28-1835
Spencer, John - Rebecca Leonard............. 11-11-1799
Spencer, Malen - Margaret Little............  5-21-1833
Spiers, Robert - Mary Buck..................  1-12-1822
Spinning, Husel - Meriam Woolley............  1-01-1832
Spinning, Thomas - Mary Woolley.............  1-19-1832
Spourt, Isack - Marian Peepel both of N. Y...  6-20-1821
Spragg, Charles - July Ann Crammers.........  5-28-1828
Spragg, Jeremiah - Mary Gaskill............. 11-28-1829
Spragg, Jeremiah - Mary Inman...............  6-26-1806
Spragg, John - Catherine Rulong.............  8-20-1818
Spragg, Jonathan - Catherine Amelia Seaman...  5-03-1841
Spragg, Joseph - Martha Reynolds............  2-17-1816
Spragg, Nehemiah - Charlotte Carman.........  8-27-1835
Springsteen, John - Susannah Smith.......... 11-18-1809
Sproul, James - Julian Walling.............. 10-23-1822
Sproul, Oliver - Sarah Dorset...............  2-07-1830
Sprouls, Joseph - Elizabeth Walling.........  6-25-1837
Sprowl, Samuel - Abigail Holmes.............  9-20-1835
Sprowles, Oliver - Rachel Dorsett........... 10-01-1797
St. Dunstan, James C. - Amanda Burs......... 10-07-1829
Stafford, John R. - Elizabeth Fell of
    Philadelphia, Pa........................  3-09-1835
Stanhope, George - Margaret White...........  6-09-1840
Staty, John - Eliza Robins..................  3-12-1816
Stell, Thomas - Charity Rouse............... 10-10-1799
Stepe, Richard - Mrs. Elizabeth Robs........  5-13-1819
Stephens, Benjamin - Clemence Lloyd.........  5-31-1798
```

```
Stephens, Ebenezer - Susan Cathcart.........  2-06-1841
Stephens, Hortia - Ann Lemon................  9-16-1830
Stephens, William -
   Cornelius Ann Hallenbroke...............  3-25-1827
Stepheson, Author - Catherine Bowker........  3-07-1839
Stepley, Derrick - Catherine Cressman.......  4-20-1811
Stevens, James - Perline Applegate..........  1834-1835
Stevens, Samuel - Desiar Cramer.............  6-02-1812
Stevenson, Abraham - June Pearce............  3-20-1826
Stevenson, Daniel - Mary Chambers........... 12-29-1819
Stevins, William - Clarissa Grant...........  4-17-1808
Steward, Anthony - Elizabeth Matthews....... 10-01-1814
Steward, George - Mary C, Pierson...........  1-02-1834
Steward, John - Agnes Young................. 12-15-1803
Steward, John - Ann Gibbins.................  4-03-1815
Steward, Samuel - Deborah Ann Thomson....... 12-14-1815
Steward, Samuel - Rebeka Herbert............ 10-13-1796
Stewart, Bashley, Alice Hopkins of
   Burlington Co., N. J....................  2-14-1832
Stewart, Charles - Ann Greggrey............. 10-12-1810
Stewart, John of Philadelphia - Mary Cox.....  7-26-1836
Stewart, Peter - Mary Tunis.................  3-18-1811
Stibs, Henry - Sarah Maxwell................ 12-16-1796
Stikes, Charles of New York City -
   Adelide ----............................  5-01-1836
Stiles, Edward A. - Margaret White..........  1-01-1833
Stiles, Isaac - Maria Seamon................ 11-12-1837
Still, Samuel - Elizabeth Clayton...........  3-10-1832
Stillfell, Daniel - Ann Stillwell........... 11-17-1796
Stillwagon, David - Ann Strickland.......... 10-27-1832
Stillwagon, Peter - Belsey Bennett.......... 10-05-1811
Stillwagon, Watson - Sarah Bennet...........  4-19-1825
Stillwell, Abraham - Ann Peas...............  2-03-1799
Stillwell, Abraham - Phebe Francis..........  2-25-1808
Stillwell, Archibald - Caroline Walling......  1-02-1833
Stillwell, Benjamin - Sarah Denise..........  7-08-1804
Stillwell, Caleb - Nellie Covenhoven........ 12-10-1797
Stillwell, Charles - Rachel Pope............  2-13-1833
Stillwell, Christopher - Dolly Herbert...... 12-14-1809
Stillwell, Elias - Lena Williamson..........  1-08-1798
Stillwell, Elias - Rebecca Hoffman..........  8-04-1799
Stillwell, Elias - Sarah Stillwell..........  6-18-1817
Stillwell, George - Gertrude Hendrickson..... 11-04-1833
Stillwell, George - Mary Bennett............ 12-06-1821
Stillwell, Jacbo - Hannah Bedle.............  6-30-1840
Stillwell, James of Illinois - Maria Rivet...  3-18-1828
Stillwell, Jeremiah - Nancy Boice...........  1-14-1808
Stillwell, Jeremiah - Rebecca Gordon........  5-21-1836
Stillwell, Job - Jedidah Vanote.............  3-27-1830
Stillwell, John - Elizabeth Elmer...........  3-08-1812
Stillwell, John - Jane Wilson...............  9-01-1839
Stillwell, John - Mary Holmes............... 12-19-1826
Stillwell, John - Mary Schenck..............  3-25-1806
Stillwell, John S. - Frances Murphy......... 10-28-1835
Stillwell, Joseph - Lois Vannote............ 11-12-1835
```

Stillwell, Joseph - Nellie Roberts........... 11-24-1799
Stillwell, Joseph - Sarah Parker............. 1-29-1824
Stillwell, Joseph M. - Hannah Conover........ 10-31-1832
Stillwell, Reuben - Ester Applegate.......... 7-08-1826
Stillwell, Samuel - Ann Conover.............. 1-19-1808
Stillwell, Samuel - Mary Snyder.............. 11-06-1814
Stillwell, Samuel - Sharlot Shreare.......... 3-20-1824
Stillwell, Thomas of N. Y. - Dinah Wittney... 2-06-1827
Stillwell, William - Ann Challender both of
    Burlington Co., N. J.................... 8-26-1822
Stillwell, William - Catherine Whitlock...... 7-28-1805
Stilwell, Forman - Mary Smock dg. of
    John R. Smock.......................... 12-13-1841
Stilwell, Joseph of Burlington Co., -
    Sarah Claypole......................... 12-10-1818
Stilwell, William - Hester Murphee........... 9-09-1820
Stines, Obadiah - Catherine Wilgus........... 12-27-1801
Stinetz, George - Jane Lewis................. 2-23-1805
Stites, John - Phebe Lacount................. 11-04-1841
Stockton, Stacy - Charity Platt.............. 2-19-1831
Stoddard, James - Ann Craig.................. 4-03-1813
Stoney, George - Nancy Cotrell............... 3-17-1834
Stoney, Richard - Sarah Freeman.............. 3-17-1841
Stoney, Stephen - Louisa Ann Bedle........... 11-12-1837
Stoney, William - Catherine Matthews......... 12-05-1832
Story, John of Burlington Co., N. J. -
    Elizabeth Wares........................ 10-12-1830
Story, Joseph - Elizabeth Singleton.......... 5-02-1811
Story, William - Mary Van Horn............... 1-23-1811
Stought, Joseph - Will Dorset................ 11-06-1818
Stout, Abraham - Catherine Bennett........... 10-15-1819
Stout, Benjamin - Deborah Irons dg. of
    Garret Irons........................... 5-04-1842
Stout, Carhart - Caroline Stout.............. 3-01-1831
Stout, Charles - Phebe Compton............... 3-05-1815
Stout, David - Isabel Curtis................. 11-17-1822
Stout, Douglass - Rachel McLean.............. 12-11-1822
Stout, Elhannon H. - Mary Lippincott......... 2-04-1839
Stout, Ethan - Mary Hurley................... 12-07-1798
Stout, Garret - Eliza Jeffery................ 2-22-1823
Stout, Garret - Sarah Jane Dickinson......... 10-24-1836
Stout, Jacob - Catherine Schenck............. 1-09-1808
Stout, Jacob - Gettey Truax.................. 2-18-1819
Stout, James - Ann Osborn.................... 1-16-1823
Stout, James - Hanna Snediker................ 2-09-1826
Stout, John - Delila Allen................... 4-22-1819
Stout, John - Martha Bealer.................. 2-08-1798
Stout, John - Rebeccah Hambleton............. 11-26-1800
Stout, John P. - Elizabeth Hulse............. 5-13-1830
Stout, Jonathan - Elizabeth Jefferes......... 12-25-1805
Stout, Jonathan - Hester Morris.............. 10-27-1799
Stout, Joseph - Amelia Falkinburgh........... 2-22-1828
Stout, Joseph - Jane Brinley (wid.).......... 3-27-1802
Stout, Joseph - Rebecca Wilson............... 5-09-1822
Stout, Richard - Ann Allen................... 2-27-1811

```
Stout, Richard - Eliza Freeman............... 10-14-1838
Stout, Richard - Elizabeth Airs.............. 8-06-1809
Stout, Richard - Hannah Stricklin............ 12-21-1823
Stout, Richard - Mary Patterson.............. 1-16-1830
Stout, Richard - Sarah Beedle................ 4-25-1812
Stout, Richard - Jaine Newman................ 6-01-1815
Stout, Samuel - Mary Packer.................. 2-06-1839
Stout, Thomas - Maria Leffertson............. 12-16-1813
Stout, Thomas B. - Amelia Walling............ 8-26-1832
Stout, Thomas C. - Sarah Ann Mc Coy.......... 10-25-1832
Stout, William - Margaret Pearce............. 11-11-1818
Stoutenborrough, Henry - Sarah Robbins....... 1-30-1814
Stoutenburrow, Daniel - Ellener Schenck...... 10-03-1805
Stratton, Charles - Mary Thompson............ 11-05-1836
Stratton, James - Margaret Peterson.......... 11-11-1832
Stratton, Samuel - Martha Montgomery......... 10-14-1810
Stricker, Elias - Nancy Posten............... 12-11-1809
Strickland, Barkalow - Abigail Bennett....... 2-02-1833
Strickland, Cornelius - Eleanor Havens....... 11-13-1839
Strickland, Thomas Jr. - Susan Loakerson..... 1-24-1833
Stricklen, Jonathan C. - Nancy Vorhees....... 7-05-1826
Stricklen, Thomas - Lucretia Barkealow....... 2-28-1799
Stricklin, Henry - Jane Vanpelt.............. 1-17-1842
Striker, Abraham - Mary Lure................. 6-21-1823
Striker, Daniel - Catherine Stout............ 2-20-1827
Striker, Joseph - Jerusha Sandford........... 3-01-1821
Stukey, Peter - Rebecca Burdge............... 1832
Stutts, Henry - Juliet Johnson............... 5-26-1838
Sulvestor, Anthony - Elizabeth Williams...... 5-30-1812
Summers, Nemiah - Mary Morris................ 9-12-1827
Sumter, James - Matila Morocco (both black).. 4-25-1829
Suphin, William - Ann Baily.................. 3-02-1820
Sutfin, Richard - Dinah Delatush............. 2-09-1804
Sutfin, Samuel C. - Harriet Solomon.......... 1-05-1809
Suthen, John - Mary Smith.................... 4-29-1815
Sutpen, John - Phebe Chambers................ 11-02-1811
Sutphen, Aaron - Jane Vorhees................ 3-14-1799
Sutphen, John H. - Elizabeth Long of N. Y.... 10-19-1831
Sutphen, William - Ann Bailey................ 1-13-1820
Sutphen, William - Elizabeth Stillwell....... 12-24-1840
Sutphen, William - Phebe Cottrell............ 12-31-1803
Sutphen, William T. - Nancy Combs............ 2-22-1821
Sutpin, Aaron - Phebe Chew................... 12-19-1798
Sutphin, Archibald - Lydia Hulse............. 3-27-1810
Sutphin, David - Eliza Rodgers............... 11-22-1816
Sutphin, George - Helen Baird................ 2-20-1839
Sutphin, Joseph - Maria Schenck Covenhoven... 4-24-1805
Sutphin, Joseph D. - Elizabeth -----......... 3-10-1819
Sutphin, Thomas C. - Mrs. Content Morris..... 1-06-1827
Sutphin, William - Ann Johnson.............. 1-13-1799
Suttan, William - Lida Mount................. 8-02-1798
Sutton, Richard - Mary Mitchell.............. 2-05-1805
Sutton, William Jr. - Margaret Herbert....... 12-10-1823
Suydam, Garrett - Hannah Combs............... 5-08-1803
Suydam, Jacob - Mary Ann Gaston.............. 7-08-1834
```

```
Suydam, Peter - Sarah Ann Lawyer............  3-09-1837
Suydam, Richard - Lydia West................ 12-14-1800
Swan, David - Sarah Wilson..................  2-12-1834
Swan, Morgan - Alice Leonard................ 12-17-1835
Swart, Mickael - Catherine Willick..........  8-31-1833
Swartz, Michael - Elizabeth Maxon........... 12-03-1836
Sylvester, Jacob - Jane Moore (both black)... 12-23-1821
Sylvester, John - Debra De Grant............ 10-05-1839
Taber, Lewis - Emmaline Morris..............  5-19-1833
Tabor, Barnt D. - Patience Thompson both of
    Burlington Co., N. J....................  4-12-1820
Tabor, John - Rebekah Tallman............... 12-14-1809
Tabour, Jesse - Harriet Isibel.............. 10-24-1815
Taleman, Samuel - Lydia Lain................  5-05-1829
Tallman, James Jr. - Elizabeth Flemming.....  5-18-1840
Tallman, Joseph - Lydia Philips............. 11-02-1813
Tallman, Samuel - Mary Tallman..............  2-05-1808
Tallman, Sidney - Belfame Brinley...........  1-29-1818
Tallman, Stephen - Deborah Slocum........... 10-06-1798
Tallman, Stephen - Mary Chandler............  5-07-1801
Talmage, John - Catherine Hogerman..........  8-20-1829
Tanner, Thomas - Lucreiesia Walgrove........ 10-19-1835
Tannley, James - Elizabeth Hankins.......... 1836-1838
Tantam, Samuel - Elizabeth Eley............. 11-17-1830
Tantum, Robert - Jane Stillwell.............  5-20-1841
Tapscott, Williand - Catherine Crum.........  5-25-1811
Taylor, ---- - Lydia Saden..................  3-12-1820
Taylor, Charles - Alice Brown...............  1-20-1816
Taylor, Charles - Rachel Layton.............  1-20-1827
Taylor, Cortland - Phebe Conk of
    Burlington Co., N. J....................  6-09-1831
Taylor, Daniel - Rachel Allen............... 12-31-1814
Taylor, Daniel - Rachel Thomas.............. 11-29-1826
Taylor, David - Caterine Suier..............  5-01-1814
Taylor, David - Jane Tyson..................  4-11-1820
Taylor, Edward - Mary Holmes................  5-09-1813
Taylor, Edward - Sarah Lloyd................  5-31-1798
Taylor, Edward (Dr.) - Catherine L. Forman...  4-13-1829
Taylor, George - Ann Cook................... 12-28-1814
Taylor, George - Emma Holmes................  3-06-1823
Taylor, Israel B. - Ann Welsh............... 10-14-1832
Taylor, Jacob - Ann Hendrickson............. 11-23-1822
Taylor, James - Lucy Morford................ 12-18-1833
Taylor, James - Rosema Vanderveer........... 10-13-1830
Taylor, James - Sophia Van Brackle.......... 1810-1811
Taylor, James G. - Sarah Mason..............  1-20-1828
Taylor, John - Ann West.....................  2-05-1817
Taylor, John - Elizabeth Covenhoven.........  3-08-1809
Taylor, John - Hester Shutts................  9-21-1797
Taylor, John - Jane Worthley................ 11-04-1824
Taylor, John - Lois Conklin.................  1-02-1835
Taylor, John - Nancy Striker................ 12-13-1796
Taylor, John Jr. - Sarah Crawford........... 12-09-1813
Taylor, Jonathan - Ussey White..............  2-02-1822
Taylor, Jonathan R. - Sarah Shutts..........  7-15-1841
```

```
Taylor, Joseph - Achsah Thompson.............    9-06-1841
Taylor, Joseph son of John - Martha Dorset...    1-03-1797
Taylor, Joseph - Mary Robbins...............     2-06-1803
Taylor, Joseph - Rebecca Ridgely............     5-30-1824
Taylor, Joseph A. - Caroline T. Holmes.......    7-05-1829
Taylor, Michael - Sarah Bennet..............    10-04-1842
Taylor, Nelson, Jane Hendrickson............     2-27-1842
Taylor, Samuel - Ann Reid...................     6-07-1816
Taylor, Thomas - Eleanor Longstreet..........    7-10-1803
Taylor, Thomas - Lydia Woolley..............     6-10-1826
Taylor, Thomas - Rachel Pitman of
   Burlington Co., N. J....................    11-18-1817
Taylor, William - Hannah Clayton............     6-06-1803
Taylor, William - Hannah Flemming...........    12-01-1836
Taylor, William - Lydia Ann Poland..........     1-18-1832
Taylor, William - Marget Van Cleef..........     6-09-1799
Taylor, William - Mary Sharp................     5-27-1811
Tealton, Lubum - Molly Sheermard............     1-19-1805
Ten Eyck, Cornelius - Mary Rue..............     8-03-1822
Ten Eyck, William - Leah Covenhoven.........     1-23-1811
Terhune, Garret - Ann Hendrickson...........    10-30-1799
Terry, Elijah F. - Mary Van Mater...........     1-10-1834
Terry, William - Cornelia Van Stryver.......     4-10-1806
Test, Jessee - Anna Milton..................    12-23-1823
Tester, John Jr. - Sophia Manning...........    12-31-1832
Tharp, David - Catherine Stillwell..........     3-17-1830
Thelings, Isaac - Susan Woodward............     1-07-1807
Thirston, Nathaniel S. of N. Y. -
   Ann Ketchum.............................     4-15-1821
Thomas, Benjamin - Kenriah Soper............    10-30-1814
Thomas, Ezekiel - Maria Runuls..............     3-07-1829
Thomas, James - Ann Brightly................     4-06-1811
Thomas, John - Sarah Emmons.................     3-09-1815
Thomas, Joseph - Catherine Shepperd.........    11-26-1814
Thomas, Onson - Elizabeth Towne (Fowne)......   12-12-1804
Thomas, Richard W. of Philadelphia, Pa. -
   Elizabeth Rouse.........................     5-22-1838
Thomas, Robert Jr. - Rebekah Kers...........     2-03-1816
Thomas, Robert R. Jr. -
   Elizabeth Boggs Thompson................     2-08-1836
Thomas, Washington - Sarah Polhemus.........    1840-1841
Thomas, William - Margaret Denise...........    10-23-1799
Thompson, Archable - Mary Waggoner..........     8-07-1816
Thompson, Charles - Catherine Reynolds.......    9-21-1822
Thompson, Charles - Mary Mc Knight..........    10-  -1810
Thompson, Cornelius - Hannah Parker.........     2-07-1805
Thompson, Cornelius - Hester Applegate.......   12-06-1801
Thompson, David - Catherine Burk............     7-11-1840
Thompson, David A. - Mary Anderson..........     1-31-1833
Thompson, Edgar - Rebecca Patterson.........     6-25-1840
Thompson, Edgar - Sophia Andrews............     2-02-1836
Thompson, Elias - Sarah Wolley..............     6-23-1798
Thompson, Elisha - Letitia Gaston...........     2-07-1837
Thompson, Ezekiel - Ann Hendrickson.........    11-11-1837
Thompson, Fenwick - Mary Mount..............     7-11-1816
```

Thompson, Henry - Elizabeth Ann Dennis....... 12-04-1823
Thompson, Horatio - Clarissa Frances
  (both black)........................... 1-05-1833
Thompson, James - Mary Ann Hendrickson....... 1-26-1839
Thompson, James - Mary Sutphin.............. 8-21-1820
Thompson, John S. - Phebe Bowman............ 1-06-1841
Thompson, Joseph - Elizabeth Warner.......... 12-30-1804
Thompson, Joseph - Lucretia Coward........... 2-06-1799
Thompson, Joseph - Mary Applegate............ 10-07-1814
Thompson, Joseph - Mary Carman............... 12-03-1812
Thompson, Joseph C. - Ann Hulshart........... 12-27-1818
Thompson, Joseph D. - Nancy Johnson.......... 11-21-1818
Thompson, Joseph P. - Hannah Conover......... 2-06-1816
Thompson, Lewis - Cornelia A. Thompson....... 1-23-1807
Thompson, Luke D. - Charlotte Cornwall....... 5-24-1827
Thompson, Millar - Mary Wilbur.............. 1-07-1826
Thompson, Nathan - Mary Laird............... 4-16-1826
Thompson, Peirson - Elinor Campbell.......... 9-11-1817
Thompson, Rosha - Mary Hendrickson.......... 1-11-1837
Thompson, Samuel - Elizabeth Hurley.......... 5-19-1838
Thompson, Samuel - Elizabeth Leaming........ 9-27-1840
Thompson, Samuel - Elizabeth Martin.......... 2-19-1799
Thompson, Samuel - Jane Smock............... 1-05-1828
Thompson, Stephen - Alice Johnson............ 6-21-1834
Thompson, Theodore - Margaret Bell.......... 8-10-1833
Thompson, Thomas - Eleanor Longstreet........ 2-21-1798
Thompson, Thomas - Eliza Eager.............. 1-12-1841
Thompson, Thomas - Lucy Applegate............ 10-20-1804
Thompson, Thomas - Sally Craig.............. 12-21-1808
Thompson, William - Ann Marlin.............. 1-28-1798
Thompson, William - Helena Pittenger......... 12-10-1827
Thompson, William - Mary Wolcott............. 12-29-1824
Thomson, James - Margaret Cheeseman.......... 5-16-1803
Thomson, John - Margaret Walton............. 1-13-1803
Thomson, Samuel - Sarah Laird............... 1-14-1802
Thorn, Edward of Burlington Co., N. J. -
  Mary Hendrickson......................... 11-19-1829
Thorn, George R. - Sarah Ann Lucas.......... 9-02-1839
Thorn, John - Elizabeth Wallen.............. 2-15-1812
Thorn, John Lawrence - Margaret Smith........ 5-29-1842
Thorn, Joseph - Fanny Newman................ 6-04-1814
Thorn, Samuel - Margaret Steward............ 9-17-1813
Thorn, William - Deborah Ann Newman.......... 7-03-1842
Thorne, Joseph - Susannah Parker............ 4-19-1801
Thorp, Aber - Mary Chamberlain.............. 2-07-1799
Thorp, Benjamin - Abigail Lippincott......... 4-24-1814
Thorp, Samuel - Susan Allen................. 11-27-1813
Throckmorton, Aaron - Nancy Ainger (wid.).... 4-28-1811
Throckmorton, Barns - Mary Jackson.......... 11-09-1819
Throckmorton, Firman - Elizabeth Morris...... 4-09-1812
Throckmorton, Gilbert - Nellie Maxson........ 6-03-1824
Throckmorton, Jacob - Elizabeth Cook......... 11-22-1837
Throckmorton, James - Abigail Warder......... 3-11-1809
Throckmorton, James - Lear Tucker............ 8-22-1816
Throckmorton, James - Mary Chasey........... 3-09-1826

```
Throckmorton, Job - Rebecca Pile.............    2-23-1815
Throckmorton, Jobe - Jane Stymas.............    2-27-1811
Throckmorton, John - Lilpha Green...........   11-04-1798
Throckmorton, John - Lydia Craig.............    2-05-1806
Throckmorton, John B. - Elizabeth Rogers.....   10-07-1829
Throckmorton, Joseph - Catherine Hulsart.....    2-16-1809
Throckmorton, Joseph - Mary Ann Lloyd........    2-25-1817
Throckmorton, Joseph - Mary Miller..........    9-11-1809
Throckmorton, Samuel - Mary Lawrence........    3-05-1832
Throckmorton, Samuel of New York City -
   Susannah Throckmorton......................    3-13-1833
Throckmorton, Thomas C. - Elizabeth Craig....   12-21-1808
Throckmorton, William - Abigail Wooley.......    6-04-1803
Throckmorton, William - Nancy Crum..........    4-30-1808
Throgmorton, John - Mary Jones...............    2-06-1817
Thropp, Lewis - Phebe Taylor.................    3-08-1810
Tice, Aaron - Deborah Cook...................    7-17-1824
Tice, James - Sarah Mathews..................    9-10-1831
Tice, John - Harriet Suidam..................   11-01-1797
Tice, John - Sara Vanbrakell.................    6-30-1799
Tice, Joseph - Jemima Bird...................   11-15-1795
Tice, Joseph - Sarah Johnston................    8-17-1822
Tice, Joseph - Sarah Vannote.................    4-02-1837
Tigert, John - Margaret Deery................    9-13-1813
Tilton, Abraham Jr. - Martha Meirs..........    1-13-1814
Tilton, Amos - Charlotte Allen..............    2-02-1839
Tilton, Amos - Deborah Lewis.................   11-03-1808
Tilton, Asher C. - Ann W. Thompson..........    4-22-1832
Tilton, Assa - ---- Eldridge.................   12-31-1829
Tilton, Benjamin - Sarah Miller.............    3-07-1818
Tilton, Calies - Deborah White..............    1-24-1832
Tilton, David - Sarah Flemmin...............   10-23-1806
Tilton, David of Burlington Co., N. J. -
   Sarah Miers................................    1-13-1825
Tilton, Edward - Rebecca Mount..............    1-25-1810
Tilton, Ezekial - Ann Maria Cook............    8-05-1817
Tilton, Garret - Jane Lewis..................    1-08-1809
Tilton, Henry - Ann K. Fleming..............   12-01-1807
Tilton, Humphrey -
   Mary Catherine Hendrickson................    9-10-1811
Tilton, Jacob - Rebecca Pearce..............    3-04-1838
Tilton, Jacbo - Sarah Story..................    1-27-1800
Tilton, James - Lydia Allen..................    1-26-1832
Tilton, Jeremiah - Sara Antonidus...........    3-15-1826
Tilton, Joel - Charlotty Letts..............    1-17-1830
Tilton, John - Aulika Emmons.................    9-14-1797
Tilton, John - Charlotte Pharo..............    3-28-1829
Tilton, John - Elizabeth Clayton............    4-15-1798
Tilton, John - Elizabeth Dickison...........    9-16-1807
Tilton, John - Mary Curtis...................    1-01-1804
Tilton, John P. - Sally Ely..................   11-19-1831
Tilton, John W. - Deborah Matthews..........    9-19-1826
Tilton, Jonathan - Lydia Ann Habert.........    1-01-1832
Tilton, Jonathan - Patience Willet..........    9-05-1826
Tilton, Jonathan - Polly Madden.............    3-05-1795
```

```
Tilton, Joseph - Althea Covert (wid.)........  11-20-1823
Tilton, Joseph - Isabella Tilton............   3-12-1829
Tilton, Joseph - Mary Scot..................  12-23-1804
Tilton, Lewis - Catherine Johnson...........   9-18-1831
Tilton, Peter - Elizabeth Morris...........   12-20-1821
Tilton, Peter - June Leming.................   3-20-1836
Tilton, Peter - Rebecah Ann Liming..........   4-25-1830
Tilton, Samuel - Hannah Conover.............  11-  -1828
Tilton, Silas of N. Y. - Ensibia Tilton.....   1-02-1833
Tilton, Silas - Mary Debeace................   1-10-1807
Tilton, Silvester - Mary Falkenburgh........   7-11-1818
Tilton, Thomas - Isabel Mount...............   2-09-1839
Tilton, Thomas - Mary Luker.................   2-05-1800
Tilton, Thomas - Mary Tice..................   1-26-1826
Tilton, William - Catherine Burins..........  11-23-1809
Tilton, William - Elizabeth Hance...........  12-15-1837
Tilton, William - Elizabeth Van Note........   7-19-1838
Tilton, William of Burlington Co., N. J. -
    Margaret Lawrence.......................  11-24-1825
Tindal, David - Elizabeth Victor............   8-09-1840
Tindal, Ezekiel of Middlesex Co., N. J. -
    Margaret Hutchinson of Burlington Co.,
    New Jersey..............................  11-06-1833
Tingal, Amos - Elizabeth Applegate..........   7-06-1803
Tise, Asher - Sarah Ellison.................   4-25-1810
Tise, John - Sara Chambers..................  10-27-1826
Tompson, Robert - Rachel Foster.............   5-09-1796
Tone, William - Phebe De Bois...............  11-18-1819
Tourt, William - Phebe Carr.................  10-09-1813
Towers, James - Mary Brown..................  11-12-1807
Towler, Joseph - Catherine Runnels..........   2-24-1820
Tracy, Francis of Middlesex Co., -
    Mary Smith..............................  12-01-1842
Trausdale, John - Emaline Hose..............   1-26-1834
Treton, Roland - Sarah Fox..................  12-07-1800
Trewex, Washington - Mary Egbert............   4-07-1833
Triley, Thomas - Elizabeth Borden...........   2-28-1810
Trowbridge, Daniel - Abigail Howland........  10-07-1824
Truas, Asher - Lydia Morris.................   2-20-1823
Truax, Abel - Catherine Hall................  11-19-1812
Truax, Corlis S. - Christian Johnson........   3-18-1835
Truax, Elias - Hannah Layton................   5-08-1809
Truax, John - Alice Rose....................   5-11-1831
Truax, John - Clarissa Swan.................  12-09-1833
Truax, John - Rebecca Fang..................   2-06-1840
Truax, Joseph - Hannah Kelsey...............   5-09-1826
Truax, Joseph - Mary Crum...................   5-08-1834
Truax, Leonard - Sarah Gant.................   4-15-1840
Truax, Salvines - Rachel Johnston...........   5-27-1810
Truax, Samuel - Catherine Osborn............   2-28-1831
Truax, Sylvanus B. Jr. - Lydia Errickson....  10-27-1838
Truax, Thomas - Deborah Morton..............  10-03-1821
Truax, William - Catherine Stout............   4-04-1839
Truckerson, James - Clarasy Woolley
    (both black)............................  11-21-1831
```

MARRIAGES OF MONMOUTH COUNTY, NEW JERSEY

Trude, Colein - Hannah Shores both of
    Burlington Co., N. J..................... 12-14-1823
Truex, Anthony - Tuity Ann White............. 12-15-1832
Truex, Benjamin - Deborah Johnson............ 1-08-1806
Truex, Goodenough - Amy Brown................ 11-22-1834
Truex, Jacob - Catherine Willet.............. 3-10-1810
Truex, Jacob - Elizabeth Johnston............ 10-23-1819
Truex, John Jr. - Marie Cotteral............. 8-11-1801
Truex, Samuel - Mary Johnston................ 6-07-1817
Truex, Samuel of Burlington Co., N. J. -
    Rebekah Nixon............................ 12-29-1832
Tucker, Brittian - Hannah White.............. 5-03-1823
Tucker, Curtis - Leutisa West................ 2-07-1827
Tucker, Ebenezer - Phebe Ridgeway............ 10-08-1801
Tucker, Samuel - Sarah Throckmorton.......... 3-21-1807
Tuckerfoot, William - Mrs. Nancy Edwards..... 2-08-1817
Tunis, Job - Rachel Swan..................... 3-26-1820
Tunis, Stephen - Elizabeth Dennis............ 12-29-1807
Tunis, Thomas - Susan Snowden................ 3-26-1831
Tunis, William - Elizabeth Cooper............ 6-23-1838
Tunison, Richard - Hannah Lewis.............. 1-09-1813
Turner, D. J. C. - Elizabeth Combs........... 2-26-1834
Turner, Tanton - Jane Taylor both of
    Burlington Co., N. J..................... 3-02-1822
Turner, Thomas - Lurrutia Walgrove........... 10-19-1835
Turner, William - Susannah Giberson.......... 2-28-1807
Twinor, William - Nancy Collings............. 4-15-1825
Tyse, Edmund - Jane Elden.................... 12-11-1817
Tyse, Peter - Jane Hans...................... 9-20-1800
Tyson, George - Ann Drum..................... 6-09-1811
Tyson, John - Jane Johnson................... 9-20-1803
Tyson, Joseph - Mercey Stillwell............. 12-18-1822
Tyson, Robert T. - Eliza Ann Morford......... 1-22-1843
Underdunk, Lewis - Mary Ann Barkelow......... 9-01-1840
Unkles, Joseph - Nancy Horner................ 12-22-1822
Updyke, Theodore - Elinor Hill............... 1-31-1838
Upham, Lucius - Deborah Clayton.............. 7-13-1831
Vallentine, Charles - Allice Woodmansee...... 12-28-1816
Vanakey, Richard Jr. - Fanny Seruby.......... 12-28-1833
Vanarsdale, Cornelius - Sarah Ann Jamison.... 12-23-1837
Vanarsdale, Nugent - Elizabeth Smires........ 11-22-1828
Van Brackle, Ruliff - Janet Lloyd
    (both black, marriage recorded).......... 8-07-1834
Van Brackle, Stephen - Ann Bedle............. 11-28-1826
Van Brackle, Stephen - Jan Morrie............ 11-04-1827
Van Brackel, Stephen - Margaret Whitlock..... 9-13-1809
Van Brunt, Albert - Mary Holmes.............. 11-24-1813
Van Brunt, Benjamin - Mariah Mc Daniel....... 3-08-1838
Van Brunt, Charles - Zilpah Ann Longstreet... 1-02-1834
Van Brunt, Cornelius - Rebecca Weeks......... 12-12-1838
Van Brunt, Cornelius - Rebeckah Ayres........ 1-02-1798
Van Brunt, Daniel - Sarah Lane............... 10-31-1815
Van Brunt, Elhanna - Elenor Malott........... 9-30-1828
Van Brunt, Hendrick - Mary Lefatra........... 1-09-1817
Van Brunt, Henry - Mirriam Wardell........... 8-25-1838

```
Van Brunt, Jacob - Sarah Craven..............  7-11-1830
Van Brunt, Joseph - Johannah Parker
  (widow of Ephraim)......................  1802-1804
Van Brunt, Joseph - Mary Ann Montgomery......  1-14-1836
Van Brunt, Joseph - Polly Plunket...........  7-05-1806
Van Brunt, Joseph - Ruhannah Haviland.......  11-06-1839
Van Brunt, Rueben - Mary King...............  5-24-1838
Van Brunt, William - Eleanor Johnston.......  9-15-1825
Van Brunt, Zephaniah - Emeline Bennet.......  12-20-1838
Van Cleaf, Benjamin R. - Rachel Van Cleaf...  1-09-1823
Van Cleaf, Daniel - Mary Merrell............  1-17-1821
Van Cleaf, John - Alice Conover.............  11-10-1822
Van Cleaf, John - Mary Van Cleaf............  5-16-1802
Van Cleaf, Joseph - Rebecca Casler..........  11-03-1823
Van Cleaf, William - Mary Van Cleaf
  dg. of William........................  5-16-1802
Van Cleave, Garret - Ann Morris dg. of
  Charles, both of Long Island, N. Y.......  11-09-1840
Van Cleave, Izrael - Elizabeth Lee..........  9-21-1825
Van Cleave, Joseph - Mary Corley............  3-06-1828
Van Cleave, Lewis - Ann Reeves..............  11-25-1837
Van Cleave, Rulef - Margaret Embley.........  8-07-1805
Van Cleef, Benjamin - Elizabeth Henry.......  3-20-1796
Van Cleef, Elijah - Abigail Lewis...........  11-10-1831
Van Cleef, Thomson - Lydia Richmond.........  1-11-1832
Van Cleef, William - Ann Nivison............  3-05-1799
Van Clef, Joseph - Mrs. Matilda Lawrence....  10-07-1829
Van Cleve, John - Margaret Van Cleve........  12-04-1819
Van Cleve, William - Mary Hulse.............  4-10-1800
Vandegrisft, Samuel - Rachel Ervingham......  8-26-1830
Vanderbalk, Cornelius - Martha Cooper.......  4-16-1825
Van Derbeek, Peter - Elizabeth N. Thorn.....  2-18-1830
Van Derbeth, Thomas - Lydia Ann Smock.......  4-07-1836
Vanderbilt, Hendrick - Margaret Ann Rosell..  1-26-1825
Vanderbilt, Jacob - Mary Poole..............  12-05-1799
Vanderbilt, John - Mary Bedle...............  11-25-1801
Vanderbilt, Joseph - Margaret Smith.........  4-04-1810
Vanderbilt, Thomas - Lydia Ann Aumack.......  4-07-1836
Vanderburg, John G. - Maria B. Dey..........  12-10-1822
Vanderbylt, Jeremia - Altia Gordon..........  11-27-1805
Vanderhoef, Elijah - Elizabeth Stout........  1-23-1829
Vanderhoef, Michael - Nelly Van Cleaf.......  9-30-1799
Vanderhoef, Peter - Mary Wilson.............  12-03-1815
Vanderhoef, Peter C. - Ann Egbert...........  2-20-1822
Vanderhoff, Thomas - Mariah Berdebt.........  7-05-1812
Vanderhoof, Samuel - Alice Holeney..........  12-19-1815
Vanderhope, Samuel - Esther Arrant..........  2-20-1825
Vanderripe, Peter - Mary Pearce.............  9-18-1837
Vanderripe, Sydney - Mary Ann Ackerson......  3-01-1842
Vanderrype, Mathias - Experience Wilkerson..  1-03-1799
Vanderveer, Abram - Susan Jemison
  (both black)..........................  6-27-1839
Vanderveer, Arthur - Alchey Barcalow........  3-07-1797
Vanderveer, Arthur - Elizabeth Trafford.....  9-14-1815
Vanderveer, Cornelius - Jane Williamson.....  12-24-1800
```

```
Vanderveer, David - Catherine Dubois.........    5-18-1802
Vanderveer, David Jr. - Eliza Holmes Ellis...   12-02-1813
Vanderveer, Domenius - Sarah Tanis..........    10-10-1808
Vanderveer, Elias - Sarah Hoffmire..........     1-27-1816
Vanderveer, Garret - Ellen Polhemus.........     1-04-1830
Vanderveer, James - Ann Matilda Hampton
   (both black)............................     5-10-1839
Vanderveer, John - Eliza Vanderveer Magee....    3-04-1840
Vanderveer, John - Hannah Bowne.............     1-17-1814
Vanderveer, John - Mary Conover.............    1834-1835
Vanderveer, Joseph - Jane Smock.............    12-06-1809
Vanderveer, Peter - Louisa Holman...........    11-05-1840
Vanderveer, Rulif - Lydia Woodward..........     1-29-1823
Vandeveer, Tunis - Getty Van Pelt...........     3-24-1811
Vandeventer, Jacob - Elizabeth Lane.........     2-11-1811
Van Doorn, Albert - Sarah Covenhoven........     3-14-1803
Van Doorn, Arthur - Harriet Van Cliff.......     1-06-1817
Van Doorn, John - Mary Covenhoven...........     1-30-1809
Van Doorn, Jacob - Getty Schenck............     2-04-1802
Van Doorn, Peter - Catherine Du Bois........     3-04-1817
Van Doorn, William - Catherine Polhemus......   11-28-1815
Van Dorn, Garret - Williampe Conover........     2-26-1821
Van Dorn, Jacob - Hannah Perrine............    12-16-1819
Van Duerson, William - Eleanor Hendrickson...   10-28-1815
Van Durren, John - Catherine Smith (wid.)....    3-23-1816
Van Dusen, Robert - Hannah Wilkison.........     9-26-1810
Van Dyke, Alexander - Jane O'Donald.........     7-11-1841
Van Dyke, Peter - Jane Gano.................    12-20-1810
Van Dyke, Sanford - Hannah Sutphin..........     1-01-1842
Vandyke, Abraham - Mary West................    12-09-1797
Vandyke, Henry - Catherine Marten...........    12-03-1812
Vandyke, Michall M. - Rebecca Brinley.......     1-13-1841
Vandyne, William - Elizabeth Bedle..........    1834-1835
Van Hise, Abraham - Margery Stepe...........    10-09-1799
Van Hise, George - Anna Truax...............     8-13-1823
Van Hise, John - Mrs. Jane West.............     7-03-1814
Van Hise, John Henry - Rachel Smith.........    11-28-1841
Van Hise, Oake - Elizabeth Stepa............     2-12-1801
Van Hise, William - Lydia Kerr..............     2-28-1808
Vanhise, Elisha - Meriba Wibles.............     8-25-1831
Vanhise, Isaac T. - Sarah Thompson..........     1-10-1832
Vanhise, John - Jane Wilbur.................     8-17-1830
Vanhise, Thomas - Rebecca Hance.............     4-28-1805
Van Horn, James - Mary Hopkins..............    11-26-1812
Van Horn, John - Alice Munyan...............    11-11-1820
Van Horn, John - Nancy Clutch...............     5-19-1819
Van Horne, Joseph - Abigail Conover.........    11-11-1797
Van Horne, Thomas - Rebeckah Pipenger.......     4-03-1824
Van Houton, John K. - Sarah C. Meeks
   both of New York City, N. Y.............     8-30-1820
Van Hove, William - Docca Ashton............     4-13-1822
Van Kerk, Peter - Catherine Schenck.........    12-16-1806
Van Kirk, Isaac - Alice Mc Coy..............     7-24-1841
Van Kirk, James - Hannah Scott..............     2-27-1804
Van Kirk, James - Sarah Reynolds............     1-12-1833
```

```
Van Kirk, Milton - Ann Haggans..............  1-12-1833
Van Kirk, Stephen - Ann Throckmorton........  3-27-1824
Van Kirk, Stephen - Elizabeth West.......... 10-10-1807
Vankirk, James - Elizabeth Brewer...........  6-11-1799
Vankirk, John - Nelly Van Brunt............. 11-29-1795
Vankirk, William - Anna Price...............  6-29-1801
Van Mater, Benjamin - Ann Van Mater.........  6-27-1799
Van Mater, Cornelius - Orpha Taylor.........  6-18-1797
Van Mater, Cyrenius - Ellen Hendrickson..... 11-13-1829
Van Mater, George - Rhoda Hendrickson....... 10-15-1837
Van Mater, Gilbert - Sarah Holmes dg. of
  John Holmes...............................  8-03-1841
Van Mater, Gilbert - Sarah Taylor...........  5-23-1836
Van Mater, Jacob - Abigail Van Mater........ 12-22-1800
Van Mater, Jacob - Mary Vanderveer..........  2-13-1804
Van Mater, John - Lucia George.............. 11-27-1816
Van Mater, Joseph - Ann Van Mater...........  9-28-1808
Van Mater, Joseph - Catherine Van Mater.....  2-28-1803
Van Mater, Joseph K. - Elizabeth Van Mater... 12-09-1800
Van Mater, Lewis - Mattie Lockson
  (both black)..............................  4-04-1818
Van Mater, Lewis (a black belonging to
  John Van Mater) - Isabell ---- (a black
  belonging to Joseph Throckmorton)........ 11-08-1835
Van Mater, William - Mary Hendrickson....... 12-20-1797
Vanneman, Thomas - Eleanore White...........  3-28-1838
Van Nest, Hanson - Rachel Dye............... 12-21-1837
Van Nest, Voorhees - Rebecca Ivins both of
  Burlington Co., N. J......................  1-29-1834
Van Noart, John - Hannah Keepers............  3-10-1796
Van Nort, William - Eliza Fielder...........  2-14-1804
Van Norwick, Christian - Eliza Gorden.......  2-21-1821
Van Note, Abraham - Catherine Gant..........  3-06-1830
Van Note, Charles - Eliza Ann Allen.........  1-18-1836
Van Note, John - Mrs. Sarah Hays............  1-22-1828
Van Note, Joseph - Elizabeth Woolley........ 11-10-1839
Van Note, Peter - Sarah Chamberlin.......... 10-18-1815
Van Note, Theodore - Mary Ann White.........  4-13-1841
Van Note, Thomas - Mary Ann Clayton.........  7-06-1834
Van Note, Thomas - Sarah Fish...............  9-01-1803
Vannote, Benjamin - Liza Woolston...........  2-09-1837
Vannote, Cornelius - Elsie Clayton..........  7-05-1823
Vannote, Jacob - Mary Ann Boud..............  8-02-1831
Vannote, James - Lucretia Miller............  4-10-1819
Vannote, Joseph - Margaret Miller...........  4-10-1808
Vannote, Polhemus - Lidia Conrow............ 12-05-1826
Vannote, Samuel - Rebecca Runyon............  7-04-1839
Vannote, Stephen - Sarah Britton............  5-13-1826
Vannote, William - Artless Wooley........... 10-19-1823
Vannote, William - Mary L. Parker...........  8-19-1820
Vannote, William H. - Orphah Stout..........  5-24-1827
Vannote, William K. - Lidia Taylor.......... 11-20-1829
Van Pelt, Alexander - Sarah Hulshart........      1814
Van Pelt, Anthony - Mary White..............  2-15-1827
Van Pelt, Benjamin - Ursula Anderson........  8-05-1799
```

```
Van Pelt, Henry - Phebe Ann Honce............  11-20-1831
Van Pelt, James - Mary Van Pelt..............   7-04-1816
Van Pelt, John - Jane Van Cleaf..............   9-25-1811
Van Pelt, John - Mary Cannan.................  12-10-1796
Van Pelt, Walter - Catherine Howell..........   1-24-1797
Van Pelt, William - Elizabeth Smith..........   2-01-1801
Van Pelt, William - Mary Conover.............   2-04-1836
Van Pelt, Winnete of Long Island, N. Y. -
   Hannah F. Morris.........................   7-31-1830
Vansant, John of Gloucester Co., N. J. -
   Lydia Anderson...........................  10-10-1831
Van Schoick, David - Emily Williams..........   2-14-1824
Van Schoick, William - Eliza Ann Hendrickson.   2-24-1830
Van Scoick, Johiah - Franisikay Forman.......   1-31-1822
Van Scoick, William - Hannah Morris..........   8-03-1810
Van Scoik, Samuel H. - Mary Craig............   5-13-1818
Vanuxam, Edward H. of Ohio -
   Lydia Drummond (recorded)................  11-08-1832
Vaughn, Robert - Artimacy Lawyer.............  10-13-1811
Vepham, Lucious - Deborah Clayton............   7-13-1831
Vermule, Richard - Mary Lloyd................  12-03-1813
Victor, John - Charity Britton...............  10-22-1814
Vincent, Isaac - Eleanor Morris..............   3-26-1835
Vincent, James - Sarah Ann Henaghan..........  11-18-1820
Vinter, David - Assenith Concklin............   1-02-1835
Voorhees, Albert H. - Lydia H. Conover.......   1-10-1824
Voorhees, John - Elizabeth Stricklin.........   9-25-1824
Voorhees, Samuel - Nancy Applegate...........  12-05-1819
Voorhees, Stephen - Eliza Laird..............   4-24-1815
Voorhees, Tunis U. - Eleanor Stricklin.......   5-28-1831
Voorhees, William - Eleanor Emmons...........  12-08-1802
Voorhees, William - Mary Gaston..............   1-29-1817
Voorhees, William Jr. - Elizabeth Pierson....   1-21-1828
Voorheis, Stephen - Eliza Laird..............   4-24-1815
Voorhies, Hendrick - Keziah Applegate........  12-04-1796
Vores, William - Abigail Laverty.............   3-04-1798
Vorhees, ---- - Hannah Smith.................   8-11-1833
Vorhees, Albert - Mary Skidmore..............   5-28-1842
Vorhees, Benjamin - Sarah Smalley............   1-19-1803
Vorhees, Garret - Rebecca Ann White..........   6-17-1838
Vorhees, John - Mary Hance...................   6-10-1798
Vorhees, Joseph - Hannah Holmes..............   4-03-1803
Vorhees, Joseph - Rachel Lucas...............   6-19-1841
Vorhees, Joseph - Rebecca Ford of
   Middlesex Co., N. J......................   1-20-1836
Vorhees, Tunis - Sarah Emmons................  11-05-1837
Vorhees, William - Matilda Pierson...........   5-24-1838
Vorhees, William - Sarah Smith...............   4-18-1799
Vreedenburg, Peter - Eleanore Brinkhoff......   4-19-1836
Vreeland, Simon - Susannah Keelan............   2-11-1798
Vunch, Joseph - Mary Clayton.................   4-30-1826
Waggoner, Henry - Kertiah Matthews...........  10-02-1824
Waggoner, John of N. Y. - Lucinda Smith......  12-01-1832
Waggoner, Robert Jr. - Huldah Newman.........   3-25-1826
Waggoner, William - Deborah Chambers.........  10-29-1836
```

```
Wainright, Holsted - Catherine Back..........  5-20-1797
Wainright, Peter - Ellen Stephens............  4-02-1834
Wainright, Peter Jr. - Sarah Phillips........  1-08-1824
Wainright, Walling - Antress Williams........  9-21-1797
Wainwright, Daniel - Ellenor Havens..........  3-01-1801
Wainwright, Ephraim B. - Catherine Taylor....  2-23-1833
Wainwright, James - Martha Brown............. 10-18-1837
Wainwright, John N. - Jane Skidmore..........       1833
Waler, Richard - Mary Ann Allen..............  2-25-1835
Walger, William - Zebah Newman...............  2-27-1840
Walker, Aron Forman - Mary Hubbard...........  2-21-1807
Walker, Emmick - Sarah Smith.................  3-21-1840
Walker, Jorge - Hannah Smith.................  9-06-1801
Walker, Peter - Catherine Moore of
  New York City, N. Y.......................  9-25-1838
Wall, John - Mary Stillwell..................  3-08-1821
Wall, Tilton - Elizabeth Curtis..............  1-03-1835
Wall, William of Ohio - Elizabeth Thompson
  dg. of Thomas.............................  4-14-1822
Wall, William - Phebe Earhart................ 12-08-1814
Wallen, Emanuel - Elizabeth Smith............  2-10-1833
Wallen, John - Ann Stoney.................... 12-02-1833
Wallen, John - Phebe Truax...................  5-28-1807
Wallen, Joseph - Anna Dye.................... 11-20-1798
Walley, William - Sarah Morris...............  1-30-1815
Walling, Abraham - Ann Baley................. 10-07-1835
Walling, Amos - Lucy Ann Hoff............... 11-28-1827
Walling, Augustus - Elizabeth Davidson.......  2-24-1842
Walling, Cornelius R. - Abigal Smith.........  3-23-1815
Walling, Daniel - Catherine Stillwell........  2-12-1815
Walling, Daniel - Ida Wilson.................  5-30-1828
Walling, Edward - Alice Walling..............  1-20-1835
Walling, Edward - Fanny Hire.................  9-30-1829
Walling, Elijah - Jane Kelsey................  2-21-1816
Walling, Garrett - Margaret Hier.............  2-01-1835
Walling, George D. - Catherine Flinn........ 11-03-1831
Walling, Gershom - Deborah Walling.......... 12-17-1817
Walling, Gershom - Elizabeth Hoff...........  7-03-1838
Walling, Holmes - Mary Aumack...............  5-07-1836
Walling, Isaac - Mary Baily................. 11-25-1829
Walling, Isaac - Mary Huff.................. 11-10-1825
Walling, John - Jane Herbert................  2-09-1836
Walling, John - Rachel Walling..............  6-21-1842
Walling, Joseph M. - Hannah Thorne.......... 12-25-1816
Walling, Peter - Rachel Atkinson............  8-07-1842
Walling, Richard - Deborah Burrows..........  3-07-1815
Walling, Richard P. - Ann Eliza Hooff.......  9-27-1837
Walling, Samuel - Ann Seabrook.............. 12-01-1833
Walling, Sydney - Cornelia Hiers............ 10-05-1842
Walling, Thomas - Ann Beedle................ 10-10-1814
Walling, Thomas - Catherine Van Cleef.......  2-28-1842
Wallis, Thomas - Alice Ralph................ 1834-1835
Walten, David - Mary Parker.................  8-23-1812
Walter, David - Ellener Prest...............  2-25-1815
Walter, John Scyler - Ann Schenck........... 10-27-1814
```

```
Walton, Elias - Lydia Brand................. 12-10-1836
Walton, Ezeckial - Sarah Gillum............. 9-03-1826
Walton, Forman - Leana Suydam............... 6-15-1803
Walton, James - Julia Beldole............... 1-22-1830
Walton, John N. - Eleanor Wilson............ 5-14-1834
Walton, Thomas F. - Sarah Laird............. 6-12-1804
Walton, William - Margaret Perrine
  dg. of William........................... 12-10-1818
Walton, William - Zilpha Hart............... 10-14-1821
Ward, James - Jane Van Pelt................. 9-06-1796
Wardell, Aaron - Mercy Osborn............... 12-24-1823
Wardell, Asher - Jemimah West............... 8-09-1800
Wardell, Asher - Lydia Heullick............. 12-30-1830
Wardell, Benjamin - Nancy Throckmorton...... 7-10-1802
Wardell, Gordon - Maria Howton.............. 8-29-1828
Wardell, Henry - Anne Bowman................ 12-24-1808
Wardell, Isaac - Ruth Cook.................. 10-30-1818
Wardell, Jesse - Mary Lippincott............ 11-02-1815
Wardell, John - Rachel Jones................ 3-20-1833
Wardell, Joseph - Mariah Robbins............ 2-18-1838
Wardell, Peter - Margaret Slocum............ 4-30-1797
Wardell, Richard - Margaret Dennis.......... 7-10-1796
Wardell, Robert of N. Y. - Jane Williams.... 12-24-1833
Wardell, Samuel - Hannah W. Maps............ 2-20-1841
Wardell, Samuel - Mrs. Margaret Hart........ 12-16-1818
Warden, Albert - Levina Headly.............. 6-15-1816
Warden, Samuel - Mary A. Hendrickson........ 10-11-1827
Warden, William - Mary Brewer............... 5-04-1816
Ware, Abraham - Sarah Reed.................. 3-14-1840
Ware, John - Ann Johnson.................... 8-28-1815
Warnar, John - Ellen Pullen................. 4-02-1827
Warner, Caleb - Elizabeth Murdock........... 4-06-1828
Warner, Jacob - Deborah Jackson............. 11-07-1833
Warner, William - Eliza Hiers............... 12-19-1830
Warrell, Daniel - Charity Morris............ 3-09-1821
Warrell, Joseph - Ann Niveson............... 12-04-1825
Warren, John - Maria Mc Cales............... 3-21-1829
Warren, John - Rebecca Winner............... 3-11-1810
Warren, Jonathan - Naomi D. Clayton......... 3-16-1836
Warren, Samuel - Hepsebah Brick............. 2-09-1827
Warrick, Derias - Elizabeth Stevenson....... 2-19-1815
Warrick, James - Mary Bennet................ 7-23-1831
Warwick, Abraham - Mary Reynold (spinster)... 4-07-1811
Warwick, Andrew - Matilda Wilgus............ 4-22-1832
Warwick, James - Harriet Hopkins............ 2-25-1817
Watson, William - Patty Fowler.............. 9-20-1828
Waydock, Francis (schoolmaster)-
  Catherine Bowers......................... 11-03-1803
Wayman, William - Hannah Morris............. 8-31-1830
Wears, John - Anne Jones.................... 6-19-1807
Weaver, Joseph - Sarah Smith................ 3-26-1837
Webb, Caleb - Ann Brown..................... 8-27-1833
Webb, Cortland - Rebecca Fenton............. 1-01-1817
Webb, Isaiah, - ---- Shinn.................. 5-04-1831
Webb, Samuel - Rachel Clayton.............. 12-31-1821
```

```
Webb, William - Acesah Blake................. 10-25-1814
Webley, John - Sarah Howel................... 2-07-1797
Webley, Joseph - Lydia Lefetra.............. 12-25-1804
Webster, Timothy - Charlotte Sprowl......... 10-23-1841
Weeb, Berman - Ann Blake.................... 4-20-1811
Weed, Hugh Mercer - Sarah Ivins............. 12-06-1804
Week, Stephen - Catherine Walter............ 1-01-1817
Welb, James - Jane Lippincott............... 7-30-1801
Welkin, Peter of N. Y. - Sarah Winent....... 8-27-1797
Well, Joseph - Elizabeth Hillyer............ 9-01-1799
Wells, Carvin - Rebeccah Woodmancey......... 5-03-1797
Wells, Hercules - Sarah Keeper.............. 4-13-1817
Wells, James - Emeline Dennis............... 2-24-1816
Wells, Joseph - Phebe Soper................. 9-19-1797
Wemple, Harmon B. - Abbie Edwards........... 10-21-1840
Wentrel, John - Fanny Brower................ 12-06-1809
West, Bartholomew - Abigail White........... 1-09-1830
West, Bartholomew - Rhoda Webley............ 5-25-1796
West, Benjamin - Elizabeth Wooley........... 6-06-1802
West, Daniel - Hellene Conover.............. 12-06-1817
West, David - Mary Lloyd.................... 2-07-1810
West, Edmund - Rachel Drummond.............. 11-07-1821
West, Edward - Elizabeth Lippincott......... 1-03-1824
West, Elias - Deborah Shearman.............. 8-27-1823
West, Elisha - Eliza Woolley................ 9-07-1831
West, Elisha - Rachel Green................. 11-17-1803
West, Gabril - Sarah Wardell................ 6-12-1827
West, George W. - Abigail Brinley........... 12-24-1818
West, Henry - Emeline Smith................. 8-25-1833
West, Israel - Martha Johnston.............. 1-07-1826
West, Jacob - Sarah Hyers................... 10-03-1805
West, James - Ruth West..................... 2-09-1826
West, John - Charlotte Emmons............... 11-07-1805
West, John - Deborah White.................. 11-11-1815
West, John - Jane Richmond.................. 4-07-1796
West, John - Lucy Ann Lane.................. 12-24-1840
West, John - Mary Johnson................... 2-24-1799
West, Joseph - Ann Pierson.................. 3-06-1823
West, Joseph - Deborah Crum................. 10-10-1807
West, Joseph - Rebecca Tabor................ 4-10-1830
West, Lewis - Mary Shearman................. 10-08-1828
West, Stephen - Aseneth Vanderveer.......... 3-05-1812
West, Stephen - Elenor Stricklen............ 3-14-1807
West, Stephen - Hannah Matthews............. 9-02-1837
West, William - Catherine Smythe............ 10-22-1800
West, William - Mary Degrot (wid.).......... 5-16-1824
Wetherell, Samuel - Cornelia Hendrickson..... 4-11-1839
Wetherill, George - Sarah Rue............... 2-18-1815
Wethers, Jeams - Elizabeth Parker........... 1-25-1814
Whare, Joel - Ellenor Wilbur................ 9-21-1814
Wheatly, Joseph - Ellen Norris.............. 9-23-1795
Wheelan, William - Sarah Ann Soden.......... 3-05-1840
Wheeler, Francis - Rachel Stout............. 10-19-1804
White, Amos - Hannah Conrow................. 3-09-1842
White, Amos - Nancy Throckmorton............ 3-17-1797
```

```
White, Andrew - Martha Walling...............  4-19-1828
White, Asher - Mary Lippincott...............  7-16-1797
White, Benjamin - Abigail Lippincott.........  9-04-1799
White, Benjamin - Ann Rivley.................  6-24-1820
White, Charles - Mehitable Hart..............  3-11-1841
White, Drummond - Rebecca Slocum............. 10-17-1829
White, Elisha - Mary Lewis................... 12-25-1816
White, Garret - Rebekah Lippincott........... 10-25-1798
White, George - Deborah Jones................ 12-03-1817
White, Goerge - Margaret Coward.............. 11-20-1833
White, Hartshorn - Ann Chasey................ 12-15-1830
White, Hendrick - Hannah Deboos..............  1-16-1813
White, Hendrick - Isabella Thomson...........  1-03-1830
White, Henry - Lydia Harvey..................  5-28-1833
White, Hugh - Susan A. Brown.................  1-06-1842
White, Jacob - Abigail Homes.................  5-03-1806
White, Jacob - Catherine Howland.............  2-09-1798
White, Jedida - Sarah Yeoman.................  7-11-1826
White, John - Eleanor Williamson.............  6-07-1825
White, John - Elizabeth Tucker...............  2-15-1807
White, John - Hannah Allen...................  2-06-1842
White, John - Jane Smith..................... 10-05-1802
White, John - Mary Golden....................  8-16-1831
White, John - Mrs. Mercy Ellis...............  3-03-1842
White, John F. - Rachel C. Sherman both of
    Philadelphia, Pa......................... 12-12-1833
White, John S. - Sarah Warner................      1834
White, Joseph - Mary Ann Matthews............  2-04-1834
White, Joseph L. - Lydia Patterson...........  9-22-1830
White, Joseph T. - Lucy G. Corlies.......... 12-02-1826
White, Louis - Lydia Niverson................  3-03-1839
White, Lyttleton - Nancy Holmes..............  8-19-1810
White, Peter - Jane Shafto...................  1-25-1834
White, Philip - Betre Bennett................  8-22-1800
White, Richard - Hannah Pierson..............  5-26-1824
White, Richard - Letitia Conover.............  8-17-1836
White, Robert - Cornelia Leonard............. 11-27-1806
White, Samuel T. - Elizabeth White...........  9-17-1821
White, Thomas - Eliza Ann Grover............. 1834-1835
White, Thomas - Esther Hankins...............  9-19-1821
White, Timothy - Elizabeth King..............  8-02-1807
White, Timothy - Hannah Crawford.............  3-19-1797
White, Tucker - Mary Jones...................  8-24-1826
White, Uriah - Mrs. Nancy Oakeson............  3-05-1817
White, William - Catherine Johnson...........  3-04-1837
White, William - Elizabeth White.............  4-15-1839
White, William - Marget Morgan...............  1-12-1797
White, William - Mary Vorhees................  2-10-1808
White, William - Sarah Letson................  1-14-1797
White, Zephema - Helena Walling.............. 10-10-1814
Whitehead, Isaac - Rachel Curtis.............  5-11-1842
Whitehead, Walter - Mariah Burdsall..........  2-18-1839
Whitlock, I. Conover - Margaret Walton.......  1-22-1824
Whitlock, Haddock - Gertrude Schenck......... 11-22-1821
Whitlock, Thadeus - Jane Ann Provost......... 12-16-1838
```

Wickoff, Samuel - Hannah Clarkson............ 1-08-1840
Wikile, John P. - Mary Aumack (wid.)......... 3-02-1826
Wikoff, Garret - Alice Holmes................ 6-18-1829
Wikoff, Henry G. - Emeline West.............. 1-13-1831
Wikoff, Peter - Elizabeth Baird.............. 10-31-1821
Wikoff, Peter - Harriet Cox.................. 6-02-1830
Wikoff, Peter - Mary Ann Imlay............... 2-12-1822
Wikoff, Richard - Jane Thompson.............. 12-07-1825
Wikoff, Samuel - Nancy Henderson............. 11-12-1814
Wikoff, Theophilus - Zilpha White............ 12-06-1798
Wilber, Dillin - Lucretia Bird............... 10-14-1795
Wilber, Edward - Rachel Phillips............. 8-19-1821
Wilber, William - Lidia Holmes............... 4-05-1821
Wilbert, Robert - Hannah Ann White........... 9-04-1839
Wilbin, James - Astemacy Skidmore............ 7-14-1811
Wilbor, James D. - Mary Applegate............ 3-29-1823
Wilbor, Reuben - Safety Robertson............ 8-08-1833
Wilbour, Gilbert - Mary Scidmore............. 6-11-1815
Wilbur, Edward - Anna Stout.................. 4-15-1816
Wilbur, Ivans - Achsa Johnson................ 12-25-1839
Wilbur, James - Catherine Tice............... 2-17-1828
Wilbur, James - Elizabeth Hopkins............ 6-26-1796
Wilbur, James L. - Mary Bennett.............. 1-05-1822
Wilbur, John - Patience Wainwright........... 7-27-1824
Wilbur, William - Rebecca Ann Skidmore....... 2-28-1839
Wilburn, John - Elizabeth Acher.............. 4-24-1820
Wiles, William - Martha Cornwall............. 4-29-1824
Wiley, Thomas - Phebe Bowne.................. 9-29-1803
Wilgus, Jesse - Sarah Bishop................. 1833
Wilgus, John - Mary Miggse................... 10-07-1800
Wilgus, William - Mary Wright................ 2-23-1804
Wilgus, William - Sarah Ford................. 3-04-1827
Wilkins, Edward - Rebecca Chamberlin......... 11-15-1838
Wilkinson, James - Nancy Lewis............... 4-21-1796
Wilkuis, John - Filey Allen.................. 8-15-1801
Willcott, Benjamin - Mary T. Spinning........ 1-20-1831
Willet, Hoseah of Burlington Co., N. J. -
    Elizabeth Chambers...................... 3-18-1820
Willet, John - Hannah Johnson................ 1-27-1832
Willet, John - Sarah Niverson................ 3-22-1832
Willet, William - Julia Ann Compton.......... 1-24-1828
Willets, Stephen - Elyda Cemonds............. 8-12-1795
Willgus, ---- - Catherine Hankins............ 11-29-1798
William - Lucy (both blacks)................. 10-26-1835
William, Elihu - Elizabeth Truax............. 5-19-1810
William, Samuel - Mary Senay................. 12-14-1800
Williams, Charles - Susan Myers.............. 4-22-1839
Williams, Cornelius of New York City -
    Mary Ann Errickson...................... 1-19-1836
Williams, Curtis - Nancy White............... 12-13-1802
Williams, Daniel - Elizabeth Layton.......... 3-18-1826
Williams, Daniel - Jane Henderson............ 3-26-1797
Williams, Daniel - Mary Tilton............... 8-02-1797
Williams, Daniel - Mary Tilton............... 12-03-1807
Williams, Daniel - Rachel Degra (black)...... 9-01-1821

```
Williams, David - Rebecca Applegate..........    11-27-1823
Williams, Elihu - Sarah Fleming..............    12-08-1809
Williams, George - Meribah Smith.............    11-02-1810
Williams, Israel - Content Potter............    12-11-1802
Williams, James - Ann Truax..................    12-13-1797
Williams, James - Rosee Ann Johnson
  (both blacks)............................     12-27-1834
Williams, John - Chairty Applegate...........     9-27-1813
Williams, John - Elizabeth Britton...........     3-15-1815
Williams, John - Elizabeth Herbert...........    12-22-1828
Williams, John - Margaret Johnson............     1-29-1797
Williams, John - Rachel Stout................     4-16-1820
Williams, Joseph - Sarah Applegate...........    12-10-1813
Williams, Peter - Delilah Flinn..............     5-11-1817
Williams, Samuel C. - Jane Coward............     9-09-1824
Williams, Smith - Rebecca Runalds............     1-21-1834
Williams, William - Jean O'Neal..............     1-07-1815
Williams, William - Mary Ann Crawford........     3-01-1827
Williams, William - Rachel Clevenger.........     1-13-1827
Williams, William H. - Martha Yeomans........     5-03-1837
Williams, William W. - Rebecca F. Andrews....    10-16-1823
Williamson, Arthur - Caroline Davison........     3-29-1815
Williamson, Cornelius - Elizabeth Erricson...     4-30-1797
Williamson, David - Margaret Leffertson......    12-05-1805
Williamson, John - Nancy Throckmorton........     1-02-1827
Williamson, John B. - Eliza R. Vanderveer....    10-15-1840
Williamson, Peter - Margaret Stricklon.......    12-07-1807
Williamson, William - Ann Paterson...........     9-20-1815
Willie, John - Sarah Updike both of
  Middlesex Co., N. J.....................     3-13-1833
Willis, Charles H. - Mary Williams both of
  N. Y. (both black)......................     9-03-1827
Willis, Samuel - Elinor Allen................     2-03-1821
Willits, Barzillai - Charity Southward.......     8-26-1802
Willock, Thaddeus - Mary White...............     6-03-1803
Wills, Isaiah - Phebe Toper..................     7-01-1798
Wills, James Jr. - Rebecka Ball..............    10-06-1793
Willson, Curlis - Sarah Soah.................     1-01-1795
Willson, Robert - Isabel Hill................    12-14-1817
Wilmans, Fredrick of Hamburg, Germany -
  Elizabeth Ivins........................    10-23-1800
Wilsie, Peter of N. Y. - Katherine Walton....    10-11-1813
Wilson, Andrew - Mary Pew....................     2-14-1825
Wilson, George - Elizabeth Applegate.........     7-24-1827
Wilson, George - Ellen Conover...............    12-14-1836
Wilson, Jacob - Mary Dennis..................     4-10-1827
Wilson, James - Adeline Walling..............     9-06-1825
Wilson, James - Ann Clayton..................     5-10-1827
Wilson, James - Caroline Fields..............     6-28-1838
Wilson, James - Elizabeth Thompson...........     3-25-1814
Wilson, James - Mary Tunis...................     2-18-1809
Wilson, James Jr. - Margaret Emmons..........    12-06-1820
Wilson, Job L. - Hette Ann Walling...........     2-05-1834
Wilson, John - Elizabeth Martin..............     3-22-1806
Wilson, Joseph - Mary Lomus..................     5-02-1831
```

```
Wilson, Lewis M. (Rev.) - Emeline Forman.....     9-13-1834
Wilson, Nicholas - Catherine Tunis...........     4-06-1800
Wilson, Robert - Catherine Jefery............    12-04-1822
Wilson, Thomas - Fany Beeby..................     9-04-1806
Wilson, Thomas - Pheby Wilgus................    11-06-1819
Wilson, Thomas - Susan Ann Card..............     5-02-1838
Wilson, William - Ann Newell.................    12-21-1818
Wilson, William - Catherine James (wid.).....    12-31-1800
Wilson, William - Elizabeth Dayton...........     2-20-1830
Wilson, William (Rev.) - Lydia Seabrook......     9-16-1841
Winant, Nicolous - Sarah Bowman..............     6-25-1809
Winckoop, Jacob - Elizabeth Brewer dg. of
    Isaac and Lyah Brewer....................     1-22-1825
Winner, Isaac - Naomi Phillips...............    10-27-1804
Winner, Jonathan - Sarah Prigmore............     7-28-1800
Winter, Andrew - Mary De Bow.................     9-05-1835
Winter, David - Asseneth Conklin.............     1-02-1835
Winter, Obadiah - Ann Dorn...................     9-30-1829
Wirl, Nickolous - Mary Brand.................     6-03-1810
Witlock, Derrick - Elizabeth Witlock.........     1-06-1798
Witlock, John - Mary Schenck.................     2-20-1810
Wolcot, Richard - Rachel Brown...............     4-12-1832
Wolcott, Benjamin Jr. - Phebe Jeffery........     4-18-1812
Wolcott, Daniel - Hannah Bowyer..............    10-19-1820
Wolcott, Henry - Margaret Bowyer.............    12-07-1826
Wolcott, Peter - Harriet Brewer..............    11-16-1830
Wolcott, Samuel P. - Hannah Bowyer...........    11-18-1819
Wolcott, William - Elizabeth Grace...........     4-12-1804
Wolley, John - Nancy Newberry................     3-28-1811
Wood, Charles - Joanner Pew..................    10-30-1827
Wood, James - Deborah Dangle.................    10-04-1832
Wood, John - Rebecca Lane....................    10-01-1805
Wood, Joseph - Sarah Chandler................    10-05-1802
Wood, Robert - Lydia Chandler................     5-19-1804
Wood, William - Margaet Covert...............     1-06-1831
Woodart, Samuel - Deborah Bird...............     5-24-1804
Woodhull, Gilbert S. - Charlotte Wikoff......    11-25-1817
Woodhull, Henry Hedges -
    Nancy Huggins Kirkpatrick................     3-17-1801
Woodhull, John T. (M.D.) - Ann Wykoff........     1-22-1812
Woodmancee, John - Harriet Platt.............     7-23-1832
Woodmancee, Stephen - Sarah Hadden...........     6-28-1839
Woodmanse, Isaac - Abigail ----..............     5-02-1806
Woodmanse, Isaac - Mary Applegate............    12-24-1814
Woodmanse, Joel A. - Disire Conklin..........    11-19-1809
Woodmansee, David - Nancy Crane..............     6-15-1806
Woodmansee, Francis - Hannah Soper...........     1-06-1805
Woodmansee, John - Catherine Marks...........    12-02-1815
Woodmansee, Samuel - Abigail Mowker..........     2-13-1819
Woods, William of N. Y. - E. J. Cook.........     7-19-1840
Woodward, Anthony - Mary D. Thompson.........    10-12-1834
Woodward, Apolio - Mariah Middleton..........     3-14-1822
Woodward, Caleb - Hannah Applegate...........     6-03-1803
Woodward, Charles - Ann Mount................    12-06-1838
Woodward, Charles - Catherine Layton.........     2-09-1843
```

```
Woodward, Charles - Martha Jeffree..........    6-11-1807
Woodward, Horatio - Clementina Lloyd........    3-03-1824
Woodward, Isaac - Elizabeth A. Thompson......  11-09-1836
Woodward, Isaac - Leah Brown................   10-25-1829
Woodward, Isriell - Clenine Woodward........    1-04-1827
Woodward, James W. (Rev.) -
    Jane G. Ten Brook......................    3-13-1834
Woodward, Nimrod - Catherine Emley...........   2-19-1814
Woodward, Nimrod - Nancy Williams............   1-03-1796
Woodward, Reben - Elinor Irons...............   1-12-1802
Woodward, Sidney - Eliner Coward............    5-11-1828
Woodward, Tilton - Susannah Woodward........    2-28-1828
Woodward, William - Ann Cook both of
    Burlington Co., N. J....................  12-29-1832
Woodward, William - Mary Hopkins.............   1-07-1832
Woolcott, Edmund - Sarah Ann Dangler........    5-27-1840
Woolcott, Jesey - Elizabeth Knott...........   10-07-1824
Woolcott, Robertson - Sarah A. Bennet........   7-28-1842
Woolee, John - Emmoline Nixon...............   11-15-1823
Wooley, Abraham - Leadya Longstreet.........    4-27-1801
Wooley, Adam - Margaret Lake of N. Y.........   2-09-1820
Wooley, Albert - Hannah Dangler.............   10-26-1837
Wooley, Amos - Ann Ellis....................    4-11-1812
Wooley, Asa - Hannah Hudy...................    1-26-1800
Wooley, Benjamin - Alice Wyckoff............    1-29-1811
Wooley, Briton - Mary Williams..............    4-15-1807
Wooley, Brittian - Nancy Wood...............    9-08-1808
Wooley, Christopher - Rebecca Chadwick.......   6-22-1799
Wooley, Clayton - Hannah Chadwick...........   12-13-1812
Wooley, Daniel - Adeline Morris.............   1834-1835
Wooley, Daniel - Elizabeth Wolcott..........    3-19-1803
Wooley, Daniel - Lydia Oakley...............    6-24-1810
Wooley, Daniel - Ruth Lane..................   10-15-1796
Wooley, Elisha - Mary Lippincott............    1-23-1839
Wooley, Elisha - Mary Throckmorton..........    4-02-1825
Wooley, George - Lydia Field Hardey.........    1-09-1806
Wooley, James T. - Rebecca Wolcott..........   11-05-1840
Wooley, Jessey - Mary Howland...............    4-18-1810
Wooley, Joel - Eliza Ann Newman.............    2-23-1837
Wooley, John - Elizabeth Sickles............   11-09-1804
Wooley, John - Johannah Williams............   11-01-1810
Wooley, John - Lydia Alner..................   10-08-1834
Wooley, John of Abraham - Lydia Borden
    dg. of Captain James Borden.............    5-31-1801
Wooley, Joseph - Sarah Lippincott...........   10-01-1803
Wooley, Joseph - Sarah Riddle...............    7-03-1841
Wooley, Judia - Elizabeth Howland...........    2-02-1799
Wooley, Ludlow - Emeline Hurley.............    2-19-1837
Wooley, Miles - Susan White.................    3-11-1815
Wooley, Robert - Julian Wardell.............    1-11-1809
Wooley, Robert H. - Sophia Forman...........    9-21-1821
Wooley, Thomas - Catherine Pettit...........    7-20-1811
Wooley, Tyley - Sarah Longstreet............    3-01-1815
Wooley, William - Catherine Emly............    4-17-1836
Wooley, William - Hannah Newberry...........   12-18-1806
```

```
Wooley, William Henry - Sarah Ann Ellison....    2-01-1838
Woolf, John - Margaret Emmons...............     6-13-1803
Woolf, Joseph - Sarah Mariat................     6-26-1803
Woolleson, Gilbert - Hannah A. Craig........     2-13-1817
Woolley, Abraham - Githy Layton.............    10-19-1820
Woolley, Adam - Nancy Clayton...............     8-03-1808
Woolley, Alan - Mary Burdge.................     2-05-1835
Woolley, Alexander - Lucy Ann Taylor........     3-05-1834
Woolley, Benjamin - Ann Emmons..............     9-05-1799
Woolley, Benjamin - Zilpha Corlies..........    10-02-1824
Woolley, David - Sarah C. Davison...........    12-08-1841
Woolley, Isaac - Hannah West................     2-05-1842
Woolley, Jacob - Deborah Aumack.............     6-11-1835
Woolley, John - Lydia Algor.................    10-08-1834
Woolley, John - Margaret Smith..............     6-24-1802
Woolley, Mathias W. - Clementine Wardell....    10-29-1829
Woolley, Robert - Lydia Williams............    12-15-1842
Woolley, Robert - Mary Wainright............     1-02-1816
Woolley, Samuel - Hannah Corliss............     4-04-1802
Woolley, Sidney - Ann R. Forsythe...........    12-17-1828
Woolley, Tucker - Ann Davis.................    11-10-1817
Woolley, Tucker - Mary Ann Throckmorton.....    12-20-1829
Woolley, Tyley - Sarah Reed.................     1-18-1816
Woolley, Usual - Phebe Austin...............     8-13-1803
Woolley, William - Abigail Newman...........    10-25-1840
Woolley, William - Elizabeth Pettit.........     2-27-1822
Woolley, William - Lettitia Radford.........    12-27-1823
Woolly, Elihu - Elinor Covenhoven...........     2-20-1812
Woolly, Montillion - Lydia Harris...........     1-25-1808
Wooly, Nathan - Ann Covert..................     6-20-1820
Worden, Albert - Rebecca Coward.............     1-22-1842
Worden, Charles - Hannah Crammer............    11-13-1819
Worden, Joshua - Susannah Knox..............    12-22-1824
Worden, William - Hannah Brown..............     1-27-1827
Worl, Tobias - Elizabeth Britton............    10-26-1824
Worrell, William - Fanney Woolley...........    11-10-1818
Worth, David - Abigail Fisher...............    10-14-1829
Worth, Edward - Hester Britton..............     4-23-1825
Worth, George - Elanenor Vaughn.............     4-06-1842
Worth, George - Lidian Robens...............     6-11-1826
Worth, Joseph N. - Mary Horner..............     5-17-1827
Worthlef, John - Elizabeth Chandler.........    10-17-1819
Worthley, Charles - Mrs. Sarah Layton.......     4-14-1811
Worthley, Garret - Hannah Borden............     2-26-1831
Worthley, Jacob - Margaret Bennet...........     6-08-1803
Worthley, Jeremiah - Margaret Morris........     3-05-1826
Worthley, John - Elizabeth Borden...........    12-23-1841
Worthley, Richard - Ann Parker..............     3-03-1831
Worthley, Richard - Delia Ann Hyer..........     2-22-1838
Wright, Caleb - Ann Ford....................     9-19-1829
Wright, Harrison G. - Sophia W. Brognerd....     3-12-1834
Wright, James (Rev.) - Mary Willets.........     9-01-1841
Wright, John - Elizabeth Cranmer............    10-20-1804
Wright, John B. - Rebecah Gragery...........     2-03-1814
Wright, Thomas - Elizabeth Steward..........     8-20-1799
```

```
Wright, Thomas - Lydia Taylor................  3-03-1800
Wright, William - Mary Ann Smith.............  12-06-1821
Wyckoff, John - Mary Sutphen.................  12-21-1802
Wyckoff, Peter - Ann Taylor..................  2-20-1817
Wycoff, Daniel - Mary T. Corlies.............  3-01-1836
Wycoff, Garret - Ellenor Laine...............  3-12-1812
Wycoff, William - Nelly Van Mater............  10-20-1799
Wykhoff, Garret - Elizabeth Vanhorn..........  3-04-1795
Yateman, Tunis - Martha Gray.................  12-28-1833
Yetman, Enoch - Hannah Pearce................  9-10-1820
Yetman, Esack - Rachel Freeman...............  8-24-1829
Yetman, Ezekiel - Sarah Boise................  10-06-1821
Yetman, Monoah - Mary Tice...................  9-29-1811
Yoeman, Jonathan - Sarah Morrell.............  1839-1840
Yong, Samuel - Mrs. Elizabeth Williamson.....  8-03-1812
Young, Abijee - Massa Clayton................  4-09-1832
Young, Edmund - Catherine Godfrey............  1-25-1816
Youngs, Edmond - Phebe Smith.................  2-11-1797
Zabriskie, George - Sarah Applegate..........  12-31-1832
Zerwick, Michael - Hannah Spragg.............  1-03-1828
Ziberson, John - Betsey Coward...............  3-19-1797
```

INDEX

121

Bailey (cont.)
 Nelly 48
Bailou, Angelina 29
Baily, Aecdery 76
 Ann 97, 100
 Mary 111
Baird, Eliza 22
 Elizabeth 34, 115
 Hannah 11
 Helen 100
 Julia 16
 Lydia 58
 Sarah 4
Baker, Charlotte 23
 Harriet 81
 Mary 89
Baldwin, Betsey S. 91
Baley, Ann 111
 Elizabeth 77
Ball, Rebecka 116
Bancker, Aletta 48
Banks, Anna 63
Banton, Elizabeth 54
Barber, Mary 65
 Phebe 74
 Sarah 62
Barcalow, Alchey 107
 Jane 27, 84
 Lydia 66
 Mary 22
 Sarah 61
Barclay, Ann 67
Bareford, Margaret 8
Barener, Mary Ann 76
Barge, Sarah 41
Barkalow, Abigail 41
 Hannah 82, 90
 Jane 69
 Margaret 46
Barkealow, Lucretia 100
Barkelow, Mary Ann 106
Barker, Ann 83
Barklow, Elizabeth 56
Barnes, Ann 33, 49
 Catherine 54
Barns, Sarah 59
Barry, Sally 54
Bartlet, Hannah 3
Barton, Sarah 51
Bassett, Deborah 50
Bates, Mary 17
Bayer, Levinah 15
Beadle, Ann E. 4
Beal, Rosanne 89
Bealer, Martha 99
Bearmore, Leah 84
Beatty, Christiana 87
Bedle, Ann 4, 106
 Elizabeth 108
 Hannah 98
 Louisa Ann 99
 Lydia 6
 Maria 42
 Mary 107
 Sarah 16
 Zimnetta 50
Beeby, Fany 117
Beedle, Ann 111
 Catherine 5
 Lydia 15
 Sarah 100
Beegle, Sarah 16
Beer, Deborah A. 16
Beers, Ann 44
 Mary 13
 Sarah Ann 90
Begle, Elizabeth 49
Beldole, Julia 112

Belis, Lucinder 61
Bell, Margaret 103
 Matilda 75
 Nancy 65
 Sarah 5
Benet, Ackey 71
Benett, Margaret 75
 Mary 64
Bennet, Adry 35
 Charity 41, 59
 Eliza 32
 Elizabeth 7 (2), 21,
  82
 Elletter 22
 Emeline 107
 Hannah 38
 Ida 6
 Mahala 17
 Margaret 119
 Mary 25, 33, 112
 Naomi 59
 Phebe 97
 Rachel 21
 Sarah 36, 71, 98, 102
 Sarah A. 118
Bennett, Abigail 100
 Achsah 60
 Amy 15, 46
 Ann 53, 83
 Belsey 98
 Betre 114
 Betsey 4
 Catherine 61, 99
 Cathern 92
 Deborah 74, 93
 Effa 64
 Eleanor 53
 Elizabeth 35, 37, 63,
  76 (2)
 Harriet 4
 Ida 80
 Margaret 96
 Marthy 92
 Mary 16, 54, 69, 83,
  98, 115
 Nancy 5
 Phebe 54
 Rachel 6
 Rebecca 70
 Sarah 15, 70, 91, 94,
  Sylvia 63
Berdebt, Mariah 107
Bergen, Eliza 10
Berk, Mary 2
Berlin, Liza Ann 64
Berry, Blainy 76
 Rebecca 58
Biddle, Mary 39
Biles, Martha L. 91
Bills, Catherine 61
 Content 40
 Eliza 32
 Idah 8
 Rachel P. 8
Billsborth, Hannah 39
Bilyer, Ellen 5
Bilyew, Elizabeth 94
Bircalo, Hanna 15
Bird, Ann 16
 Catherine 57
 Deborah 117
 Elizabeth 63
 Henrietta 17
 Jemima 104
 Lucretia 115
 Mary 78
 Mary Ann 81
 Patience 39

Bird (cont.)
 Phebe 12, 18
 Sarah 2
Birdsall, Betsey 14
 Maria 85
 Martha 76
Bishop, Ann 67
 Eleaner 27
 Sarah 115
Blackman, Elizabeth 9
Blackwell, Margaret 85,
  87
Blake, Acesah 113
 Ann 80, 113
 Ann Marie 54
 Frances 73
 Lucy Ann 52
 Margaret 20
 Sarah R. 63
Bogart, Charlotte 29
Boice, Alice 73
 Margaret 39
 Maria 89
 Nancy 98
 Sarah 27
Bois, Sophia 26
Boise, Sarah 119
Boker, Lydia 75
Bolling, Yanne 27
Bonbath, Elizabeth 54
Bond, Elizabeth 5
 Mary 57
Bongart, Ann 93
Bonnell, Hannah 18
Bonnet, Sarah 59
Book, Sarah 92
Booth, Dinah 90
Borden, Ann 44, 78, 92
 Beuley 10
 Caroline 44
 Elizabeth 24, 105, 119,
 Elizabeth W. 44
 Esther 31
 Hannah 83, 119
 Lydia 118
 Margaret 60
 Mary 5, 9, 14, 31, 55
 Nancy 58
 Nany 44
 Rachel 62
 Susannah 65
Bordon, Hariet 52
Boucie, Elizabeth 95
Boud, Hannah 40 (2)
 Jane 69
 Mary Ann 109
Boude, Nancy 75
Bound, Eliza 6
 Sarah 3
Bouth, Ann Mount 75
Bower, Ann 85
 Sarah 25
Bowers, Catherine 112
 Margaret 33
 Mary 37
Bowker, Ann 11
 Catherine 98
 Elizabeth 27, 62
 Hannah 97
 Mary 28
Bowles, Rachel 50
Bowls, Leah 35
Bowman, Anne 112
 Charlotte 88
 Esther 75
 Phebe 103
 Sarah 117
Bown, Delilah 9

122

124

Conk (cont.)
Joan 8
Mary 30
Phebe 3, 101
Williampe 49
Conke, Amie 24
Conkley, Asseneth 47
Conklin, Asseneth 117
Disire 117
Lois 101
Rachel 97
Connars, Sarah 54
Connet, Mary 1
Sarah Ann 79
Conover, Abigail 108
Alice 47, 77, 107
Anitha 50
Ann 34, 52, 55, 88, 99
Ann B. 6
Caroline 21, 25, 52
Catherine 21, 39, 72, 74
Catherine G. 71
Deborah 22, 79
Elinor 27
Elizabeth 42, 51, 64, 83, 95
Ellen 63, 116
Frenchy 22
Gertrude 8, 26
Hannah 19, 35, 64, 99, 103, 105
Helen 34
Helena 82
Helena A. 1
Hellene 113
Idah 48
Jane 40
Julianna 91
Leah 28
Letitia 114
Letty 1
Lucy Ann 6
Lydia 27
Lydia A. 19
Lydia H. 110
Margaret 37, 67
Mary 16, 81 (2), 108, 110
Mary Ann 63, 86
Mary S. 62
Rachel 58
Rebeca 14
Rebecca 23 (2)
Rebecca H. 71
Rintha 80
Sarah 80
Saryann 6
Williampe 108
Conrow, Frances 17
Hannah 113
Lidia 109
Mary 45
Rebecca 29
Sarah 44
Cook, Achsah 41
Ann 23, 25, 61, 71, 101, 118
Ann Maria 104
Caroline 40
Catherine 58
Charity 31
Cornelia 70
Deborah 25, 92, 104
E. J. 117
Elizabeth 103
Elizah 97
Ellen 52

Cook (cont.)
Hannah 18, 20, 47
Harriet 14
Jane 23
Keziah 8
Lydia 72
Margaret 75
Martha 31
Mary 25, 59
Mercy 41
Rachel 14, 20 (2), 86
Ruth 112
Sally 16
Cooke, Harriet 35
Mary 57
Cool, Lydia 32, 60
Coombs, Elizabeth 53
Rebecca 66
Cooper, Abigail 75
Anna 51, 56
Elizabeth 67, 76, 106
Helener 68
Lydia 74
Martha 107
Mary 70
Sarah Ann 26, 68
Zilphy 19
Coperthwaite, Mary 18
Cord, Eliza 95
Margaret 90
Corley, Mary 107
Corlies, Allice 29
Charlotte 52,
Elisabeth 25
Lucy G. 114
Lydia 66
Mary T. 119
Nancy 25 (2)
Sarah 6
Zilpha 119
Corlis, Hannah 19
Luce 72
Sarah 13
Corliss, Hannah 119
Cornelius, Elizabeth 63
Margaret 2
Mariah 82
Rebecca 12
Sarah 38
Cornell, Anne 10
Charity 39
Cornwall, Charlotte 103
Martha 115
Sarah 86
Corolen, Sarah 1
Cossel, Meribah 80
Cotral, Mary 12
Cotrell, Nancy 73, 99
Sarah 35
Cotteral, Ann 44
Eater 6
Hannah 70
Marie 106
Pollina 48
Cottrall, Matilda 19
Cottrell, Amanda 96
Catherine 6
Elizabeth 79
Gertrude 49
Hannah 2, 72
Lydia 88
Mary 96
Phebe 21, 78, 100
Sarah Ann 93
Susan 86
Covener, Nancy 35
Covenhoven, Alice Ann 19
Ann 91

Covenhoven (cont.)
Anne 31, 90
Elinor 119
Elizabeth 26, 101
Ellener 49
Gesha 41
Hannah 89
Jaein 79
Jane 22, 41, 84, 91
Leah 102
Ledia 80
Margaret 52, 91
Maria Schenck 100
Mary 55, 79, 108
Meriah 3
Nellie 65, 90, 98
Nelly 73, 90, 91 (2)
Sarah 26, 47, 108
Covert, Althea 105
Ann 16, 119
Elizabeth 10
Julian 29
Lydia 45, 67
Margaet 117
Mary 70
Rebecca 53
Sarah 23
Coward, Alice 89
Betsey 119
Eliner 118
Elizabeth 34, 58
Jane 116
Lucretia 103
Margaret 114
Rachel 58
Rebecca 119
Sarah 78
Susannah 60
Theodocia 78
Cowenhoven, Elizabeth 32
Cowperthwaite, Rebecca 63
Cowperwaite, Charity 45
Cox, Almira 3
Ann 27, 89
Catherine 48
Hannah 18
Harriet 115
Mary 38, 98
Perthene 64
Phebe 55
Sarah 77
Sarah Ann 71
Craddik, Deborah 69
Craddock, Elizabeth 78
Lydia 48
Craft, Hester 44
Rosetta 77
Craig, Ann 99
Catherine 55, 91
Elinor 91
Elizabeth 104
Ely 23
Hannah A. 119
Lydia 104
Lydia B. 93
Mary 110
Phebe 47
Sally 103
Sarah 10
Crainer, Elizabeth 81
Cramer, Desiar 98
Elizabeth 22, 27, 92
Mary 25
Massey 36
Nancy 94
Crammer, Bulah 59
Edith 81
Eliza 65

Dunnison, Mary 31
Dunsee, Mary 31
Dunton, Rachel 17
Dunwell, Mary 75
Dye, Anna 111
  Harriet 33
  Martha 51
  Rachel 1, 109
  Sarah 38
E---, Jane 11
Eager, Eliza 103
Ealy, Lucy 12
Earhart, Phebe 111
Eastman, Martha 12
Eastmond, Mary 51
Eayres, Deliah 77
Eddy, Elizabeth 95
Edward, Ann 18
  Nancy 24
Edwards, Abbie 113
  Abigail 24
  Catherine 51
  Eliza 33
  Elizabeth 77
  Elizabeth W. 52
  Mercy 94
  Nancy 106
  Phebe Corlies 54
Egbert, Ann 107
  Catherine 70
  Mary 105
Eggleston, Catherine 55
Ekbulk, Elizabeth 65
Elberson, Hannah 26
Elden, Jane 106
Eldridge, ---- 104
  Ann 61
  Mary 31, 38
  Valaria 94
Eley, Elizabeth 101
  Mary 92
Elison, Hannah 88
  Mary 68
  Susanah 88
Elliot, Elizabeth 42
Ellis, Ann 118
  Catherine 62
  Eliza Holmes 108
  Mercy 114
Ellison, Eliza 47
  Elizabeth 43
  Martha 73
  Sarah 105
  Sarah Ann 119
Elmer, Ann 74
  Deborah 55
  Elizabeth 98
  Phebe 7
Elsworth, Mary 81
Ely, Belinda 75
  Elizabeth 38, 93
  Mary 53
  Rebecca F. 5
  Rebecca M. 22
  Sally 104
  Sarah 57
Emans, Mary 8
Embley, Margaret 19, 107
Emens, Alice 14
  Catherine 45
  Williampe 22
Emley, Catherine 118
  Henrietta 11
  Patience 7
  Rebecca 43
  Rebekah 46
  Sarah 20
Emly, Catherine 118

Emly (cont.)
  Jane 2
Emmans, Hannah 79
  Rhoda 97
Emmens, Ann 53
  Catherine 73
  Margaret 3
  Nancy 2
Emmons, ---- 7
  Ann 119
  Anne 67
  Aulika 104
  Aultye 70
  Cate 72
  Catherine 9, 35, 56, 69
    (2)
  Charlotte 113
  Deborah 68
  Eleanor 110
  Elenor 48
  Eliza 2, 51
  Elizabeth 5, 22, 29, 66
  Ester 94
  Esther 20
  Eunice 59
  Jane 35, 71
  Louisa 41
  Lydia 9, 69
  Margaret 37, 39, 116,
    119
  Mary 38, 42, 53, 69
  Mary Ann 21
  Phebe 20
  Rachel 37
  Sarah 66, 102, 110
  Unice 53
  Zilpha 57
Emmos, June 25
Emons, Isabella 67
  Jane 37
  Mary 62
English, Ann 13
  Jane 47
  Lydia Ann 35
  Mary R. 49
Erickson, Ann 39
  Jedidah 5
  Jerusha 82
Erixson, Elizabeth 60
Ermine, Margit 88
Erricson, Elizabeth 116
  Mary 80
Errickson, Catherin 5
  Jane 75
  Lois 22
  Lydia 105
  Margaret 34
  Mary 39
  Mary Ann 50, 115
  Phebe 21
  Sarah 42, 66, 97
Ervingham, Rachel 107
Erwin, Katherine 53
Esla, Lydia 31
Eslick, Dinah 46
Estel, Hannah 39
Estele, Sarah 56
Estell, Rachel 49
  Sarah 69
Estie, Jane 80
Estile, Catherine 52
  Rachiel 54
Estill, Ellen 40
Estle, Emeline 16
Estol, Anne 12
  Elizabeth 59
Estory, Jane 31
Evengrim, Hope 15

Everingam, Elizabeth 19
Everingham, Alchy 3
  Ann 54
  Mahala 13
  Permelia 62
Everngam, Elizabeth 70
Evernham, Lucy 36
  Lydia 56
Ewing, Nancy 1
Falkenburg, Nancy 47
  Phebe 43
Falkenburgh, Hannah 77
  Mary 105
Falkinburgh, Amelia 99
Fane, Lidia 36
Fang, Rebecca 105
Fanny, Rosetta 39
Farrow, Mary Ann 49
Fell, Elizabeth 97
Fenton, Charlott 16
  Mary Ann 5
  Rebecca 112
  Susan Mary 39
Ferguson, Eunice 68
Fewts, Sarah 37
Field, Mary 16
Fielder, Catherine 40
  Eliza 109
  Eliza Ann 90
  Mary 22
  Sally 69
Fieldley, Cornelia 41
Fieldor, Mary 83
Fields, Ann 22
  Caroline 116
  Catherine 19
  Elizabeth 28
  Lucy 93
  Rebecca 37
Fiffer, Sarah 30 (2)
Finison, Sarah Jane 72
Finly, Margaret 11
Firman, Eleanor 12
  Mary 87
Fish, Catherine 77
  Esther 70
  Sarah 109
Fisher, Abigail 119
  Catherine 48
  Elizabeth 85, 91
  Hannah 14
  Margaret 90
  Mary 68, 71
  Rebecca 46
Fitsimonds, Mary 89
Fitzemmons, Margaret 16
Flat, Rebecca 41
Fleming, Ann K. 104
  Anna 94
  Eliza 73
  Maria 13
  Rebeckah 34
  Sarah 32, 116
Flemmin, Sarah 104
Flemming, Elizabeth 101
  Hannah 102
Flemmon, Elizabeth 83
Flin, Sarah 88
Flinn, Catherine 111
  Delilah 116
  Maria 23
  Rachel 41
Ford, Ann 89, 119
  Caroline 81
  Elizabeth 43, 54
  Harriet 88
  Lidia 55
  Rachel 69

Hains, Martha 82
Halaway, Sarah 76
Hale, Mary Ann 9
Haleman, Mary 10
Haley, Eleanor 96
  Eliner 3
Hall, Catherine 15, 105
  Cornelisann 78
  Elizabeth 42, 81
  Luhana 79
  Margaret 48
  Maria 87
  Martha 25
  Mary Ann 3, 90
Hallenbroke, Corneliusann
  98
Halloway, Rebecah 76
Halsey, Getty Ann 71
  Lydia 11
Hambleton, Rebeccah 99
Hamilton, Catherine 66
Hammell, Acsah 97
  Harriet 55
Hampton, Ann 14
  Ann Matilda 108
  Elizabeth 53
  Gertrude A. 24
  Gertrude Jane 90
  Hannah 48
  Lydia 56, 67
  Mary 4, 53
Hance, Ann 42
  Elizabeth 44, 105
  Ellis 25
  Emiline 8
  Heather 44
  Mary 110
  Rebecca 108
Handlin, Elizabeth 89
Hanes, Frances Lucretia
  43
  Margaret 62
  Mary 54
Hank, Amelia 67
Hankenson, Elenor 74
Hankerson, Ann 91
Hankings, Nancy 11
Hankins, Ann 50
  Anne 25
  Catherine 115
  Eliza 35
  Elizabeth 101
  Esther 3, 114
  Fanny 29
  Hannah 11
  Mahala 45
  Mariah 83
  Mary 75
  N. 62
  Phebe 36, 54
  Rebeca 21
Hankinson, Deborah Ann 80
  Eliza 85
  Fanny 51
  Hannah 49
  Hannah A. 43
  Nelly 20
  Sarah 19, 92
Hannah, Isabel 40
Hans, Jane 106
  Margaret 26
Harbart, Masey 65
Harbert, Mary 5
Harbor, Ann 92
Hardey, Lydia Field 118
  Hannah 30
  Susan 43
Harent, Margaret 29

Haring, Catherine 61
  Christeana 6
Harkell, Elizabeth 21
Harker, D. 2
  Damarias 51
  Mary 91
Harkinson, Nelly 17
Harley, Phebe 75
Harling, Anna 59
Harman, Eliza 9
Harmer, Phebe 47
Harres, Amy 42
Harris, Ann 76
  Catherine 58
  Elizabeth 23
  Hannah 26
  Lauretta 6
  Lydia 119
  Mary 59
  Rebecca 74
Hart, Catherine 89
  Elizabeth 44, 49
  Margaret 112
  Mary 9
  Mehitable 114
  Zilpha 112
Hartman, Ducretia 73
  Mary Ann 96
Hartshorne, Elizabeth
  8, 88
Harvey, Anna 52
  Catherine 31, 55, 61
  Elizabeth 3, 52, 75
  Hannah 39
  Jane 32
  Lydia 114
  Margaret 31
  Maria 68
  Mary 9, 76
  Phebe 7
  Sally 80
Hatfield, Sarah 78
Haughawout, Elizabeth A.
  88
Haveland, Ann 43
  Eliza 69
Haven, Elizabeth 61
Havens, Ann 12
  Anne 48
  Catherine 59
  Deborah 77
  Eleanor 100
  Elizabeth 27
  Ellenor 111
  Fetry 61
  Hannah 81
  Jane 59
  Lidia 58
  Lindia 53
  Margaret 60
  Maria 83
  Mary 10, 39
  Rebecca 34
  Sarah 58, 96
Haviland, Catherine 66
  Lidia 65
  Lydia 43
  Mariah 43
  Martha 76
  Ruhanna 107
Hawker, Alithael 45
Hayden, Ann 83
Haymen, Elizabeth 60
Hays, Catherine 81
  Elizabeth 45
  Gertrude 3
  Lydia Ann 97
  Margaret 84

Hays (cont.)
  Mary 67, 71
  Mary Ann 8
  Sarah 109
  Sarah Jane 59
Haywood, Abigail 90
  Elizabeth 81
  Nancy 9
Hazelton, Deliverance 6
  Mary 55
  Mary Ann 81
  Sarah 41
Headdon, Leah 88
Headley, Blumer 25
  Hopy 84
  Rebeckah 80
  Sarah 9
Headly, Ceany 47
  Levina 112
  Mary 54
Heaveland, Jane 55
  Lavinea 31
Heaviland, Eleanor 18
  Sarah A. 43
Hebberson, Theodosia 81
Heirs, Merriby 22
Helmore, Catherine 80
  Lenah 80
Helsey, Catherine 28
  Eliza 67
Henaghan, Sarah Ann 110
Henderson, Catherine B.
  24
  Eliza 14
  Hannah 40
  Hope B. 38
  Jane 115
  Mary 42
  Mary Ann 57
  Matilda 8
  Nancy 115
Hendickson, Rachel 20
Hendrickson, Alice 3, 48
  51
  Altea 36
  Altie 77
  Amy 58
  Ann 2 (2), 14, 78, 101,
    102 (2)
  Catherine 25, 48, 52,
    54, 61, 96 (2)
  Charity 52
  Cornelia 113
  Coziah 43
  Diadame 64
  Eleanor 108
  Eliza Ann 110
  Elizabeth 5, 16, 48,
    52
  Ellen 109
  Francineka 27
  Gertrude 98
  Hannah 45
  Helena 88
  Jane 47, 102
  Lydia 8, 11, 37
  Margaret 20, 45
  Mariah 95
  Mary 40, 74, 103 (2),
    109
  Mary A. 112
  Mary Ann 103
  Mary Catherine 104
  Nancy 45
  Nellie 52
  Patience 77
  Rebecca 26, 83
  Rhoda 109

132

140

141

Witteny, Dinah 99
Wolcott, Elizabeth 118
  Hannah 2, 73
  Lydia 11
  Mary 103
  Rebecca 118
  Sarah 63
Wolley, Sarah 102
Wolston, Rebecca 30
Wood, Abigail 94
  Amelia 17
  Margaret 27
  Nancy 118
  Rebecca 94
Woodhull, Matilda 21
  Sarah 38
Woodly, Mary 8
Woodman, Abigail 15
Woodmancey, Rebeccah 113
Woodmancy, Hannah 83
Woodmanse, Amy 84
  Edith 94
Woodmansee, Allice 106
  Amelia 17
  Patty 27
Woodruff, Mary 36
Woodward, Achsa 53
  Clenine 118
  Eliza R. 59
  Elizabeth 48
  Ellen 81
  Lucy 25
  Lydia 108
  Margaret 44
  Margaret B. 46
  Martha 17
  Mary 86
  Rebecca 19
  Sally Ann 17
  Sarah 6
  Susan 102
  Susannah 118
Woohiver, Julia 19
Woolcote, Edna 53
Woocott, Elizabeth 55
  Jane 90
  Marobah S. 61
  Sarah 7
Wooley, Abigail 104
  Ann 1, 41, 78
  Anna 77
  Artless 109
  Caroline 52
  Catherine 64, 74
  Deborah 26
  Elizabeth 59, 113
  Getty 34
  Hannah 16
  Margaret 80
  Maria 46
  Mary 61, 78
  Ruth 43
  Susan 33
Woolf, Esther 49
Woolley, Adeline 60
  Allice 41
  Amy 73
  Ann 30, 37
  Clarasy 105
  Constant 42
  Deborah 24
  Eliza 113
  Elizabeth 1, 14, 52,
    60, 63, 72, 109
  Fanney 119
  Hannah 24, 68
  Jemima 40
  Lucy 42

Woolley (cont.)
  Lydia 102
  Mary 26, 76, 97
  Mary Ann 25
  Meriam 97
  Patience 59
  Rachel 24
  Rebeccah 44
  Rebecca 95
  Sarah 43, 55, 62
Woolston, Liza 109
  Sarah 28
Wooly, Lecritia 70
Woordell, Deborah 24
Wordell, Lydia 5
Worden, Mary 50
  Sarah 16, 50
Wordle, Ann 59
Worth, Harriet 57
  Jemima 46
  Lydia 18
  Mary 10
  Rachel 71
  Sarah 25, 52
Worthington, Mary Ann 72
Worthley, Ann 60
  Elisabeth 17
  Jane 101
  Sarah 65
Worthly, Harriet 92
Wright, Fanna 2
  Jane 88
  Mariah 74
  Mary 115
  Sarah 85
Wyckoff, Alice 118
  Ann 74
  Louisa 75
Wykoff, Ann 117
  Emeline 33
  Grace 50
Wynant, Elizabeth 57
Yearling, Amelia 78
Yeoman, Sarah 114
Yeomans, Martha 116
Yetman, Catherine 25
  Hellen 26
  Margaret 53, 70
Youmans, Hannah 52
  Rebecca 74
Young, Agnes 98
  Ann 37
  Catherine 84
  Margaret 37
  Rachel 13
  Sarah Ann 35
Zenas, Amey 71
Zutphen, Elizabeth 3
Zutphin, Catherine 26